Robin Woods

ROBIN WOODS

An Autobiography

SCM PRESS LTD

British Library Cataloguing in Publication Data

Woods, Robin
Robin Woods: an autobiography.
1. Woods, Robin   2. Church of England
—Bishops—Biography
I. Title
283'.092'4   BX5199.W/

ISBN 0–334–02424–2

First published 1986
by SCM Press Ltd
26-30 Tottenham Road, London N1

Phototypeset by Input Typesetting Ltd
and printed in Great Britain by
The Camelot Press Ltd, Southampton

Contents

List of Illustrations

Foreword

by His Royal Highness the Duke of Edinburgh, KG

King George VI had made his country home at Royal Lodge in Windsor Great Park. At the time of his death, we did not have a place in the country, and it was only after we had been using rooms at Windsor Castle for some months on a temporary basis, that we finally decided to install ourselves permanently in the Castle. This brought us into much closer contact with the Castle community, and particularly with the Dean and his family. We therefore took rather more than a passing interest in the appointment of a new Dean when Eric Hamilton died.

In this book Robin Woods describes how he came to take up this appointment. We had stayed with Robin Woods' father while he was Bishop of Lichfield, so that he did not come as a complete stranger, but it was only during the period when he was Dean of Windsor that I got to know him and his family, and to appreciate his wise advice and his considerable gifts of leadership and organization.

In the short time we had been resident at Windsor, it had become abundantly clear to us that the Chapel and College of St George's were facing serious problems. As with so many other institutions, the normal process of change and development had been interrupted by the war, and both the economy of the College and the fabric of the Chapel and the Canon's Cloisters were in dire need of repair.

In the first part of this book Robin describes his early life and the wide variety of church appointments which came his way. A chaplain with the Eighth Army during the war, followed by a spell of duty in Singapore, and then into a completely different task with the Industrial Community in Sheffield. With this background it is easy to see why Robin could not have been a better choice for the daunting and challenging task that awaited him at Windsor.

In the years that followed he achieved far more than simply to repair the fabric of the Chapel and Cloisters and to re-organize the College. He succeeded in giving the whole of St George's an entirely new and eminently practical direction for the future. His imaginative concept of creating a small residential centre where consultations between lay and church leaders could take place in a quiet and peaceful atmosphere, has proved to be highly successful. Robin was kind enough to discuss his plans with me and I found the whole process of developing the structure and programme for St George's House entirely fascinating.

Robin would certainly not have been able to succeed in this task if he had not been a committed reformer and improver. He was always looking to the future, and while he had the vision to see how the ancient purposes of the College could be adapted to contemporary and future circumstances, he was also determined to help the church to use its human and physical resources as effectively as possible in the rapidly changing conditions of the second half of the twentieth century.

We were naturally very sad when the day came for him to leave Windsor but we were also delighted that he had been elected Bishop of Worcester. This new appointment gave him new opportunities for service in the wider responsibilities of a diocese as well as in the higher councils of the church and Parliament.

This book is one man's story, but that story happens to coincide with one of the most interesting periods in the development of the Church of England. Robin Woods will certainly be numbered among those who helped to point the way ahead.

Preface

The tradition of my family to keep a daily diary or journal covering events is one that I have kept up from my schooldays to the present day and it has proved extremely useful in writing this book. In addition I have been greatly helped not only by members of the family but also by friends and colleagues from different partnerships over the years. In particular I thank His Royal Highness the Duke of Edinburgh for his encouragement and helpful advice, Admiral Davies for giving me detailed records relating to my time at Windsor and Bishop Oliver Tomkins, author of the life of my Father, for his watchful eye on the book as a whole.

Any formal dedication of this book is replaced by offering it primarily to my children and grandchildren. I had always hoped to leave some account of these years for the family, and it was with that intent the book was originally undertaken.

Tirley, Gloucester   Robin Woods
February 1986

Acknowledgments

The publishers are grateful to the following for permission to reproduce photographs: Barnabys Picture Library, 94, 146; Berrows Newspapers Limited, Worcester, 268; Evening Mail, Slough, 192; Leicester Evening Mail, 80; National Coal Board, 121; Sunday Telegraph, 208.

=== [1] ===

The Story of a Family

The story of my life is – perhaps to a much greater extent than is usually the case – the story of a family. It is the story of grandparents and parents, brothers and sisters and children, but it is also the story of an even wider family than that. From the very beginning it is also a story of the church family. To talk of the church as a family affair has by now become glib and sometimes almost meaningless, but that was not always the case. Throughout my life the narrower family has constantly opened out into the church, and sometimes it has been hard to tell where one ended and the other began. All that I have experienced within the family I have experienced only to a slightly lesser degree within the church. In the church of my time, as in the church of my parents' day, bishops and archbishops were men who had grown up in the same environment, who went to school and university together, and who appreciated one anothers' strengths and weaknesses. They may have differed in churchmanship, but common loyalties were never in question. And it was the same in the academic world. That is not so apparent now: not only are the church's work of sustaining the religious life of the nation, the life of the academic world, and the pursuit of knowledge becoming separate in an atmo-sphere of distrust and tension; each of these spheres individually is becoming less coherent. And it is the same internationally, even in the ecumenical movement. As I grew up I found myself in a community of clergy and laity where all the leading figures in the different churches knew one another. Today relationships and movements within the churches and society are more fragile, almost brittle.

It is as though my life has come at the end of an era, or at least at the end of a distinct period in the English church. Within that setting I can see how as a young man I was brought to the crest of a wave

[1]

which in later years I watched breaking and dispersing.

When I retired from full-time activity in the Church of England, I was Bishop of Worcester. My retirement also marked the end of a chapter in this story. Without a break, for more than sixty years, from 1917 to 1981, Woods had been bishops in the central councils of the church. From being Vicar of the huge parish of Bradford, my uncle Theodore was made Bishop of Peterborough in 1917 at the age of forty-two. He took a strong lead in the last years of the Great War and the period of adjustment which followed, particularly in the field of industrial reorganization. Translated to the great diocese of Winchester in 1922, he was more at the centre of the church, and in the House of Lords. Edward, my father, having worked with William Temple in the Life and Liberty Movement which led among other things towards the 1919 Enabling Act, was made Bishop of Croydon in 1930 and of Lichfield in 1937, in which capacity he served fifteen years in the Church Assembly and in the preparatory work for the British and World Councils of Churches. Frank, my oldest brother, overlapped with Father; he was made Bishop of Middleton in the Manchester diocese in 1952 after serving on Church Assembly soon after the war, and in 1971, the year in which he became Primate of Australia, I became Bishop of Worcester.

Many and varied factors had played their part in bringing the Woods into their senior positions in the church. My mother was a descendant of John Gurney of Earlham. The family had established itself near Norwich in the eighteenth century, where it became known for its strong Quaker traditions, its keen sense of Christian responsibility among the poor and labouring community on the land and for its strong sense of the stewardship of money and resources. This led to the Gurneys of Earlham becoming the trusted bankers of the area. Much has been written about them, principally because the daughters of the house, who married round about the year 1800, carried their convictions into wider spheres. Elizabeth Gurney became Elizabeth Fry of prison reform fame. Her younger sister, Hannah, married Thomas (later Sir Thomas) Fowell Buxton, who worked with Wilberforce for the liberation of slaves. Ellen, the daughter of their second son, Thomas Fowell Buxton, who made his home at Easney, near Ware, married Robert Barclay, of the Bank, and they were my mother's parents. The ties between the Gurneys, the Buxtons and the Barclays were close and interwoven. As landowners and as strong believing Christians, the families formed an intimate partnership, partly as a result of their inheritance of land in East Anglia but more because of their common religious and social convictions. They not only led the Society of Friends in their area but also readily joined up with and became committed to the rising evangelical movement in the Church of England. Religion, social concern and responsible financial dealing owed much to these descendants of the Gurneys.

It seems to be the case more often than not that mothers do the remembering of the family ancestry and pass the traditions on to the children much more readily than do fathers. Mine was no exception; she was constantly aware of our family in the past and would tell of its significance for new generations.

Mother, born Clemence Barclay, daughter of Robert Barclay and Ellen Buxton, was not so much proud of her Gurney, Buxton and Quaker inheritance as aware of the responsibilities and opportunities that followed from it. She would tell us about the activities of Elizabeth Fry in Newgate Gaol and elsewhere; she would want us to know how the slaves became liberated not only in Africa but in the West Indies; she had been rightly encouraged by her father and mother to place Bible reading and the wonder of the expanding church in the forefront of her interests, and she passed this on to us. Her parents with their four sons and four daughters had moved out from an earlier home near the city of London to High Leigh, a large and comfortable house that they built for themselves in the heart of their new estate between Hertford and Hoddesdon. At this home the children enjoyed the freedom of a spacious upbringing and were also able to keep up with their many cousins in Norfolk and Suffolk. They also had a pleasant house on the cliffs at Cromer as their summer home. At the same time there was to be no doubt in the Barclay household of the family's strong Christian allegiance, which was characterized by an intelligent approach to religion and a sense of their social and 'missionary' duty, together with a deep piety. There were family prayers every morning before breakfast with the menservants and the maidservants.

The atmosphere of High Leigh was a mixture of the severity of the head, Robert Barclay, and the generous care of Ellen and her household and the ever-widening interests of the eight children as they came to marry and work, either at the Bank or in the missionary service of the church. Robin Barclay, Robert's oldest son, who led the next generation at the Bank, was well read; he thought deeply about his own and the nation's faith and later gave much to developing Christian movements. The next two brothers were both ordained into the Anglican ministry and the youngest, Gurney Barclay, worked first with the Bank and then with the Church Missionary Society in Japan. The four sisters all had strong and distinctive characters; the two youngest became missionaries. Clemence, who was the second daughter, was good-looking and had beautiful golden-red hair. She never went to school, but with the help of governesses she became knowledgeable in history, literature and art.

At Cambridge, Gurney Barclay had met Edward Woods, and they had become close friends. Gurney Barclay brought him from Cambridge to High Leigh, where Edward met Clemence Barclay. They soon found that they had mutual interests, and the bond was strengthened further by the fact that they even had ancestors in common, since Edward, too, was a descendant of John Gurney of Earlham by a different line.

The Woods family was related to John Gurney through Elizabeth, his third daughter. She had married her husband, Joseph Fry, in 1800. They were soon to settle in London, first at Ham Common and then at Plashet, where Joseph established himself as a private banker. This did not prove successful and he was constantly in financial trouble; added to which, they had eleven children to look after. While bringing up the family and caring for her husband, who at one stage became bankrupt, Elizabeth Fry became concerned with the plight of those in prison, particularly the women in Newgate East. Her pressures on the authorities became legendary and her influence in prison reform soon stretched across Europe. In the meantime Joseph had to establish a simple and more frugal way of life for the family. Alice Octavia, the eighth child of the oldest son of Elizabeth and Joseph, married Frank Woods, a clergyman, and so left the Quaker fold for parish work. They became a powerful and much loved pair in their parish of Hereford, where Alice is commemorated in a fine window, and then at St Andrew's Nottingham, where Frank had a great ministry, among other things establishing a life-long friendship with the two Player brothers in their tobacco shop. He died a young man, at the age of forty-five. It is said that the hearse, pulled by black horses, was followed by a funeral procession a mile long. Two sons, Theodore and Edward, went to school at Marlborough and then entered Trinity College Cambridge; of the three daughters, Evelyn, Richenda and Josephine, two married clergymen and the third a missionary. Theodore and Edward, separated in age by some six years, had become very devoted to their parents' ministry and both resolved to follow on in it at an early age. Theodore was ordained first and became deeply involved in ministry to the drab industrial mill area around Huddersfield. On ordination in 1901, Edward was appointed chaplain to Ridley Hall and curate of Holy Trinity Church and thus had a place in the pastorate of Cambridge University. In these roles he greatly enjoyed both training young men for the ministry and at the same time taking up the opportunities for evangelism and group work among undergraduates and shepherding successive generations of students; it suited his gifts perfectly. His ardent, joyous faith, his gift of making friends easily, his love of sport and his attractive personality were all extended to the full.

Whereas Mother was a wonderful story-teller and was always ready to recall her ancestors and their interests, Father was much more reticent, and we came to know more of his life only later, through a meticulous diary. Were it not for these daily narratives maintained for fifty years, we would not have known of his feelings or the details of the friendships he kept up throughout his life. And it was he, in that diary, who gave a graphic account of his meeting with Clemence Barclay, their courtship and engagement.

It was during the August of 1902 that Edward Woods began to record his love for Clemence Barclay:

> ...Up to Easnye... Cousin Ellen (Buxton) gave me a warm welcome, then left Clemency and me to go into the wood... ***** (he marks the row of stars) back before lunch – most loving and touching reception from them all... The aftn. and evening we just wandered in 'our' wood... the Lord bringing it home to us by degrees... growing every minute.

Such a record of this private joy can properly be made more public, for the rest of Edward's life is not understood apart from realizing how deep was the mutual love between him and 'my Clemency', and how completely it was held from the beginning in happy submission to the overarching love of God. Their devotion to each other was complete. She was utterly loyal to him and yet she maintained her individuality, with many personal idiosyncrasies of dress and behaviour in later life that led to much amusement.

My grandmother Alice, after the sudden loss of her husband and therefore her home, had decided to take her growing family back into the areas of Hertfordshire and Essex in which she had been brought up. Buntingford village was situated in the vicinity of many of the old family friends: Gurneys, Frys, Buxtons and Barclays. The Court at Buntingford became the home of the Woods family for nearly thirty years. Because it was so near, it was not hard for Edward to court Clemence Barclay at High Leigh, only a few miles away. They married in 1903, immediately to share each other's family to the full, enjoying from the start their common ancestry, their mutual interests, and above all the life and wide resources of the Barclay family. Bicycling in the summer and shooting in the winter were the recreations of the time. The Woods family clearly enjoyed expeditions to the Barclays at High Leigh or to the Buxtons at Ware, since both had estates which were well endowed with woodlands. They were also sufficiently close to Cambridge and Suffolk to keep contact with their many cousins in both places.

Their first home on getting married was a little house not far from Ridley Hall, where Edward's happy and varied ministry continued, but now in a new and wonderful partnership. Cambridge at that time was a stimulating place to be in. A strong Christian concern among students, which had begun in the latter half of the previous century, had gained a rapid impetus there as a result of the spectacular programme of the Cambridge Seven, a group including C.T.Studd, Captain of the Cricket XI and leader of a famous victory against the Australians, and Stanley P.Smith, the stroke of the Cambridge boat, who with five others announced their intention of being ordained in order to serve abroad as missionaries in 'evangelizing' China. Their example had led to the foundation of the Student Volunteer Missionary Union, a select group whose members had pledged themselves to serve the church abroad, God permitting, and also to the creation of a wider circle of Christian Unions in the universities generally.

After the first halcyon days, during Edward's time, difficulties were arising. Thinking Christians, in a period when science seemed to be encroaching more and more on religion, were unhappy with the intellectual shallowness and narrow-mindedness within the Christian Unions; concerned that Christianity should take a prominent and respectable place within the university and should welcome outsiders, they had also become unhappy with the aim and basis of the Christian Unions, which restricted membership to those who personally confessed Christ as saviour, thus posing difficulties for honest searchers. This conflict, which was to recur time and again in university settings and still has not been resolved, was most prominent in Cambridge, rather than Oxford or elsewhere, and it was there that

[6]

the issues of belief and mission were being hammered out on the anvil of university life.

In fact, in 1907 a break was to come between the conservative Evangelicals in the Christian Unions and those with a more liberal approach, who eventually moved away to become the Student Christian Movement. Student conferences abounded to discuss serious issues at this time, and Edward took a lead in them. Under the inspiration of the American John R.Mott, President of the recently formed World Student Christian Federation, this whole development led to the famous World Missionary Conference in Edinburgh in 1910 and popularized the slogan 'The Evangelization of the World in Our Generation'. With men of the stature of Scott Holland and the young Kenneth Kirk on the one hand, and William Temple, William Paton and Jo Oldham, later architects of the World Council of Churches, on the other, it is not surprising that the treatment of the major issues of world mission and the unity of the Christian enterprise was profound. It was to prove vitally important for the years of the First World War and the 1920s and 1930s that a group of men was formed who embraced the great doctrines of the Bible and the church while allowing a breadth of interpretation and a wide variety of response.

However, all this was not something that Edward was to be involved in for much longer, since he was soon to be removed forcibly from the scene. To his surprise, and to the grave concern of Clemence and the family, in 1907 he was taken ill: the diagnosis was that he had fairly advanced tuberculosis in both lungs. He was ordered to stop work, and advised that if he hoped to recover at all he had to put himself in the hands of experienced continental doctors in the air of the high Alps; even then the cure might only be partial.

It was a tremendous blow to him. His diaries show that everything seemed lost: his home, his ministry and his wide circle of friends. And by now there was not only Clemence to consider. They already had their first child, Priscilla, and Clemence was expecting another. However, there was nothing for it; off they went with all their possessions to Switzerland.

We have more than Edward's diaries from which to assess his mood. Much later, in 1941, in the dark days of the Second World War, he gave a series of broadcasts in the 'Lift up Your Hearts' series, entitled 'Things I Live By'. The last of them was called 'Chastening Accepted'. In the guise of the third person he looked back on these years in his opening words:

[7]

I know a man who, some time ago, had a serious breakdown in health and was obliged to go abroad for some years. It meant the break-up of his home, the abandonment of useful and interesting work, and the future looked black. On the Channel crossing he found running in his head the title of Tolstoy's tales, 'Things Men Live By', and he wondered if his present disaster was one of the things he had to learn to live by. In the event he found it was so. The thing took indeed a lot of learning, and there were kicks against the pricks; but the time did come when he could honestly thank God for what had at first seemed sheer calamity.

Indeed it took time: Edward spent the next seven years in and out of the Schatzalp sanatorium above Davos. For two years he was largely confined to bed, but then his strength began to return: he was allowed to walk, and then could even skate (eventually, before he left, he became so good that he won the championship for figure skating in 1913). When his health allowed he became official chaplain to the Anglican commmunity and was in charge of the little church in the lovely valley in which the town is set. Clemence was with him and made a home not far from the sanatorium. German became a second language. The family increased; Priscilla had been born while Edward and Clemence were still in Cambridge and Frank was born in Davos quite soon after their arrival. Clemence would go home to High Leigh regularly, and Samuel and Janet were both born at the other Barclay home at Cromer. It certainly was a credit to Clemence that she raised children, managed a home in Switzerland and kept in close touch with her own family in England for those long years of Father's illness. It must have been hard to think of everything all the time, and sometimes she did not quite succeed. On one journey home she had to change trains at Basle. She established her luggage and what she thought were all the children in a carriage on the new train across the way. However, twenty minutes after the departure she discovered that Janet had been left in a bassinette on the platform. Urgent consultation with the conductor led to cables being sent, and arrangements were made for the infant to follow in the next train to Calais. In such a situation Clemence may well have been worried, but she was never found wanting for resourcefulness.

By 1913 Edward was remarkably recovered. He had come to see the long years of illness as providential. He had experienced great anxiety and severe illness; he had looked at an unknown future. Moreover, he had recovered miraculously when others had died, and all this brought him a maturity of faith and confidence in God's promises which he was always ready to pass on to his family and friends. Clemence, in the meantime, having children at regular intervals and looking after an invalid husband, had become very dependent on her parents, Robert and Ellen Barclay, at High Leigh. Without their home and material help matters would have been very different. As it was, the Barclay parents provided a base for our family throughout the years of Edward's illness and convalescence. In 1913, he was nearly ready to return. However, the chaplaincy at Lausanne was vacant, and he was advised to do a final year there, in touch with his doctors, and without too arduous a duty. It was during the months of the chaplaincy that I was born, the fifth child, in 1914, a few months before the outbreak of war. When I was two days old, Father noted in his diary, 'he is not nearly so ugly as they usually are at this age'. I was baptized Robert, and Robin Barclay was one of my godfathers, a fact which was to have important consequences in the future.

In the meantime, Theodore had moved on to curacies and parishes in Southwark, Kersall and Bishop Auckland. He was as forceful a preacher as he was a good parish priest, and he soon became known as someone who was able to initiate new ventures among the mill workers and was particularly good with young people.

His rather narrow experience and training at Cambridge had rapidly given place to a vigorous liberal position. Well-versed in Hebrew and Greek, he was a very much better scholar than his younger brother Edward. With many others at the time he argued for the symbolism of the Bible rather than its inerrancy and verbal inspiration. He preached a gospel of social care as well as a strong message of personal salvation. He was a man of heavy build, with a faith to match his energy. At that time he was undoubtedly the more dominant of the brothers, but their ministries, though so different, were complementary.

Theodore held remarkable missions on the Sands at Blackpool and later amongst the miners in County Durham. At the time one of his parishioners wrote:

> He was a friend who, like his Master, went in and out into the highways and byways of the parish. He knew all the poor people, and had a smile for everyone he met, stopping to shake hands with the road-sweepers and never forgetting to ask about their wives and children. For long afterwards they used to ask me, 'Have you

heard anything of our vicar?' So many rich and poor heard the voice of God through his teaching; or it may have been at some mothers' entertainment when he played 'My grandmother went to Paris', or sang 'Cockles and Mussels', to the great delight of his audience and, as we always felt, to the glory of God.

It was during Theodore's incumbency at Bishop Auckland that King Edward VII died, in 1910. Theodore was a royalist and throughout his life maintained a firm faith in the monarchy, and he felt the King's death as if it were almost a personal bereavement. He never forgot the Coronation festivities of the following year – the great service in South Church, the procession through the town and a huge meeting in the market place for which, as he wrote, 'I had the heads of my address printed in large letters so that if the crowd could not hear, they could at least see what I was talking about – a day of Unity, of Loyalty, and of Responsibility.' After these functions he went to Portsmouth to stay on HMS Good Hope for the Naval Review, and to preach on the following Sunday. He loved pageantry of all kinds, especially the pageantry of the sea, and his experiences both at the Review and in the Sunday services afterwards thrilled him. 'A celebration of holy communion in the casemate of one of the guns, the most remarkable church I have ever been in!', was a real highlight. In 1912 he became Vicar of Bradford and for the next five years threw himself into the work involved.

Early in June 1914, Edward and Clemence came home on leave from Lausanne; at that time the clouds of war were rapidly gathering. Two months later Edward reported to Bishop Taylor Smith, the Chaplain General, in the expectation and hope that he would be sent to the Front. However, he was ordered to report to the Royal Military Academy at Woolwich; by the late autumn he had moved in as one of several chaplains serving young artillery and engineering officers in training. Once again, he was at home among young men;it is clear from his diary that he spent most mornings preparing addresses for church parades, from which the cadets had no way of escaping. He was happy, but found it increasingly worrying, and evidently very hard work after his years of illness.

It was the Student Movement that was to bring him renewal. In his diary he records his gratitude for times with John Macleod Campbell, Bill Paton and Robert Wilder at SCM conferences. He still hoped to be posted to active service in France, but his TB record prevented that. Instead, in mid-1915 he was moved to the Royal Military Academy at Sandhurst, where the family joined him, to live in the chaplain's house at 5 The Square.

Among the many cadets in training over whom he had pastoral insight was the Duke of York. Edward's acquaintance with the Duke, later to become King George VI, was to lead, as we shall see, to regular visits on which he would preach to the Royal Family. This established a connection which would continue over the generations. However, Edward's immediate concerns were of a much less happy nature. In his diary he records that by May 1915, after only eight months of war, 10,955 officers had been killed, many of whom had passed through his hands – not to mention the 250,000 men in the ranks who had already been lost. It weighed heavily upon him to have young men in his care for some two or three months when all he could really do was to prepare them to die. He kept records of those who were commissioned, hundreds and hundreds of them, and then of those who never came home. He would write to bereaved parents, wives and fiancées with deep feeling. Some of the entries in his 'Spiritual Diary', which he kept spasmodically, in addition to his own daily record of events, reflect both the influence he felt he might be having on others and the cause for it.

One such entry in November 1915 reads:

If I am to speak to others of 'Revival' and the Glory of the Lord, and the coming of new life to the church, there must be more of it – a new beginning – in my own life.

And in January 1916:

Thrust back upon prayer, as the only force to achieve great spiritual ends. Many interested and friendly, and in their way Christian: but I long to see some fairly gripped by Christ, and set on fire for his kingdom. Must not God wonder at the lack of Intercessors, in view of the fact that his mightiest works are manifested only in the pathway of unselfish and persevering intercession? The history of the church and Christian experience show conclusively that the workers and leaders who have accomplished most in extending and building up the Kingdom of God have been those who gave to prayer for others the foremost place in the use of their time and strength.

Later, he went on to say:

Two great needs in my life (not new ones):

1. Discipline, including more regularity and order in prayer and all work for God. This discipline must be self-imposed; for there is no one else to impose it.

2. Sacrifice. Find room somehow – search for ways and means, for living life marked by the cross, 'marks of the Lord Jesus'. In these days all men sacrificng comfort, convenience, life itself for the nation. Shall I, Christ's ordained minister, do less for him and his cause?

With no bishops to oversee or advise on ministry; no sustained lay partnership in assessing the value of preaching or pastoral care; and with only the security of being called by God to get on with his work in the face of the unseen enemy, ministry had to be worked out on the basis of other people's need. This became archetypal for the family: it was for Theodore, and it became so for Frank and myself a generation later.

Edward saw tens of thousands of cadets through his hands between 1914 and 1918; thousands lost their lives. As they left to join their regiment, he gave them a little booklet he had written and had printed, *Knights in Armour*, a title which speaks of the romantic imagination of a generation that was reading Tennyson and Rupert Brooke. To boys of eighteen, who were quite likely to be dead by the time they were twenty, it spoke of daily living and of the life beyond, in language that they could understand. It is a measure of the distance we have travelled to read Edward's booklet today: the simple virtues then fairly readily accepted are no longer part of our vocabulary or our experience. Such a summons to courage, unselfishness, chastity and loyalty is harder to present in our modern situation. It would seem that the task of preaching and counselling then was much more simply defined when seen in comparison with the role of the chaplain or parish priest today.

Simplistic Edward's approach may have seemed, but it must not be forgotten that he was regarded as a radical at that time, and that factor, coupled with the question mark over his health, meant that he had no promotion in four years. On the whole the Church of England made a sorry showing in the First World War, as Alan Wilkinson's account in *The Church of England and the First World War* (SPCK 1978) shows all too clearly. However, this was largely because of the nature of the official establishment of chaplains and their superiors who were already in uniform as commissioned officers in 1914, and the attitudes of senior church leaders who were too much swayed by the slogans of the state. It is interesting – and important – that the figures who come out of that period best are those in the liberal, questioning tradition to which Edward now belonged: F.R.Barry, later Canon of Westminster and Bishop of Southwell; B.K.Cunningham, one of the finest trainers of Anglican priests; and indeed Theodore himself, who after his vigorous activity as Vicar of Bradford had been appointed by Lloyd George to the bishopric of Peterborough at the early age of forty-two. Their contribution was to discover the needs of the Englishman committed to a war to end all wars. That these few were unable to make more than a small mark on the situation is not surprising. Nevertheless, their contribution was considerable. They noted and acted on the social injustices in the treatment of munition workers and they identified themselves with the men in the trenches; they prepared those in the fight also to win the peace, and they gathered around them a band of candidates for the ministries of all the churches which stood the nation in splendid stead over the next two decades and more.

Edward, still a chaplain, was permitted a period of visiting the troops in the line in France in 1917, and there he gave talks in the base areas on the main social issues that would be facing the returning soldier. With the good will of Llewellyn Gwynne, the Chaplain General of the First Army, he introduced discussions on future society – home life, education, wages, employment and much else. He also realized that there was a further ferment in the minds of the troops which concerned the future of the church itself. Writing home he records:

> They were evidently delighted to have someone from England whom they are pleased to regard as more or less representing the church at home and into whom in such representative capacity they could pitch to their hearts' content. Quite a new role for me, who have little use for the church *as it is*! But if I'm a reformer, they are revolutionaries. There is no doubt that out here, continually face to face with all the realities of life and death, and perforce driven to unity and cooperation with other Christian bodies, they are further on than we are at home and longing with an even deeper longing for Life and Liberty in the church. As in the industrial world, so in the church, it will be *too late* to start reconstructing when the Armies come home. It is absolutely vital to get on to the work now – and people out here have grave fears that we at home do not sufficiently realize the urgency of the situation.

[13]

The reference to Life and Liberty needs some further comment, since it was a cause to which Edward was to devote himself, outside his normal duties, for more than twenty years, and does much to explain the tone of his comments.

In March 1917 William Temple had resigned from the rich living of St James's, Piccadilly, to give his whole time to the cause of reform in the church and work as executive chairman of the Life and Liberty movement. He borrowed the church of St Martin-in-the-Fields, where Dick Sheppard was vicar, both because of its independent attitude through the years and because of its national standing. He summoned there a group of friends, including Father, to look at the future of the Church of England. The gathering consisted almost entirely of younger men, and no bishops were present. It resolved that both church structures and church membership should be overhauled. In the first place they unanimously agreed that they must concentrate on the church's own abuses and shortcomings. Action had to begin in the church, and the church had to set its own house in order before it could hope to catch the ear of the nation. The anomalies of church patronage, the inexcusable disparity between clerical incomes, which seemed to bear no relation to the work involved, the conditions of tenure and the lack of pensions for superannuated clergymen – these and other abuses in the life and organization of the church militated against its witness and stultified its message.

If reforms were to be put in hand, Parliament first had to give a degree of freedom to the church. Neither Temple, Dick Sheppard nor Father was prepared to go as far as disestablishment and disendowment in order to obtain liberty for the church, but it was soon agreed that the first thing to press for was an element of self-government. All this led, amongst other reforms, to the Enabling Act of 1919. Up till then any changes in the life of the church, its finances, its management of property, parish boundaries and the smallest alteration in the Prayer Book were subject to Parliament, where the pressure of ordinary business was invariably so great that ecclesiastical matters were crowded out. The old 'Convocations' of bishops and clergy, after being suppressed by the Crown for nearly two hundred years, had been revived in the middle of the nineteenth century, but they provided no place for lay membership or lay consultation; they did little more than review theological issues and tinker with parish endowments.

In this situation, with many a parish freewheeling and the church much in need of the participation of clergy and laity in its government, the Enabling Act was passed by the Commons and, rather grudgingly, by the Lords. The measure authorized the setting up of the National Assembly of the Church of England and gave the church a limited but real internal control of its resources: property, finance and manpower. Those days in 1917, in close partnership with his friends, were a turning point in Father's ministry. They identified both the causes and the individuals which would influence the established church in the post-war years.

Before Father returned from France he was allowed two days in the Front Line under the guidance of a friendly officer. That he was allowed to go and look at all was a concession at that time. Trench warfare had become the dreaded issue facing the Government, bringing as it did such continuing frustration and so many casualties. Over several days he was invited to conferences and meetings behind the lines before his few hours with the infantry where he saw the 'hell-inspired dreariness' of trench warfare and the miles of blasted wasteland. To see the human and physical desolation of Ypres was an experience for which Edward was deeply grateful and it was firmly imprinted on his mind when he returned to conclude his ministry to the young officers who were to face it themselves.

Over the years at Sandhurst Mother had not only made a happy home at 5 The Square but had also carved out for herself a place in the care of the young officer recruits. She was able to share with Father in her own way, as a young wife, the fears and hopes of the men. She could adapt to the needs of all comers, and her country background and wide circle of family and friends made her someone whose personality seemed particularly rich and fulfilling. Having arrived at Sandhurst as an infant, I was nearly five by the time the armistice was declared. Over those years I had come to love our house, the horses, the band, the parades and the colourfulness of the Royal Military Academy. I still have a clear memory of the ceremony that was held with all the cadets, staff and instructors lined up to hear the official news of peace. The relief was immeasurable; that those present would not go off to trench warfare was unbelievable. Celebrations were the order of the day, and talk turned at last to 'civvy' life and normal matters. For my parents, after seven years of illness and four years of war, there was now the hope of a settled ministry, perhaps at a college, perhaps in a parish.

═ [2] ═

A Coat of Many Colours

There was an enormous amount of jostling for jobs once the First World War was ended, and Father, too, was thrown into the mêlée. His future was quite unknown, so it was uncertain where we would now live. He was invited to go abroad, but his health ruled that out; others suggested different parishes to which he might go for further experience. However, what seemed truly to be his call was a proposal that he should return to Cambridge and be Vicar of Holy Trinity Church, near the market place and most of the colleges, which was deeply committed to working with undergraduates. So to Cambridge the family returned, to live at 7 Brookside, off the end of Trumpington Street.

There the parents soon established a home for us six children and an open house for anyone who came within the scope of their ministry. Both Edward and Clemence had strong individual characters, but they proved to be superbly matched, and at home neither dominated the other. The fact that both of them were at home for so much of the time proved a most important factor; there were none of the disadvantages which arise when one parent is away from the house for much of the time. We children had a great admiration for Father; we never called him Dad or Daddy, though our respect was tempered with some affectionate nicknames. For me, Father became affectionately known as 'Booker', after our little terrier, for complicated reasons. We were, of course, especially dependent on Mother, who influenced all of us, but each in a different way. As I look back on it, perhaps Mother was disproportionately attached to us boys and Father to the three girls, but that is natural anyway, and the difference in emphasis was only marginal. Hardly an evening would pass without Mother quoting the Psalms or talking about figures from the

Old Testament as part of our bedtime ritual. The call of Samuel and the old hymn 'Hushed was the evening hymn, the temple courts were dark' and other memorable verses from *Golden Bells* were part of a natural and continuing commitment to Christian service that she passed on. All of us were given a remarkable freedom to think and pursue whatever interests attracted us. Our religious upbringing was based upon the Bible stories and the person of Christ. There was no fear in the religion that was implanted in us, no guilt complex of the kind which is sadly to be found among some evangelicals, and no sense of failure if church did not meet our own particular need. Many factors made the nearly ten years at Cambridge from early 1919 to 1927 a wonderfully happy and formative time, especially for me.

Holy Trinity Church became a very happy centre of ministry and preaching to an ever-widening circle of men and women enjoying first demobilization and then the easy expectancy of the 1920s. A new dimension of congregational friendship was established there in which we as a family took full part. The Cambridge Inter-Collegiate Christian Union (CICCU), then as now the evangelical and fundamentalist rallying point, was partly based on Holy Trinity, but its concerns were to find little place in Father's ministry or in our family faith: this was a disappointment to the older generation of Buxtons and Barclays. In its place there developed a much more open religion, the knowledge of a God whose demands were real, but not alarming or pernickety, and of Christ and his church, requiring and offering salvation not so much through the imagery of Christ's 'saving blood' or through the rigours of sacramental discipline as through a gentle and persuasive atmosphere created by a personal relationship with Jesus of Nazareth. This led to sympathy for doubters and provided a meeting place for those men and women who wanted to bring Christian values and Christian actions into the social and professional concerns so prominent in the university, now that it had been set free from war. It also led to an enormous strengthening of the Student Christian Movement, from which I was eventually to benefit.

Help was needed at home with a large household and a house that had four storeys and many stairs; moreover, the care and friendship of successive generations, no longer of cadets, but now of undergraduates and others within the wide circle of the university, called for a good deal of entertaining. So we had a succession of domestic

servants. Some of them we children liked and made at home, and others we didn't.

The garden proved a happy place for us to play; it had to accommodate first donkeys and donkey carts, and later a succession of bull-nosed Morris cars, which arrived when the older brothers were allowed to drive. Neither of the parents ever learned to drive a car. However, we rode bicycles constantly, and much enjoyed the flat Cambridgeshire landscape on bike-rides with Father. Although grandmother's home at Buntingford was some twenty miles away, we got out there by bicycle during most holidays.

As a small boy I seem to have proved something of a handful. My first school was the kindergarten. I remember being reprimanded one day when I got home from school for having made my teacher, Miss Borrer – I can see her still – cry before I said sorry. The way from home to school passed a conduit building, which still stands in Trumpington Road, that controlled the flow of water down the Cambridge streets. In an attempt to exercise some discipline over me, my father's curate, Bill Anderson, told me that this curious domed structure was a prison and that my naughtiness would one day land me inside.

My early reluctance to learn meant that I did not stay put at any one school very long. All three of us boys were sent to the New Beacon at Sevenoaks, a prep school at which all of us were miserable. The train up to Liverpool Street on the way there was bad enough; the school train from Charing Cross was hateful. To be fair, the fault did not lie with the school; at that time it was considered right for those in the tender age group between seven or eight and twelve to be subjected to being away from home and a pretty hard discipline. I expected to follow both Frank and Sam to Marlborough, but by 1925, when I was eleven years old, both Father and Mother were clearly disenchanted with my progress and with the traditional public school. I was to be given a fresh start at Gresham's School at Holt in Norfolk, first of all in the junior department.

The correspondence between Father and the headmaster of the New Beacon makes it plain that my parents were moving away from the establishment image of public schools and towards a greater freedom in education. Poor old Norman of Sevenoaks! He felt that it would be a lasting injustice to me not to have been at Marlborough or one of the front-line public schools; but Father held to his new convictions and was determined that I should not be tied and bound by formal religious or social standards, but free to think and choose.

◁ *Early days*

He was right. I found Gresham's School, Holt, a liberal and radical foundation in the great sense of those words, and would not have been anywhere else.

At one stage I had what was probably routine tooth and gum trouble, but Mother made it the occasion to keep me at home for a whole term before starting at school afresh. I can still remember the unconditional joy and freedom of being by myself with the parents for those months. Whether or not eleven is an impressionable age, it was a personal and private pleasure to be the only child at home. We would have an early supper before Father went out to his meetings, and then Mother would read aloud to me from the novels of Henty, Robert Louis Stevenson or Scott. Simply to watch Father was a source of confidence – an encouragement to be outgoing which I did not have at school. We children did not suffer from the consequences of the outgoing personalities of our parents; on the contrary, we came to see their readiness to meet with all and sundry as the norm. Both Edward and Clemence loved their work, and they managed to communicate this love to us.

Christmas at Cambridge brought the whole family together, as it was to do for years to come. We did not buy much extra to give as presents, but we took enormous pains over making and wrapping and presenting our gifts. Christmas Day began with all of us children singing 'Christians, Awake!' outside the parents' bedroom, and undoing our stockings in their room. On Christmas morning the church service amounted to little more than carol singing, since traditionally Holy Trinity was not a church where there was a deep attachment to sacramental worship. This was, of course, at a time before the eucharist attained the central place in church life which it has today. We would then spend the afternoon playing mixed hockey with other families. The day concluded with Christmas dinner with a 'Higham' turkey sent each year from the Barclay estate and much pleasure over the flaming pudding, all to be followed by an evening of home-made music in which we would tackle parts of *Messiah* or secular madrigals with a variety of voices and instruments. Each of us made quite a creditable contribution to it.

To be sent to a school where scholastic progress could be slow without disadvantage and where examinations would not be a recurring hurdle to cross certainly proved more of a success, if formal education can be measured in such terms. At Gresham's I found myself among masters, mistresses and contemporaries whom I came to respect, and from whom I learned as much outside the classroom as in it. J.R.E., as Eccles the headmaster was universally known, certainly had a remarkable influence for good. He developed a voluntary system of discipline and an 'honour' system of personal responsibility as a normal part of school life: it proved unexpectedly successful for succeeding generations of boys. There was virtually no corporal punishment; and those who objected to games or the Officer Training Corps could go off looking for local seabirds on Blakeney Point, for wild life on the heathlands, or even for ancient churches. As a result of that I have enjoyed a working knowledge of birds, flowers and the world of nature that my brothers never got at Marlborough or my sons at Winchester. Hundreds of boys – and their parents – benefited from the controlled experiment of an open school which was quite unique in the 1920s and 1930s, and which established a new dimension in education at the time. Everyone in the family, however young, was familiar with talk of COPEC, the Conference on Christian Politics, Economics and Citizenship, and Life and Liberty, since these were Father's main preoccupations during the 1920s. The reshaping of the government of the Established Church which had been begun in 1919 was going ahead, and it was as a result of this that inter-church conversations like the one at Lausanne were beginning. Father was deeply involved. However, his concern was not with ecclesiastical joinery but with bringing the kingdom of God into the social and domestic life of the time. It was also the concern of Theodore and one in which he was very active from his position as a bishop. From the last stages of the war he used the weight of his episcopal status in connection with many social and political issues: the housing and employment of those returning from the Front, and the organization of working people along with the emergence of trade unions which were vocal in their demands for a 'country fit for heroes'. He was one of the main protagonists of the new social concern which was growing in the life of many a congregation and in the structures of all the Christian denominations. He was fond of saying that 'we are all Christian Socialists nowadays', and shared with many of his clergy and friends the simple hope that the principles and practices of Christian fellowship would contribute the most hopeful remedy for the ills of the 1920s and 1930s.

In addition to his varied activities in this area Theodore was also an original diocesan bishop, and he developed methods and ministries that were often well ahead of his time. For example, because he wished to understand the outlook and pace of life in the countryside, he hit on the idea of pilgrimages: he would walk through whole tracts of countryside over a week or ten days. His first pilgrimage was in Northamptonshire, in July 1920; he would meet people on village greens or by arrangement at informal gatherings in the country churches, and he felt able to stop and talk with those whom he met. In particular he visited the homes of the people and was careful not to be always entertained in the big houses of the neighbourhoods through which he passed; he wanted to familiarize himself with the problems of his clergy and of ordinary people. Such pilgrimages caused a great sensation whenever they took place, and his example was to be followed by others.

It is small wonder that although he was only forty-five at the time he was made secretary and administrator of the 1920 Lambeth Conference. It was there that he joined George Bell of Chichester in drafting the famous 1920 Lambeth appeal to all Christian people, which put forward the vision of a truly Catholic church into which each separated church would bring its own contribution of life and organization.

In 1922 he was appointed Bishop of Winchester. He continued to be involved in the social issues of the day. During the coal dispute and miners' strike of that same year he stated publicly that nationalization of the whole industry was not only a just solution for the mining community but also an inevitable development. Here he was thirty years ahead of his time. From his time at Peterborough, the first stop for express trains to the north-east, with its prominent engine sheds and railway workshops, he took a great interest in the railways, and in his new diocese he had Eastleigh, the home of the Southern Railway, so he became known as the railwayman's bishop. It was an apt title: he was most concerned to support improved working and social conditions and at the same time enjoyed riding regularly on the footplate of express trains. In connection with the railways, too, he spoke out in favour of nationalization years ahead of his time. In the field of medical ethics he led the Church of England into a careful study of birth control, which led to their acceptance of it.

In 1924 Theodore was appointed joint chairman, along with Archbishop Söderblom of Sweden, of the World Conference on Life and Work at Stockholm, the first representative gathering of Christians from Europe since the Edinburgh Missionary Conference of 1910.

That same year he and Father were involved in COPEC at Birmingham; they had been responsible for the preparations for it. The gathering set the tone for a strong Christian social movement; we as a family became identified with it, and it certainly left a mark on us children. There were in fact those who regarded COPEC as a climactic point in English religion, before disillusionment in society brought a return to obsessions with narrowly ecclesiastical matters and doctrinal rigidity. This tradition directed me in later years towards a social gospel which I felt to be just as important as personal religious experience.

After I had been at Gresham's a couple of years, in the summer of 1927, when I was thirteen, Father took me as someone who could at least carry his bag to the World Conference of Faith and Order at Lausanne. This was the first occasion in history that brought together leaders of all the main non-Roman churches with a view to finding reunion. I was glad to go to see the place where I was born, and for me the gathering was a memorable mixture of business and pleasure. I became interested in watching the preparation of the minutes and departmental reports, which were Father's responsibility. He had been appointed administrative secretary along with John R. Mott, who by then had joined the International Missionary Council. William Temple joined us to play in the evening or go rowing on the lake below the town. Many lasting friendships were established at Lausanne that summer.

As for Life and Liberty, Father was given leave of absence from his parish to travel round the country in the cause. It was probably at this stage that at times life at the vicarage in Cambridge became almost too busy for pleasure, and imposed increasing strain on Mother, a strain which was not to lessen as the years went by. The side-effects on us children, though, were not wholly unpleasant: for whole periods in school holidays we three younger ones were left very much on our own. With Priscilla at work, Frank a curate in Portsmouth and Sam at Trinity, we enjoyed our own company and our own arguments.

The latter years at Gresham's laid the foundations for much that was to prove important in later life. I began to keep a diary in the same way as Father kept his, but I found it difficult to maintain regularly. In place of a day-to-day record of events I found it more interesting and in retrospect more useful to keep a journal of interesting events in the week, of books read and people met. If you are a collector, as I was, it is also a pleasure to collect experiences in a notebook. Art lessons at school became increasingly fascinating. My teacher was interested in those of us who wanted to draw and encouraged sketching. This had been an activity of the family over many generations. My ancestor Joseph Woods was an architect of distinction and made drawings of buildings and landscapes quite beautifully in the 1810s and 1820s. He took lessons from John Sell Cotman at Norwich and indeed provided his own landscapes of Greece so that Cotman, who could not afford the journey, was able to do his famous series without ever visiting the country. The ability to draw and readiness to sketch remained in the family, and it was in my mother's family as well; the large collection of water-colours in our successive homes bears testimony to considerable ability in the past. Father had a remarkable gift for drawing animals – horses in particular. Having been able to share his interest in art I found myself well grounded in the disciplines and methods of perspective and colour work. I have enjoyed drawing and painting ever since.

Gresham's was also a marvellous place for what proved to be my prime interest, music. The senior music master at that time was Walter Greatorex, a composer of no mean ability. It was during his time in Holt that he wrote 'Woodlands', a tune now widely sung not only to Montague Butler's 'Lift up your hearts', but also to Timothy Dudley-Smith's 'Tell out, my soul, the greatness of the Lord'. He taught me not only to enjoy music but also to enjoy making music and indeed to compose. We were doubly fortunate in those years, since Benjamin Britten arrived as a new boy in the upper school in the same term as I did. His quiet enthusiasm and obvious gifts, not least his powers of conducting, singled him out even then as someone quite exceptional, and whether I was a playing a flute in the school orchestra or the piano or organ for school prayers, I was enormously stimulated by him. He and I not only arrived together but left together. At one of our last morning assemblies we accompanied 'Praise, my soul, the King of heaven' at the piano with four hands. Ben announced his plan: he would improvise between the verses and modulate in such a way that each verse started a semitone higher than the one before. C major for the first verse was easy, C sharp not so straightforward, D major was about the right level, and E flat a bit high for the voices – and quite a strain on me! However, the three hundred boys voices responded superbly. Although we did not often meet, my friendship with him continued, and duets were to be played again later with him in a very different setting.

Mother used to arrive at school unexpectedly, particularly if I had a cold or was in any way laid low. She would also send cooked sausages through the post for fear that I might be hungry. Holidays in those days were particularly memorable: we went to Pembrokeshire, the Lake District or, later on, to Scotland, to meet our Barclay cousins. At those times Theodore would come to join us. I have vivid memories of playing golf with him each day on the funny little course at Fishguard. There we talked freely and endlessly about all that he and I were doing.

In this way we all grew very close as a family, living and learning together. To be able to develop a love for the countryside, an appreciation of music, art and natural history, as a part not only of school life but also of family life, was an inestimable privilege. It gave me a wide range of interests that have been a joy to keep up and enlarge ever since. In the latter years at school and afterwards at Cambridge one man, however, came to influence me considerably. My mother's oldest brother Robin Barclay, vice-chairman of the Bank and a public servant in several ways, became a real friend. As my godfather he met all the expenses of my education from preparatory school to taking my degree, thus helping my parents considerably. But he was more than a benefactor: he invited me to spend time with him at his home near Bishop's Stortford; he took me salmon fishing at Helmsdale and grouse shooting on his island of Raasay year by year. He was well-informed politically and had a keen sense of social issues which he was ready to share. From his position of responsibility he gave unstintingly of his time and resources to the church, local government and agriculture. Although he had had a narrow religious upbringing, Uncle Robin became a thinker and reformer; he appreciated new scholarship in biblical studies and understood the aspirations of those who had adopted the new scientific and secular outlook.

In addition he had become the honorary treasurer of both the Student Christian Movement and the Church Missionary Society at a time when they were both developing into major voluntary movements in support of Christian witness. This had brought him, too, to share the wider insights and religious concerns of William Temple and others. As a result of all this his outlook moved to a strong liberal but firm churchmanship, and he became involved in work for reunion and inter-church activities. This estranged him quite considerably from many of his more narrow evangelical family and friends. It was his experience with SCM that led him to play a crucial part in the purchase of The Hayes, in Derbyshire, later to be known to thousands of students as Swanwick, which became the centre of great SCM Conferences from the 1920s on. Indeed, in 1924, when he sold his Scottish estates, with great insight at the same time he gave High Leigh for the ecumenical service of the churches.

It was while I was at Gresham's that the family moved to Croydon. Father had been appointed vicar in 1927. Croydon was so near to London, with a fast electric service from the station close by, that we children were able to get used to London and had a good deal of personal liberty to enjoy. However, the proximity to London and thus Father's greater availability also added further to his work, and increased the strain on the family, especially on Mother, which had been already becoming evident in Cambridge. The parish was a large and demanding one; at the time it had four curates. Although Father started by being just vicar, he soon became rural dean, and was then appointed archdeacon, with some forty urban parishes to care for. Nor was that all; within three years, in 1930, he was made suffragan bishop and assistant to the Archbishop of Canterbury, with all that that entailed. He enjoyed all this increased responsibility, but Mother certainly did not. It was not easy for her to settle herself and the rest of the family into a smaller house in a rather cramped urban setting, and the mounting pressures over those years came very near to breaking her. She always insisted that her job in life was to keep 'Edward on the road'. She never forgot his illness in early years and waited on his every need year by year. However, such care took its toll. Mother became a chronically bad sleeper and often being up at night was easily tired out by day. Still, she never showed it; rather, she presented the picture of being a woman of great individuality and wide interests.

That period made an enduring impression on me. They were great days in the life of the flourishing churches, and considerable crowds made up the congregation at Croydon Parish Church at the eleven o'clock morning service and in the evening. However, it was the regular early holy communion at eight o'clock that became the quiet and unassuming foundation for the spirituality of our family and, indeed, for that of the parish. In those days there was a real mystery about the service that made it all the more wonderful: there was no side or ceremony there, no eucharistic vestments or music, but a weekly occasion of renewal for those at the heart of parish life. The modern parish communion which has assumed pride of place in Sunday worship these days may have much to be said for it, but the disappearance of the quiet early morning communion from congregational life has led to a loss of discipline and wonder. Not least, the balance achieved between it and the teaching offered at morning prayer led to the existence of a laity that was much better instructed in the faith than it tends to be today.

The evening services were great occasions for large numbers of people and the sermons given at them were well-prepared and substantial. I would regularly walk the mile from home to church arm-in-arm with father, and largely in silence. It was his final preparation for meeting a huge congregation which was receptive to Christian experience and teaching. People had to be there half an hour early if they did not want to sit in an aisle, and the church was packed with a congregation of several hundred, Sunday by Sunday. The organist regularly allowed me to sit by him at the console whenever I wanted to, and it was there that I went on learning the art of choir training and leading congregational singing – for there were some forty boys and thirty adults in the evening choir. It made a great circle of friendship as well as a solid base for public worship.

I was confirmed at Gresham's. All that I can remember about it was that Father came to school and, now being a bishop, was allowed to take the service in place of the Bishop of Norwich. Much more vivid in my memory are the confirmations at Croydon Parish Church. Since it was one of the largest churches in the Canterbury diocese, the Archbishop of Canterbury, Cosmo Lang, would come in person. When he arrived at the vicarage he would be served scrambled eggs and milk pudding, which had been ordered by his secretary in advance. He would then proceed to the service in his gaiters and top hat. He was certainly a severe figure to us children until we got to know him as a friend, and in due course we even managed to thaw him out a bit. One one occasion Janet and I got him out of Lambeth to go to a ballet – a totally new experience for him!

In church the impression he gave was of a distant but very great man. He would wear a black train, which needed two choirboys to carry it. Sitting in his robes, he would confirm a hundred or more, four at a time – I can still hear the measured tones of the words 'Defend O Lord, this thy child...' which he used. Of course a eucharist was never combined with the service. By the end he would be showing marked signs of weariness, but there was no mistaking his tremendous presence, and although there was little personal contact between bishop and candidate in those days, Cosmo left one with no misunderstanding of what he came for.

A close relationship grew up over those years between Cosmo, Edward at Croydon and Theodore at Winchester, and all were involved in the Lambeth Conference of 1930, in which they took a leading part. Though only sixteen, I went to the closing service in Westminster Abbey – those hundreds of bishops assembled together were not easily forgotten.

One regular event at that time in which we were never involved, but about which we were always fascinated, was Father's annual weekend at Sandringham with King George V and Queen Mary. Such visits, the origin of which goes back to his contacts with the Duke of York during the First World War, occurred regularly over some twelve years; after each of them we would be given a full account at home. Father usually brought back an occasional table made by the King's ex-service cabinet makers; we still have Sandringham tables in the family.

Those were happy times, but in the midst of them tragedy struck. At the age of fifty-two, early in 1932, Theodore died. His death was not only unexpected but, in retrospect, quite unnecessary. On Remembrance Day the year before he had caught cold, and then developed pleurisy. Antibiotics had not yet become generally available, though that same winter they were given to King George V in a last desperate– and in fact successful – attempt to save his life. For four months Theodore lay seriously ill, grew weaker and weaker, and never recovered.

I found his sudden departure from the scene bewildering. I was allowed away from school and to this day can see his coffin draped with his cope and mitre lying lonely in Winchester Cathedral. We felt that there had been a kind of amputation in the family. He was very close to us, for he and aunt Nina had no children. He had brought much laughter with him; he had shared our interests, enriched our musical activities, joined in our holidays, and even more, had shared his faith with us and given us an insight into the real meaning of churchmanship. I felt especially bereft. It was hard to see the providence of God in the fact that at that very moment he had been taken from the church, when he had done such valuable work and might well have been in line for York or Canterbury.

But it would be wrong to end an account of my schooldays on a note of grief. For all the tragedy of Theodore's death, what stands out is the way in which as a family we had grown together, each in his or her own way, in understanding, respect and dedication. For the boys in particular, Father and his generation had been a vital model. He had shared much with us – not least his power to laugh at himself and his ministry and his keen eye for the essentials. He was a real source of inspiration, and Frank had already left Cambridge for ordination, with Sam following on in the same hope. I was coming into my last autumn term at school, and before long the question would arise: 'What was I to prepare to do?'

=== [3] ===

Getting My Feet Wet

As I entered my last year at Gresham's, it was fairly clear what the next stage of my life was going to be. Like my brothers, I would be going up to Cambridge the following autumn. I would have to do 'little-go', the qualifying examination, since my school results had not been good enough to exempt me from it, and then finish the academic year. However, there was a surprise for me in store.

Father almost never visited us at school, and of course we never went home for a weekend break. However, one Saturday in October 1932 he suddenly arrived, by train. The visit proved to have two purposes: first to thank the headmaster and staff for all that they had done for me, and secondly to tell them then and there that he felt that it was best for me to leave school in December and complete the rest of the year travelling and working overseas. This was a far-sighted decision. At that time there was no Voluntary Service Overseas, nor any other similar agency for young people, but Father had concluded that to help an underprivileged community was a necessary part of growing up, a useful preparation for university life and selecting one's future work.

Consequently, after a bare week at home over Christmas, I was sent to London, where I met Wilson Cash, at that time head of the Church Missionary Society. He and Father had hatched the plan that I should travel with him to Egypt and that he should introduce me to the Mission School in the heart of the poorest area of Old Cairo. Two things would seem to have influenced his choice of that particular area. First, the Bishop of Egypt and the Sudan, Llewellyn Gwynne, a most remarkable man, was an old friend of Father's from Cambridge SCM days and the War. And secondly, Christina Barclay, mother's younger sister, had done a short spell of work there.

After spending two days at Rapallo with an aunt and uncle, I met up with Wilson Cash at Genoa, where I carried our bags on to the Lloyd Triestino boat, which took some four days to reach Alexandria. From there we went on by train over the delta to Cairo. There were few better ways of getting to know one's companion than sharing basic accommodation on a leisurely journey, and with Wilson Cash I set up a friendship that lasted till he died. He was marvellously kind, and over many hours introduced me to the intricacies and difficulties of maintaining missions and churches in Egypt, Africa and further afield. He was enormously knowledgeable about the religious and social situations confronting the younger churches at that time, and immediately I found myself being treated as a mature adult and given some insight into the responsibilities of Christian leadership.

We spent two nights with Llewellyn Gwynne, who had homes in both Cairo and Khartoum. In 1933 Egypt was under a British mandate, and through close links with Europe was developing education and medical services. The church in the Nile valley, particularly in the Sudan, was growing substantially, with whole tribes in southern Sudan embracing the Christian way of life. Between the two World Wars Bishop Gwynne encouraged developments in the Nile valley; he was much trusted by the Sudan Civil Service, a fine example of colonial administration, and both Egyptians and Sudanese came to hold him in high regard. I wished I could travel with that remarkable bishop, but he had rightly planned for me to do some real work in the poorest area up the Nile from the city. At first I was to live in the CMS mission hospital, but the school at Old Cairo provided more suitable accommodation. I settled down in a room, with a huge jar of water and a basin to wash in, and made the place my own for the next eight months.

The terms of my appointment were that board and lodging were to be provided in exchange for what work I was able to do. There were two sessions each day at the Old Cairo Boys School, from 6 to 10 a.m., and again from 3.30 to 6 p.m. This meant a short night and a long midday sleep. With no qualifications or experience I was given several classes of little boys, to whom I was to teach English and physical education and whom I was to supervise in out-of-school activities; this included running the school Scout troop. Since the boys only talked and worked in Arabic, it was all something of a hit or miss experience. Slowly I was to become involved with a number of very poor homes and families drawn from the crowded areas of Old Cairo.

[31]

Nearby there was a splendid mission hospital, the only medical centre of its kind at our end of the city, and there again I was allowed to share in the caring and teaching work, which also embraced the families of those who were sick. In those days food was not provided by the hospital, but brought in by relations and friends. Many would squat down for days and nights in dusty corners of the town and our small Christian community would try to minister to them as well as to the hospital patients.

Up the road in Cairo City were two remarkable missionaries. S.A.M.Morrison was an Arab linguist who over the years developed both Anglican and Presbyterian missions. He established the Near East Christian Council, to help the churches from Beirut in the north to Khartoum in the south. Few people did more than he to make the Christian mission to the Arab world both understandable and accepted, without antagonism on either side. Constance Padwick, who worked with him, had a mastery of Arabic and a deep understanding of Arab culture based on the Koran which made her uniquely acceptable to the thinking Muslim. These two had inherited and sustained the contacts with Muslims which had been started so remarkably twenty years earlier by Temple Gairdner. Gairdner had left a promising academic career in Cambridge to share his faith with the Muslim world. For many years, which also covered the period of the Great War, he had identified himself with educated Muslims, to the extent of being able to teach in Arabic at the Al Azhar university. He became an Arabic poet of renown and composed prayers for the use of Muslims as they came to understand Christ. He was a unique and very great missionary. He and Sam Morrison broke down the widespread notion that the Muslims were wholly evil, and had opened up ways of entering into dialogue with their thinkers. The devotional leaflets that they produced, in Arabic, which enabled Muslims to enter into Christian spirituality and Christians to understand Muslim prayer, were a unique contribution to mission. The friendship of Sam Morrison and Constance Padwick, and the patience and understanding with which they treated a young man as ignorant as I was in this field of mission, was to become a turning point in my subsequent choice not only to enter the ministry but also to go overseas to help to spread the gospel.

Constance Padwick, with her simple flat open to Egyptian callers and enquirers of all types, made a very striking contrast with the headmaster of the Old Cairo Boys School. Canon Toop was an old-fashioned 'converting' missionary, and kept up that image rigidly, with his black suit, tall clerical collar and topee, which never gave place to wear more suited to that lovely and constant sunshine. Perhaps because of this the senior boys seemed glad to have someone as youthful as me to be with them. Moreover, I had the wherewithal for some out-of-school excitement. Christina Barclay had left behind an old Model T Ford, built in 1922, for the mission. It had no gear lever and was probably among the most elementary mass-produced petrol vehicles ever built. I soon learned to drive it, and so was able to get around the city and its superb mosques, or the delta villages, and above all go into the desert with the hills and wadis beyond the Pyramids. Moreover, I could take boys for outings who otherwise never left the crowded streets.

In a letter home in February 1933, I wrote:

> One's first impression of the Pyramids is from sitting in a tram going over the railway bridge at Gezer. They appear quite immense, even from this distance six miles away. One alights at the foot of the desert where the road suddenly winds up the 200 feet on to the plateau above... The Sphinx was a surprisingly long way off, ten minutes' walk: by daylight it appears more of a monstrosity than an object of beauty, but by moonlight its disfigured face is lost in the darkness and its beautiful design, the damaged nose, lips and deep-set eyes, stand out in their real beauty. The Colossus at Memphis wins for sheer size, and the Step Pyramid of Sagara and its surroundings, standing unmolested in the desert, makes one realize what the past civilizations were like. Moses paid a visit to these tombs as a sightseer and Herodotus remarks on a stone table that has survived that he thinks it a disgrace that people are getting into the habit of writing their names on ancient monuments!

However, my letter of 19 March shows more concern for my work:

> I have been taking a gymnastics class. They are all boys between eleven and fourteen and I now know enough Arabic through listening to my interpreters to take them myself. Since they are all clothed differently – and in rags at that – it is awfully hard to make them appear harmonious. I said that I would take Scouts in their first-class cooking test. By the way, no Egyptian is punctual, so I am becoming unpunctual because I know they will not be there... I sent them to buy animals that they could kill and make edible. That is the test. They returned with white rabbits. I then had to

watch each in turn being slaughtered and prepared for the pot. They were such sweet rabbits that I longed to keep them.

Every morning I go to Boulac and say Shalom to an old beggar woman, too dirty for words, who sits on the river bank. She has two children, a girl and a boy, and has been divorced several times from Mohammedan husbands. Her daughter was the hope of the scene. I saw her and got her into our ragged Sunday School: she helped her mother every day. One day I returned to find the old woman with a cloth over her head wailing as hard as she could and beating her breast. I went up and tapped her on the back and said, 'There, there, what's the matter?' She replied, 'Mefeish Saida' (there is no greeting). I discovered that the girl had fallen into the Nile and been allowed to drown in front of a whole crowd of people. This is just to illustrate to you the utter hopelessness of Islam. Mohammed made a remark in the Koran to the effect that since Egypt depended on the Nile, God controls it. The result is that if anyone falls in they will offend God and the Spirit of the Nile if they attempt to get them out! It's continually happening. No one attempts to save them because they mustn't deprive the River of its children.

I could go on for ever telling you about customs out here. One day I passed a house with a crowd of the dirtiest and most dreadful women sitting outside. I asked the missionary who they were and discovered they were professional wailers. That evening I heard piercing shrieks from the same direction and realized that the good person inside the mud house must have died. If someone is going to die in your house you have wailers ready who will do the shrieking and crying with no feeling at all. I must stop now, though I have a lot to say. I have been at two Arabic services and each time the little church is packed full. Isn't it splendid? I really think after Cambridge I must come out here to work.

At Easter I had a short vacation in Palestine. After crossing the Suez at Kantara by rowing boat I had to run after a train that had already started and jump into the guard's van. And in that way I eventually reached Jerusalem. Four pounds in my pocket were all I needed for ten days in the Holy Land! I visited Nazareth, Galilee and the Jordan valley, and this turned the familiar Bible stories into a historical reality in a way which otherwise would have been very difficult to achieve. To be able to walk around Jerusalem and take the city in, as it then was, still with a peacefulness and simplicity of life, proved to be a source of the deepest inspiration. Places have always meant a great deal to me, and some of my deepest feelings are associated with them. But perhaps nowhere has meant more than the early morning on the Mount of Olives or walking by the lakeside of Galilee, for it was there that the ministry and passion of our Lord and all that they meant came home to me. And it was there that I began to realize more and more that when I went home and went to Cambridge, it would not be in preparation for accepting Robin Barclay's invitation to enter the Bank. I would be preparing to become a missionary.

Because of this, when I returned to the heat of Cairo for a further few months, it was with a more realistic approach to the opportunities and pressures surrounding the CMS mission there. I began to spend a good deal of time with Bishop Gwynne, and also learned of the enormous developments in the Sudan and among the Nilotic tribes, and all that still needed to be done. And I began to wonder how I could help. I left Egypt full of hopes and ideas for the future.

Then, in October 1933, I went up to Trinity College, Cambridge, as an undergraduate. I had already lived in Cambridge for years, Frank was established as chaplain at Trinity, and Sam had just completed his time there, so I had long since come to know and appreciate the place. However, familiarity did not breed contempt. I easily slid into university life with a ready-made circle of friends and advisers; here I had a great advantage over hundreds of others who came up to a strange new situation. Since rooms were being vacated by a member of the family, I was allowed to live in college my first year; at that time this was quite unusual, since freshmen were obliged to find lodgings to begin with – at a time when in fact they most needed collegiate life.

The corner staircase in New Court, where my rooms were, was well placed, conveniently close to the Backs and to Trinity Lane. There were disadvantages as well as advantages in having a brother as a don and on the staff: one could know too many people too quickly at a time when it was important to be identified with newcomers. However, it was natural that I should support Frank in the life of the chapel, attendance at which had only recently become voluntary. Nor was this just brotherly loyalty; those years at Croydon and months in Egypt had given substance to my religion, and I was conscious of going up to university not as an immature schoolboy but in order to test out my attitudes and vocation.

I was fortunate to have John Burnaby as my tutor and adviser; he helped me not only then but for many years afterwards. A classical scholar by training, he had very wide gifts of learning; he became a leading light in the acting world and led amateur dramatics in the university; he was a good musician and a ready entertainer. It was about that time that he turned his attention to theology and began to influence the college and university by his fresh approach to biblical and moral issues; however, what mattered most to undergraduates was that he had time for people and especially for the younger generation. He had just taken over as junior tutor in succession to Winstanley, who had been at Trinity a generation before, as had Dr Stewart, the Dean of Chapel, and old Dr Parry, a tutor in Father's day. The Master was Sir J. J. Thompson, an enormously erudite physicist who shared with Rutherford and Arthur Eddington in the discovery of nuclear fission. At that time the college was at the height of its scientific eminence: six of its residential fellows had been awarded the Order of Merit, an honour limited to a total of twenty-four throughout the country at any time. I came to know the Master only very slightly; his household was a formidable one. Even undergraduates invited to dine at the Lodge were expected to wear a white tie and tail coat. When a freshman turned up one evening in a dinner jacket, Lady Thompson greeted him with, 'Well, Mr Smith, you will know next time what to wear when invited to the Lodge.'

I had opted to read English literature and do the Part I Tripos in that discipline, rather than history, which tended to be the degree most people fell back on. However, there were complications. John Burnaby told me that there was no one in Trinity who could supervise the English Tripos, although ours was by far the largest college. Such was the scientific leaning of the high table just then. So he sent me to King's for my supervisions. 'Dady' Rylands, the Dean, took me on, and guided me through the work. He was a superb interpreter of the written language, a very fine critic of poetry and prose alike, and one whom I could admire. F. R. Leavis was dominating the critical school of English Literature just then, and Sir Arthur Quiller Couch continued to lecture at a great age, smoking a large cigar at the same time. It was through Dady Rylands that I was able to develop a real love of seventeenth-century and later literature; we did not bother with the mediaeval era! His link with dramatic and musical life in the university enabled me to get parts in the productions of Handel's *Jephthah* and other oratorios. Since I had already taken up rowing for exercise and recreation, not to mention organ lessons, my time was full.

In retrospect, I hardly find it surprising that, with so many interests and an increasing commitment to the religious life of the college, after three terms I failed to pass my 'Mays', the first-year examinations. However, after a caution from my own tutor I did manage to pull off a third in the Tripos. Dady Rylands had been an excellent antidote to my other interests; he was a superb teacher, and he made it a fascinating course to follow. For anyone who could not take advantage of a broad classical education, the English degree was a very good alternative.

Towards the end of my first year I was approached by Lesslie Newbigin, later to make a great name as Bishop in South India, and at that time a graduate theological student. Would I accept the presidency of the university SCM? At that time the Movement, with about 1500 signed-on members within the colleges, was a healthy influence on the life of Cambridge. Virtually every college had good groups of undergraduates both supporting the churches and pursuing the important task of thinking out the implications of the Christian faith. The SCM was the most effective arm of the churches in helping the rising generation of Christians to understand the demands posed to belief by current developments in society and the scientific world. Within SCM, the Student Volunteer Missionary Union, with about 150 members, still continued to be a vital force. With my background in this tradition it was natural for me to accept, and as a result I immediately found myself in direct touch with senior dons and supporters such as Charles Raven, then Regius Professor of Divinity and one-time Vice-Chancellor, and Max Warren, then Vicar of Holy Trinity Church. Further afield in the life of the church, William Temple, at that time Archbishop of York, Wilson Cash, head of the Church Missionary Society, and Neville Talbot, who after being Bishop of Pretoria was then Vicar of St Mary's, Nottingham, all of whom had long associations with SCM, were ready to help in any Christian developments in the university world.

More important in guiding my thoughts as president of SCM was, however, in the first place Robert Mackie, General Secretary in London. A Presbyterian minister of great charm and ability, he had taken over from Tissington Tatlow, the effective founder of SCM as we knew it. Robert Mackie became one whom the student world trusted and admired and whom theological leaders in the nation respected. He was also a very good guide to young men in lay or ordained work. The ecumenical movement was increasingly guided by him into Inter-Church Aid, World Service and the wider cares of the World Council of Churches. Then there was William Paton, head of the International Missionary Council and one who also had the ready hearing of the student world. In the 1930s he interpreted the international situation in a particularly inspired way. Through these two I also came to know and respect the great reformed denominations in England and abroad. My opposite number as SCM president in Oxford was David, son of William Paton. He was considerably more knowledgeable than I was as an undergraduate, and had the care of a large branch of the SCM. We met regularly to compare progress in our two places and work out a strategy for the church in our two universities. He and I have stayed in league ever since, though our ways have taken very different directions. The wealth of Christian leadership associated with SCM in the 1930s was unprecedented and has never been matched since; the absence today of a strong open Christian movement in the colleges is a main factor in the decline in numbers and quality among candidates for the ordained ministry and the narrowing of experience within our churches.

Of course there was also in Cambridge at that time the alternative sphere of the Christian Union (CICCU), with its narrow biblically-inspired thought and its pious community life. As has already become clear, by this time there were quite major differences between the Christian Union and SCM on fundamental matters. However, in the 1930s there was no hostility, as there is now, between the liberals and those who were more narrowly evangelical. We existed side by side to meet the particular aspirations of the student population. At the same time as I became president of the university SCM, my close friend and contemporary at Trinity, John Taylor, later to become head of CMS and then Bishop of Winchester, became head of CICCU. We met regularly for prayer and discussion and were each concerned to forward the Christian witness in the colleges. However, there is no denying the width of the gulf between those who held to a narrow view of the verbal inspiration of the Bible and the more positive attitude to varieties within Christian vocation which were to be found among members of SCM. As before, in the first decade of the century, and as still today, there is tension between those who have the gospel as a sure possession and those who go on seeking for the truth in Christian experience and service. Any period of war or severe economic and social pressure seems to encourage the narrow approach to religion, but the future must surely depend on both traditions being integrated into the body of the churches.

[38]

It is hard to stress too much the importance for the rest of my life of the friendships made at Cambridge in those years. Indeed, they had wider significance than that. Although in later life all of us would go our different ways, bonds still remained which enabled contact to be maintained between individuals with differing temperaments, backgrounds and beliefs – to the great benefit of both church and society. That open companionship in the churches does not appear so common in later generations – to our considerable loss. Other Cambridge friends included Miles Phillimore, with whom I shared rooms in the Great Court, who then did years of service with the Oxford Group; Gilbert Hort at Queens, who died as a priest working in Delhi; Richard Howard at Jesus, who became a missionary doctor; David Say, later General Secretary of the British Council of Churches and Bishop of Rochester, at Christ's, and Davis McCaughey, a theologian who has ended up as Governor of Victoria. Nor were the ties limited exclusively to Cambridge. Year after year SCM held large summer conferences at Swanwick, to which many hundreds of members came from old and new universities, teacher training colleges and polytechnics, to meet one another, study and grow together, discuss, and listen to prominent figures not only from the churches but from politics, the arts and other walks of life.

Near to Swanwick SCM sponsored work camps for students and unemployed. These were not easy to manage as the voluntary projects of turning the slagheaps into children's playgrounds were seen by the unemployed as something the nation should pay for; they proved occasions by which those of us privileged enough to enjoy university life could meet with and understand those suffering from economic forces entirely outside their control. I am afraid that the undergraduates gained more in experience and social knowledge than the miners and their families gained in benefits.

This is not the place to enlarge further on the healthy enthusiasm of SCM during those years. However, one event, which still remains vivid in my mind, is worth recalling. After much thought we agreed that one of the main emphases in our 1934 activity in Cambridge should be on encouraging men and women to serve the growing life of the younger churches in Africa, India and the East. We were bold enough to invite no less a person than the Archbishop of Canterbury, Cosmo Lang, to address a university meeting, and we took the risk of hiring the Guildhall. Since I was president of the SCM and a personal friend, I went to the railway station on a chilly November evening. Things did not get off to a very good start. As he entered the taxi, the Archbishop banged his head quite badly, knocked off his top hat and sank back into the seat saying that he was weary. Earlier that day he had conducted the wedding of the Duke and Duchess of Gloucester. 'I have joined a very fine jewel,' he remarked, 'to a very rough diamond.' Moreover, as we approached Clare College where we were to dine, he admitted that he felt unprepared. What should he talk about? I felt nervous that he would let us down, but he listened as I talked about the situation and made notes on the back of an envelope. He kept the cab waiting at the college gate as he sat there to finish writing, though the Master of Clare and Charles Raven, the Vice-Chancellor, were standing there to greet him.

I need not have worried. When we arrived, we found the Guildhall full to capacity – 1500 or more were already seated. Of course Cosmo Lang was a very accomplished public speaker, but little did I realize that he could hold such an audience in rapt attention for fifty-five minutes. He gave us not only a vision of world-wide service in the church, but also a great many relevant facts to remember. Many laughed at my taking the chair in the presence of the Vice-Chancellor, heads of colleges and the Bishop of Ely, but it was an undergraduate occasion sponsored by what was then the strongest undergraduate movement in the country.

What stands out from my early Cambridge days is the memory of two vacations spent with William Temple at York. The parents were in Africa and 'home' was shut, so I found myself invited to come up to Bishopsthorpe. To be allowed as an undergraduate to share William Temple's home and his thinking, to walk, talk and play duets with him, gave me a highly privileged insight into a great mind and memorable personality. I learned from him that faith was dependent not on proof texts or a sequence of historical events but on grasping the very personality of God in Christ and discerning God's purposes for mankind in and through Jesus of Nazareth. The lead given by him to his generation, as to me, was based on the emphatic conviction that God is love and love needs that to which it may give itself, as was shown on the cross. I remember William Temple saying at the time that 'the essence of Christian religion is not a theory any more than scientific laws concerning electricity are the essence of a flash of lightning or of an electric shock'. He insisted that the church was the only society that existed for those who were not its members. That mattered far more than arguments over scripture, sacramentalism or the church. What he conveyed to me was more formative than any academic training.

Under these influences at Cambridge and outside I came to see the faith as both an experience of new life and power and a way of living born out of a changed attitude and involving changed relationships. This not only posed an immediate problem of discipleship, but also indicated the necessary ground plan of a transfigured world order within which humanity would be able to grow to its full stature. It is difficult to convey the confidence of those days: victory was always sure; the final outcome, although perhaps tempered by judgment, would be the fulfilment of the personality and the fulfilment of society. It was a time which, despite the Second World War and the many crises and setbacks which were to follow, has sustained my outlook and ministry for over half a century.

Although it had a hundred dons, Trinity had proved incapable of teaching English. Nor could it readily teach theology, which I opted to read for the second part of my degree. The result was that I was allocated to a philosopher of enormous mental ability and national standing, F.R.Tennant. Although he had been ordained, he almost never went to chapel, and although he was Christian in the broad sense of the word, he doubted most of the major tenets of the creed. He was a thinker in the tradition of the Cambridge Platonists and a teacher of what was then pure moral philosophy. However, he listened with patience to essays on biblical criticism, church history and doctrinal issues; he became a good friend, but made very few comments.

Other distinguished theologians of the time taught us the basics of Christian doctrine and experience. Charles Raven never allowed us undergraduates to lose sight of the wonder of nature or the scale of material knowledge as we studied theology. He was the great advocate of natural theology and pursued religion as if it were a matter of personal commitment to scientific research; here he was the mentor behind the liberal movement in the churches. We as a family – for Frank and Sam were also taught by him – owed a great debt to his teaching and his basically humble and understanding personality. I also got to know C.H.Dodd well – that New Testament scholar and biblical linguist who is one of the great figures of modern scholarship. His lectures made the Gospels not just narratives but also the basis for a logical and unassailable faith in Jesus and the coming of his kingdom. I visited him regularly in his home on Parker's Piece, and we became real friends. Like Charles Raven and so many other leading theologians of the time – T.R.Glover was another of them – he was also deeply involved in SCM, so both work and my other activities were closely connected. In a way it seems curious that in reading theology it was from the great Free Churchmen that I learned most – from H.H.Farmer and Newton Flew as well as from Glover and Dodd. Men like this in the theology faculty were representatives of a gospel of personal experience, but at the same time they taught us to communicate it to what at that time was becoming an increasingly unbelieving generation.

As I entered my final terms at Trinity I handed over the student leadership of SCM to Davis McCaughey. The Movement continued to thrive, and I was to undertake a number of journeys on its behalf, but at that stage in my degree course John Burnaby made it quite clear that I was to work and work hard. Things were made easier by a move into lodgings in Jesus Lane, where I had time to myself and could get to lectures, libraries and tutorials without the interruptions of voluntary societies.

Tennant was still my supervisor. One day, when I had read my essay to him, he remarked that there was a prize which would be awarded to the best New Testament scholar in the College. The Dealtry Greek Testament prize was quite valuable and also brought with it a supply of new books. Since there were no other candidates for it that year, he thought that I had a chance of winning it. So I sat a three-hour paper alone in his rooms. He cogitated for a while, and then announced that I was College prizeman that year. Quite a new experience!

It was also in 1936, my last year at Trinity, that Father and Mother left Croydon for Lichfield. This meant a major change in our family pattern of work and home. For Father it was a real relief to conclude his long and arduous period as vicar, rural dean, archdeacon and suffragan bishop of the large town of Croydon. He had carried the responsibility of the group of parishes that formed an island in the diocese of Canterbury surrounded by Southwark and had shared in giving the borough some standing in the South London area; this happened at a time when the metropolitan airport was at Croydon, a fact which helped to bring it into prominence. The move to the Palace at Lichfield gave my parents a sense of scope and welcome new opportunities. The house, though large, was manageable; the garden was a pleasure; and having a staff inside and out meant a much greater degree of independence for them both. Lichfield proved a happy home for Gabrielle, my youngest sister, and me; all the others had left, Priscilla to Winchester, Frank to Portsmouth and then Wells Theological College, Sam to New Zealand on ordination and Janet to her musical studies in London. For me this was a time of close association with Father as he came to grips with some six hundred parishes, and as he built up his staff of suffragan bishops, archdeacons and secretaries. His episcopate was to last nearly twenty years, and over that time his local ministry and national powers of leadership came to be greatly appreciated.

It was a relief to walk across the street to Westcott House for my post-graduate ordination training. Trinity had meant much to me, as it had to my grandfather, father, uncles, brothers and relations over many years, but it was like reaching the end of a rather rough voyage to enter the tiny community of men learning together under the leadership of B.K.Cunningham. Father had been at Ridley Hall, but it was he who guided all three of us sons to Westcott House.

The House had been founded towards the end of the nineteenth century by Brooke Foss Westcott, an eminent scholar and Bishop of Durham, in order to enable men to receive some training in pastoral care, ethical judgment and above all spirituality. The little chapel was the centre of our daily life, as it was central to the quadrangle of our rooms. Then as now, the college was largely for those who had their degree, but it drew men from all walks of life – although 'B.K.' himself was an aristocratic Scotsman. He conveyed a deep sense of personal care for each of his men over nearly thirty years at the college; thus his influence over the Anglican ministry for a generation or more was enormous. Up to his coming, Cuddesdon or Ridley Hall had been the seed-beds for bishops; under his leadership Westcott House overtook them both, not just in producing very good clergy but in giving them a wide and outgoing outlook.

The Vice-Principal was John Collins, later known as Canon of St Paul's Cathedral for his association with CND and Christian Action. As my tutor he certainly saw to it that I was as much a theologian as he could make me, and without his help I would have remained ignorant of the essential doctrines basic to the ordained ministry. My debt to him was real and our friendship down the years was never impaired by our differences of opinion over politics and social matters. I was influenced most in my thinking, however, by B.K. Cunningham himself. He made it quite clear that he was anxious that I was taking my ministry too much for granted, that my knowledge of the historic and Catholic inheritance of the church was too scanty, and that I would exercise too easy a ministry, off the cuff. He gave me, as he gave so many others, an astonishing grounding in the essentials of the priestly ministry, and right up to the time when I left he took enormous pains to see that I was ready.

It is important to remember that at that time selection and preparation for ordination were still very arbitrary, and even those of us who were privileged to be at Westcott House were thought of as needing primarily time to think and pray. We very much made our own way with the personal help of those who taught us. 'God has given you your personality,' B.K. was fond of saying; 'you have come here to learn how to use it in his service.' I was not inclined to any stereotyped churchmanship, and Westcott House gave me an adaptability, a generous attitude towards other churches, and a will to work hard. And above all, the atmosphere of the place had stamped on all of us a deep commitment to prayer and the sacraments.

From schooldays on travelling had delighted me, and going abroad to meetings was as much preparation for the ministry as Westcott House. By this time tension was rising in Europe and there was an air of uncertainty in society and in the churches with the rise of Hitler. My vacations brought me much first-hand experience. Perhaps the most memorable was a visit to Bulgaria in 1937. Father had been invited to be part of a delegation to a World Student Christian Federation conference which was to take place at Chamcoria, near Sofia, in order to gather Christian students and staff from the universities of Eastern Europe, where there were already pressures from the Fascism of Germany on the one hand and the Communism of Russia on the other. He was also to bear greetings from the Archbishop of Canterbury to the Orthodox and other church leaders whom he would be meeting. They, too, were beginning to be under severe political pressures which inhibited the life of their churches. I went with him.

We joined a Danube passenger steamer at Passau and proceeded for several days, with stops at Vienna, Prague and Budapest. As the ship paddled its way through sleepy waters or down the narrow, fast-flowing Iron Gates, Father spent his time either with his notebook and pencil drawing the banks, catching the peculiar shapes of Balkan cupolas and towers, or immersed in theological conversation with men of all races to whom he felt a calling in helping them understand the movement for the reunion of all the churches.

The gathering we attended and to which Father spoke on the Bible each day left a profound impression on me. I realized for the first time the real threats that Hitler on the one side and Stalin on the other were posing to the whole fabric of European society and to the Christian community within it. By listening to each other, praying together and committing ourselves to God's cause, I believe we did strengthen the struggling Christian movements of Eastern Europe, and we maintained links with them over the years to come. That was one side of the international picture. Another vacation I attended a short course at Union Theological Seminary in New York City, listening to Reinhold Niebuhr, after which I went to an SCM gathering in Toronto. North America provided the very opposite picture to that of Eastern Europe.

Like my contemporaries at Cambridge, I fully expected to be ordained to a curacy and to work under a good vicar. However, things worked out differently. To my surprise I was approached by Robert Mackie, who at that time was about to resign from the General Secretaryship of SCM, and Billy Greer, who was about to take over from him. They invited me to join the staff of the Movement in London. For the purposes of ordination I could be nominally attached to All Hallows, Lombard Street, but my job would be that of missionary secretary to the national Movement. I would be responsible in that role for encouraging students to commit themselves to service overseas or on an international basis, in view of the urgent need of the developing younger churches, and to take up the opportunity that lay before the Christian churches to influence the developing situation in Africa and the East. It was indeed a challenge, but also an honour to be asked to join the staff of the Movement. I did not accept the offer lightly, but after consultation with Father and others thought that it was the right thing to do. Moreover, time was against the churches, and the openings for evangelism and Christian education in the large student conferences already planned were there before me. It was hard to think of a more useful thing that I could do. B.K.Cunningham warned me against going my own way, but admitted that it was an opportunity for ministry that could not be put on one side.

I left Westcott House at comparatively short notice and reported for work at the SCM headquarters at Annandale, Golders Green, in the week after Easter 1938. Billy Greer, an Ulsterman of great sympathy and religious insight, was in effect my very first 'vicar'; he taught me method in my ministry, and discipline in matters of work and timing, proving an example I was more than ready to follow. He later became bishop of the enormous see of Manchester and one of the most reliable statesman-bishops of the century. We remained in close touch over the first twenty-five years of my ministry. There was also Dick Milford, a thinker and writer who became Master of the Temple; Alan Richardson, later Professor of Christian Theology at Nottingham and then Dean of York; and Oliver Tomkins who, after a long stint with the World Council of Churches, became Bishop of Bristol. It was into this team of men, with some twenty others on the staff, that I was introduced. In partnership with them I became involved with colleges and student groups all over the country. Together with Dorothea Ferguson, my counterpart on the women's side, I took a full part in planning and carrying through what would now be regarded as very large student gatherings, particularly at Swanwick and High Leigh, recalling each time I went back to the latter my grandparents and my childhood. To spend six months as a layman on the staff was a salutary experience: I was able once again to watch others who could be models for my ministry, and I learned to appreciate what ordinary Christians wanted of their ministers, rather than going into the priesthood expecting to exercise authority over a congregation.

As a result of all this, ordination, when it came, involved no dramatic change in the direction of my life or employment: perhaps it should have meant more. My academic standards were adequate, my mind was made up and I was already identified with a field of propagating the faith rather than administering or maintaining it in a parish. More than that, my work meant being fully identified with others in the cause of Christ. I had been warned against ordination as going into the family business, but that is exactly what it was – my father, grandfather and two brothers were examples of it. Why should I not be in it too, seeing that I had the same hopes and aspirations? Moreover, by ordination I would be joining a great company of friends and contemporaries who were prepared to shape the Church of England into a force that mattered. Winnington-Ingram, the Bishop of London, agreed to ordain me without further ado. As he wrote to me:

Of course I will ordain you with pleasure. The more Woods we have in the ministry, the better. But unfortunately we have no Lent ordination, so it will have to be either Advent or Trinity. It will be nice to have you here and I will do my best to back you up.

The winter of 1938 brought more travel. I was invited to represent the British SCM at the International Missionary Conference at Madras over Christmas, and found myself seconded to the personal staff of William Paton, at that time the General Secretary of the Conference, with Jo Oldham, working on the preparations for a World Council of Churches. The assignment meant that I would spend some six months in India.

At Delhi I lodged with the Cambridge Brotherhood, and at Poona I stayed at the Franciscan ashram with Father Algy Robertson. In both places I found myself in the company of C.F.Andrews, the personal colleague and helper of Mahatma Gandhi. He was the real missionary, identified with the Indian people at a time of dangerously rapid change. Leaving the ashram after only three days, I joined up with Bill Paton at Nagpur and travelled on with him to Madras to assist in the arrangements for welcoming some three hundred delegates from younger and older churches alike. Under the chairmanship of John R.Mott, and under the theological tuition of Hendrik Kraemer, the Dutch missionary-theologian of the East Indies, the whole gathering studied, consulted and worshipped, expecting a great forward movement. This gathering soon became one of the main occasions that led up to the formation of the World Council of Churches. The Asian and African participants trusted the leadership of Jo Oldham and William Paton, and both men had the confidence of the European churches. Among other things I was pianist for the daily services – the one on Christmas Day was particularly memorable; this also brought me into close personal contact with the leading figures of the conference. Among them was Theodore's successor at Winchester, Cyril Garbett, later to become Archbishop of York, and his chaplain, Gerald Ellison.

Further travel in South India, where I spend some weeks with Leslie Brown at Alwaye, gave me a deep insight into the significance of Christianity in that country for students and the church at home. I spent the pleasant voyage home preparing to become much more fully involved in the life of the SCM, the missionary societies and the colleges.

However, the work was cut short. War seemed inevitable, and

foremost in our minds was the problem of contacts with the Movement in Europe and further afield, which were proving increasingly difficult. The work of the junior secretaries in the colleges was supervised by Billy Greer and Alan Richardson; they kept us aware of religious and social issues. The prophetic insight of both these men was well ahead of the views of the average clergyman, and we were expected to exercise the same sort of prophetic yet pastoral ministry among the students in those uncertain months.

I was ordained priest in St Albans Cathedral by Mike Furze, the Bishop, in the month in which war broke out. The London diocese went partly out of commission in the confusion of wartime threats and as I had been living in one of the lodges, belonging to my mother, on the old High Leigh estate, I found myself in the diocese of an old friend. The retreat in his care and the ordination by so outstanding a man of God were humbling and helpful. He delivered the charge out of the Book of Common Prayer, two pages long, without once looking at the text.

The autumn of 1939 changed everything. On the Sunday morning when war was declared, I was assisting at Hoddesdon Parish Church, nearby; the sirens wailed to warn of an air raid and the congregation evaporated with little more than a quick Amen. Gurney Barclay, Mother's brother and still Father's closest friend after forty years, was present at church that morning. He was a sage adviser on our new and alarming situation. Since he lived nearby, we walked to his home together along the empty roads and lanes.

Immediately war broke out we had a council at Annandale. We reduced our staff a little and planned for all contingencies. It was agreed that my sphere of work should largely include pastoral care for the students at London University: in those days there was no chaplaincy service other than that voluntarily supplied by our SCM staff. Those were odd days in London. We expected bombs at any minute, and waited for convulsing and upsetting action, but nothing happened. I shared a flat for the year in Bloomsbury with my sister Gabrielle, who was working in London for MI 5. SCM held on to its London headquarters, whereas many organizations moved out. The vast University of London dispersed to Cambridge, Oxford, Bristol, Nottingham, Wales and elsewhere. In view of this we reorganized ourselves so as to be able to cover the new situation. As well as remaining missionary secretary for the whole Movement I was made responsible for Nottingham, Derby, Leicester and Loughborough

University colleges, which together with the then London colleges numbered several thousand students.

Neville Talbot, yet another close friend of Father, offered me a home in his vicarage in Nottingham, which proved a happy and convenient arrangement. He knew the work of SCM and was quickly adaptable to the demands of a wartime crisis for his parish and the city. My memory of him is of a huge man wringing his hands in both despair and in prayer. He became a godsend of a colleague in those months of 1940, so full of uncertainty and with constant air-raids. When the Blitz came in the summer of 1940 the ministry in the parishes and among students, hospitals, prisons and much else rapidly changed. I was asked by Billy Greer, still the General Secretary of the Movement, to take over from David Paton, then leaving for China, and to add to my student parish the university and medical schools now centred upon Birmingham University. One memory stands out more vividly than any other. I was driving across from Nottingham to Birmingham in my Morris Eight the very night that Coventry was blitzed. I stopped on the high ground near Nuneaton and watched the blazing city from a very safe distance. It was a terrifying experience. As I reached Birmingham the streets were deserted, and I found my way to Selly Oak in the pitch-dark of the blackout.

The easy partnership of the SCM staff soon gave place to an isolated and difficult ministry. Fortunately I had a good base in Birmingham. Edward Cadbury, chairman of the chocolate firm and a good friend of SCM, local churches and Selly Oak Colleges, had added to his generosity by building a chapel and Christian centre for the university. With a little office there and good meeting rooms, hard by the students union, I re-established and reorganized my work in the universities and colleges of the Midlands. Edward Cadbury's generosity extended even further, since he had made my my post possible by personally paying the salary of the SCM secretary. I embarked on rather more than a year of trying to meet the needs and anxieties of hundreds of young people as they completed their university courses or were called up for military service. I was fortunate in having Raymond Priestley as Vice-Chancellor: over all those months he was a great support to our work.

As I preached regularly in the chapel, I came to realize afresh the way in which, for the people of the Old Testament, the significance of God's covenant was understood through the depths of uncertainty and defeat. And I began to see that preaching the crucified Christ was a demand that had eluded us in the days of peace.

As the war went wearily on, with the fall of France and setbacks in North Africa, I inevitably began to wonder whether I was doing the right thing. Should I not be serving as a chaplain in the forces? Father had felt the same in 1914, and Frank had been called up in 1939. He had served with an artillery regiment stationed near the Maginot Line, had retreated with his unit across France and had landed on the beaches of Dunkirk – fortunately being rescued across the Channel just before the final capitulation. Though I had had little contact with him since he had been a chaplain, it was enough to weigh on my mind when I realized what our troops were enduring and how our chaplains were meeting the situation. Although I was like many other junior clergymen serving in the parishes, I felt that I had not responded sufficiently to the demands of the time. So I wrote to the Chaplains Department, since I felt more called to the army than elsewhere. However, in the middle of 1941 I was told that my work among students was a matter of priority, and that if the situation demanded it I would be considered in 1942.

The next year was inevitably burdened with the difficulties of travelling between my five university centres and the absence of a local back-up ministry in the parishes concerned. And so many of the young people in my care were burdened with the anxieties of the call-up and the unprecedented situations that they faced. Eventually, in the spring of 1942, things changed. I was officially notified by the War Office that I should report for interview with the prospect of joining the Royal Army Chaplains Department in September. It was not easy to leave the universities of Birmingham, Nottingham, Loughborough and Leicester, not to mention parting company with Billy Greer, who had advised and sustained me over the first years of ministry. Of course there was no one to replace me in the work that I had been able to do, and so I left the sustaining and secure partnership of the university world with a real sense of sadness.

Nor by that stage did I have only myself to consider. Through Edward Cadbury I had come to hear about Park Hall, the home of his sister and brother-in-law Kenneth and Isobel Wilson. It was more directly due to Christopher Wharton, who had been up at Trinity with me and now was a house surgeon at the Queen Elizabeth Hospital, that I paid my first visit there. He had been a close friend of the Wilson family over the years and suggested that I should go to Park Hall with him to meet them. Kenneth Wilson's family, strongly

Quaker in tradition, had come from Kendal, his mother being a
Pease from Darlington. He had inherited both the family home near
Kidderminster and the management of Albright and Wilson, the
growing chemical works at Oldbury. Isobel his wife, sister of Edward
Cadbury who had given me much help, was the oldest daughter of
the great George Cadbury, head of the long line of Quakers in
Birmingham. It was he who had moved the chocolate factory out of
the city to Bournville and it was due to him that the garden village,
the social centre, adult schools and day continuation courses for
the workers were established. All this, together with the founding of
the Selly Oak Colleges, had played a large part in the childhood and
upbringing of Isobel and the family of eleven sons and daughters.

It was with a knowledge of their background that I was taken to
Park Hall to meet Kenneth and Isobel and their family one afternoon
early in 1941. There I found the four Wilson sisters coming in from
hunting. I got to know Henrietta quite quickly and appreciated her
strong Quaker inheritance and many interests that coincided with my
own. Although she had little working knowledge of the Church of
England, and of course had been neither baptized nor confirmed,
with my ancestry so closely allied to hers in conviction we soon found
that there was little trouble in our relating our traditions in Christian
service. Any differences certainly did not prevent us from falling in
love. I could not have hoped for a better wife. Strange though it may
seem, after meeting Clemence Barclay Father entered afresh into a
Quaker tradition and was privileged to share its resources. Henrietta
with her Wilson and Cadbury background did much the same for
me. We took any opportunity to meet that was allowed by her nursing
shifts at what was then a military hospital in Bromsgrove, and by my
work in the universities. Increasingly we enjoyed not only each other's
company but also our interests and our respective families.

Park Hall, a Georgian house of beautiful proportions, soon became
a second home for me, and I was able to get out there increasingly
frequently. Kenneth Wilson, Henrietta's father, rapidly became a
close friend and adviser and remained so till he died. As a man of
wide responsibilities, a magistrate, a borough and county councillor
and head of an enormous manufacturing company, he exercised a
considerable influence over my thinking at the time. My future
mother-in-law was kindness itself to me, but took longer to accept the
idea of an Anglican priest in the family. As the situation became clear,
they were both an unfailing help. An added bonus was the welcome

given to my parents at Park Hall; they too came to love Henrietta and her family as I did. However, the war did not encourage being in love or hopes for the future. There was a sense of unease in the air, as things were going badly for the allies; moreover there was uncertainty as to where I would be serving, or where I would be required to go if I became a chaplain. Nevertheless we became engaged over Whitsun 1942 and were married in August when my SCM appointment was at an end.

We were married in Churchill Church, the parish church of Henrietta's home and estate. The wedding was conducted by Father, Bishop Neville Talbot and Wilson Cash, my old friend from CMS days who by that time had become Bishop of Worcester. There was barely room for three tall bishops in the tiny sanctuary, and hardly a seat in the small village church for all the many cousins and friends from both our large families. Although the war was so depressing, we had a great party and were made very happy by our families on that day. Since there was no petrol to be had, we made our way by train to Inverness and and enjoyed a brief honeymoon by the side of Loch Ness. It passed all too soon, and we returned together, for me to get fitted out for the army and for Henrietta to return temporarily to her nursing. We had already been together long enough for all decisions to be taken together. From then on, 'we' replaces 'I' and my story becomes our story.

◁ *Wedding day at Churchill Church, August 1942*

=== [4] ===

With the Eighth Army in Italy

For hundreds of those who were married in the middle of the war almost immediate separation was inevitable. Henrietta and I were more fortunate. The Royal Army Chaplain's Department required a month's training under their guidance at what was then the Teachers Training College at Chester. Square bashing was so minimal as to be a joke, and the remaining rather drawn-out periods were directed towards the acquisition of such elementary military knowledge as map reading. The way in which the requirements of a soldier's religion were presented tended to make me thoroughly impatient with the church in my new environment.

However, training was soon over. To my surprise I was posted to the large Royal Signals Training Centre at Prestatyn in North Wales, where I found some three thousand troops housed in a holiday village of chalets by the sea, being systematically taken through crash courses in radio, line telegraph, despatch riding and all the other forms of communication required by a modern army. It was a well-managed unit and they welcomed the services of a padre. There was clearly an enormous amount to be done, not only in providing good Sunday worship – for church parade was still the rule – but in helping hundreds of young men and women to come to terms with their first separation from home and loved ones, and the discipline required of any community life.

The CO, Brigadier Hitchins, was a very traditional senior officer, always to be found in breeches, immaculately polished Sam Browne, and top boots. He was in very distinct contrast to the more dishevelled appearance of the well-educated and often radical recruits who tended to be drafted into a technical corps.

To have been an SCM Secretary was no bad introduction to an attachment to such a branch of the army. However, there was a great difference between the two spheres. The biggest change was the move from the inevitably adolescent atmosphere of the student world into the hard and adult world of the war itself. However, there were compensations in finding oneself immediately committed as a minister to those who needed the gospel and were glad to receive the assurances of the faith. For me, as for hundreds of other clergy, the army was to prove a sphere where we learned our real job. Here were the people the church was looking for and willing to serve, and whom the Lord came to recover and set on a new way. Could we offer a religion that was sensible and related to their need? As I re-read the sermons and booklets prepared by Father for the cadets in the First World War, I realized at once what a distance we had travelled in outlook from those times.

Of course there were similarities, but the ministry in the Second World War had to take account of new attitudes. The social and religious revolution that had conspicuously started in the trenches of the First War was still in progress. No longer could men be seen as 'Knights in Armour', as Father had once named them. My parish of signallers, both officers and men, was a thinking group of people. Of course they were as anxious about their personal future as the rest of us, but they were also critical of the politicians and those who had mismanaged Europe between the wars. In addition, the years of appeasement, followed by the phoney war of 1940 and then the set-backs in Europe, in North Africa, in Singapore and the Pacific made participation in any sphere a depressing prospect. Battles had taken place and we had lost them; wounded were being brought home, and indeed we were in earnest, preparing for a long and frightening war. Frank was one of those who had returned across the beaches and with the help of small craft from France, with the remains of his Field Regiment of the Royal Artillery. He was able to pass on not only advice but something of the despair of the war in Europe.

Soon after settling in at Prestatyn I was lucky enough to find part of a furnished house on the hill looking down on the holiday camp. Henrietta was then able to join me and we made the best of it. It was a difficult old house with an oil stove for a cooker and a coal fire in the living room, but it was somewhere where we could not only live together but also have friends and visitors. Before too long we moved down into a house by the sea much nearer the camp, and it was there that we made our first real home. Here was a place where our parish of troops could come and find us. It was from that house just under the shingle bank at the back gate of the 'Holiday Village by the Sea' that for most of 1942 I became increasingly involved with my own and other units dotted about Snowdonia.

In the camp Tommy Tomlinson, a keen young teacher, became my chapel steward/churchwarden. With the encouragement of the CO we set about forming a choir, developing study groups and preparing good voluntary services. He, like many others whom I was to meet later, brought to church life the layman's approach of which the civilian parishes were so desperately starved. Before long the hut which served as our chapel had proved too small for all the activities which were now going on. Some thirty years later, I found Tommy at Droitwich in my diocese as lay vice-chairman of his deanery synod.

However, what was most needed at Prestatyn, as overseas, was the personal and pastoral care of men and families, and here having a house of our own was invaluable. It is impossible to over-emphasize the advantage of it. Henrietta turned what were very poorly furnished lodgings into a real welcoming home in which we were able to entertain and share our amenities.

Looking further afield than my own unit, I joined two or three other chaplains in making a plan for our large training area. However, progress proved very difficult, as throughout the ministry there were priests who showed little adaptability in spite of the enormous opportunities. I seemed to have been spoiled by my membership of the SCM staff with its strong leadership and powers of sustained teaching. However, we were able to develop well-planned 'Padre's Hours'. We shared in voluntary adult education programmes and through them introduced the religious and moral aspects of the war to the men. But not all my time during that year was spent at Prestatyn. I went on officers' and NCOs' courses of various kinds, including a despatch riders' course that required me to drive a 350cc Matchless over the foothills of Snowdon and through the rivers on its slopes. In a way it was all too pleasurable, but as the newness wore off and I came to compare notes with others, I felt that I was in a backwater and out of the wider context of the developing war.

Since Lichfield was within reach, Father and I were able to keep in touch and compare notes on our respective ministries. After about a year, and towards the end of this posting, Rachel, our first child, was born, and like all soldiers in similar circumstances I was given compassionate leave to spend a few days with Henrietta and her at Park Hall.

The North African campaign and the war in the Far East were bearing the brunt of the fighting and consuming our war effort. Not unnaturally those at home were eager to join the forces overseas. Frank and his gunners, having recovered from Dunkirk, were already in Egypt, and most of my friends were in fighting divisions. I constantly wondered whether I was going to miss out altogether. However, I need not have worried. Over Christmas 1943 the training centre was ordered to move to Catterick and I was instructed that my next posting would be elsewhere. Sure enough in January I was given embarkation leave; we cleared up our first home, to which we had owed so much, and Henrietta returned to her parents with the baby.

The drabness of the troop train pulling out of Marylebone station in the gloom of the blackout and the total uncertainty in our minds about our destination left those of us in the train somewhat deflated. However, our feelings were nothing compared with the agony experienced by wives left behind on the platform. Like so many others, not only was Henrietta dreadfully alone, but left totally in the dark in all senses of the word. At least I was sharing a common experience with all the others on the train on that day, confronted with the unknown destiny of an overseas posting.

The train wound its way first to Bedford, and then to Sheffield, where we waited interminably. On we went to Manchester and then, rather to our surprise, fetched up on the dockside at Liverpool: the betting had been that we would go to Glasgow. We boarded the troopship in even greater ignorance of our destination, with forecasts ranging anywhere between South Africa for training and the Middle East, but with the strongest bet on Burma.

We set sail, and late that afternoon found ourselves off the coast of Northern Ireland awaiting the formation of our convoy. Against the setting sun and then in the evening light ships appeared and one by one took up their stations. By the next morning we were still anchored, but the whole array of twenty ships was in formation, a most magnificent and somehow deeply moving sight.

How often had I spoken on Abraham's obedience and his willingness to consent to travel on, not know where he was going! Now here we were, doing precisely that – though I am not sure how willing most of us were. Whether we were also to be involved in the sacrificial

[57]

side of the Abraham saga was also a thought that was very much in my mind. Certainly during the voyage I had opportunities to talk to both officers and men about the true meaning of sacrifice, the promises of faith and the Christian expectations for society and the nations who were at war. The chaplains were allocated a corner of the ship as a meeting point. Three of us, of different denominations, would meet each morning for prayer and discussion, and on the Sunday there was a communion service in the lounge. We all had a love-hate relationship to that journey. There was something in us that wanted to go, but we were unsure, and some of us had very conflicting feelings. There was nothing like the uncertainty of wartime postings, I remember thinking, to bring relevance to biblical religion.

After travelling west and zig-zagging in mid-Atlantic for a whole week, we arrived unexpectedly in sight of Gibraltar and proceeded on through the Straits. The whole ship's company was much relieved, and evening entertainment took on a new joviality: Burma wasn't on. It was clear that we would be obliged to stop somewhere in the Mediterranean, as the Canal was blocked. In the event we docked two days later in Algiers.

The easy relationships and fairly happy community that had come into being on board ship were soon lost when we all found ourselves dispersed into the labyrinth of British and US army, air force and naval transit camps which were sprawling along the coast east of Algiers. Several hundred thousand men were in process of being identified, classified and allocated to the units that already had a million or more troops in southern Italy. The scale of the war effort was both impressive and daunting.

In Italy our armies were commanded by Field Marshal Alexander. General Montgomery had gone home to prepare for the Second Front, leaving nearly a million British and nearly as many Americans to 'sort out' Italy and southern Europe. We were a substantial force of three army corps, each with two or three fighting divisions consisting of about 20,000 men each. The average division had three brigades, each consisting of infantry, artillery, signals, medical and ancillary regiments or companies, and these divisions not only became real communities but had their own traditions, lists of honours won, and a sense of membership that was greatly valued. After spending nearly a week in a camp with a lovely bathing beach, my name came up and I discovered where I was to be posted. I was ordered to join the Fifth Indian Infantry Brigade, part of the Fourth Indian Division of the

Eighth Army, commanded by Gertie Tooker, a much respected general. This notice reduced me to silence. The few other chaplains were all allocated to field hospitals, base camps and LOCs (lines of communication). Would I not have been better off well behind the lines!?

Little did I realize at this juncture the advantage and indeed the privilege of being attached to a fighting unit with a great name, and sharing the inheritance of the Indian Army. At that stage I could find out practically nothing about my future colleagues, and was given no time to try and do so. However, transport was available, and I was to board the troopship *Derbyshire* the next day and proceed from Algiers to Naples, from where I would report to the transit camp at Caserta. The morning before we reached Italy I held a service. Again I was among men suffering from anxiety. I at least could formulate my thoughts and live with them, but there were others who needed to have their thoughts articulated for them. I tried to do this, conscious of the depth of responsibility any chaplain had. After all, he was the only one involved directly in terms of human feelings and relationships.

By then it was March. In the event I had to spend some time waiting in the transit camp at the rear HQ of the Eighth Army at Caserta. The battle for crossing the Garigliano was on. A severe set-back at Monte Cassino had thrown out the Allied plans: the weather had proved unexpectedly wet and cold, and if both the First and the Eighth Army were not exactly in confusion, they were certainly in process of realignment. So for nearly two weeks we waited, since movement up to the line was very limited.

However, the delay gave me some time to meet those who were to be in my division and brigade. As I did so, I discovered a good deal from the British element in the Indian army about our role in the battle. I was taken to our HQ on the very night of the final assault on Monte Cassino, when our division, together with General Freyberg's New Zealand Corps, was thrown against the treacherous hillside in an assault in which the monastery was finally destroyed and captured, with very severe loss of life. My immediate introduction to the Italian campaign proved to coincide with the tragic destruction of one of the historic Christian centres of Europe. Once the objective of Monte Cassino had been captured, the US army was left in the Front Line and we were ordered to retire to a rest area many miles to the south, near Benevento. It was during that journey, with hundreds of vehicles on a road already crowded with civilian refugees, that I found the Brigade HQ to which I was officially attached and the First/Fourth Essex Regiment with whom I was to live and work.

The Fourth Indian had been a well known and respected regular division of the Indian army for many years. By the time I joined it, it had distinguished itself in North Africa, particularly at Tobruk and in Tunisia. Within it were three brigades, each containing two Indian or Ghurka battalions and one British battalion, an artillery regiment, anti-aircraft units and all the necessary servicing and medical arrangements. The Fifth Indian Brigade was to be my 'parish'; I soon learned that it was the senior brigade of the whole Indian Army. It consisted of the First/Fourth Essex Regiment, the First Field Regiment, Royal Artillery, and various signals, anti-aircraft and medical units, together with the British staff at Brigade headquarters. All the officers in the Indian Infantry Battalions, Gurkhas and Baluchistan Rifles were British – many of them very fine and dedicated Christian men. To keep in touch with them in their isolated non-Christian communities was a real responsibility.

We were some three thousand British and four thousand Indians in the brigade, and there were three brigades in our division: no small force when armoured and heavy artillery units were added. After a very fine and long record in North Africa, the division was held in high esteem in the army, and indeed they proved a remarkable body of men with whom to spend the remainder of the Italian campaign. Gertie Tooker, the general, was invalided during the Cassino battle and I only came to know him in later years. He proved to be only one of many victims of months of strain.

We reached our rest area at Benevento on Palm Sunday, late in the evening, in the cold and wet. There was no possibility of any worship, though I was deeply aware that it was Holy Week. My experience and training thus far in the ministry had shown me that this week was an essential time for renewal and enrichment of faith. Though I could make time to think and pray, only a handful of men were aware of the meaning of those special days in the Christian year, especially as after only twenty-four hours we had been warned to be ready to move back into the line at the end of the week – this time on the east coast in the area of the river Sangro.

On Good Friday we were packing up, and Easter Day found the division on the road again in convoy, moving to our new battle area.

To make anything at all of Easter for those who wanted an act of worship, I combined the Good Friday and Easter themes in a few small gatherings for communion – they made a quick way into providing a meaningful religious life for the unit. On Easter Eve I took a special evening service for a sad group of deserters, forty or fifty in number, who were being held pending court martial – a constant problem for every unit. Anxieties over marriage or family had broken their will to continue after three or even four years of separation.

It was not for another week, when we settled in our new positions as a fighting force, that we celebrated Easter properly. Although the men were scattered in small groups, they fully expected that Easter should be marked in some way. By the time I had conducted seven short but happy services on the Sunday after the festival in various areas of the line, chiefly amongst the companies of the First/Fourth, I had made a new beginning with my parish. It was strung out in farmhouses and scattered hamlets in typical and very lovely Italian countryside. The countryfolk, the *contadini*, were glad enough to have us, but all too aware that they were squeezed between us on one side and German and Italian units on the other.

My battalion commander was Tony Noble. Not only was he a splendid support in all my duties, but he also became a friend and adviser. Once again, I was to have it brought home to me how the parochial ministry so often failed because the clergy did not acknowledge or accept advice that could be given about the priorities of ministry by a dedicated layman. Sadly he was wounded and left us all too soon.

The company commanders and those at Brigade HQ could not have been more helpful to a chaplain arriving as green as I was. For many months we were committed to a rather grinding campaign, exercising pressure on enemy positions. With the officers and senior NCOs I was involved in the unending but important task of coping with the pastoral needs of the men. I set up a close and invaluable partnership with our regimental doctor, Roy Pellow, when we were in action. Every day I would make the Regimental Aid Post my base, and be as available as he was. Every evening we would be told of the company or platoon that had been selected for patrols that would be testing the enemy positions. Often we would wait all night for the men to return. Usually they did, but it was rarely without casualties. Many a time we were heavily pressed in the RAP with the wounded and the dying. For me it was a matter for real thankfulness that the doctor and some of the medical orderlies were believing Christians. As the wounded were brought in they would always fetch me across the makeshift surgery when a soldier was beyond their powers to save: I would hear the words, 'Over to you, Padre.' Much morphia would have been given, but the man was usually aware of the end of his road. It was a privileged, but also unnerving task to help one who was dying with assurances for himself and, more importantly, with assurances about his wife and family. Sadly, the latter were to prove somewhat hollow: the long-term continued care of war-widows by the nation was all too inadequate.

I soon got to know my units. I kept careful lists of men separated off or on dangerous forward observation posts. Like other chaplains, I found myself responsible for burials, and with that task went the care of the few possessions of those who had been killed and the task of writing letters to their families. On a Wednesday towards the end of April the weather had improved and the prospect was encouraging, when the whole of C Company HQ was blown up by a booby trap left in the farmhouse into which they were moving. The notebook which I kept records that twenty-four men were killed – only two were recovered alive, and they died very soon afterwards. I played my part in sorting out the rubble and digging temporary graves, as I had done on other occasions, before sending off the inevitable letters. Among those killed that day was Stuart Mallinson, the company commander, a splendid officer in every way. Nearly two years later I was able to visit his parents in Woodford Green, to leave with them some impression of what he had done for the cause and of the love and respect in which he was held by his men.

Four months of slogging line warfare took us up fom the Arno to the coastal area of Forte Caldaria and San Polo. After the severe strain on the division in North Africa and around Monte Cassino this proved comparatively quiet but none the less demanding, with constant changes of personnel and a regular stream of casualties on the one hand and soldiers going sick or getting into trouble on the other. In these circumstances I made lasting friendships, and gradually a community of committed Christians emerged. Differences of denomination or church allegiance were totally ignored. The CO, Major Beckett, 'Doc' Pellow and several NCOs were with me in Christian hope and trying to discern the will of God for ourselves and the cause in hand. Near Monte San Sepulchro we ran into heavy enemy opposition. For some weeks in the face of a crack German division we sustained losses and made only minor advances. Morale was low, and made much worse by one of the very rare occasions when the RAF misjudged their target. They dropped a string of bombs marginally short of the enemy lines and too close to our patrols: we lost several soldiers. I remember a company signalman, Billy Bristow, dying as I tried to sustain him – typical of so many casualties that meant sadness and bereavement at home.

I did feel that it was within my calling as chaplain to find the very rewarding groups of men, perhaps at a Company HQ, in a well-led platoon, isolated on an Ack-Ack gunsite or in the rear echelons, where questions were being asked about what the war was all about and what we would make of the peace when it came. It was in small and regular contacts with such men that I tried to confirm the credibility of the Christian position. There were still minefields of misunderstanding to be lifted – largely relating to the church. There were complaints about the Archbishop of Canterbury being paid £15,000 a year, the vicar at home who would not help, the Bible thumper who inoculated people against true religion. These were typical of the obstacles to religious progress: Woodbine Willie had found the same thing in the First World War. When William Temple died in the autumn of 1944 there was an extraordinary sense of loss among hundreds of non-churchgoers. He had related the faith to personal and social needs and they knew it. And of course he had taught our generation that the church must never claim too much for itself; rather, we must be humble and rebuild from the expectations and experiences of a nation at war.

The loss of the Archbishop at that stage was as difficult for me to accept as being within the providence of God as Theodore's death had been, but we lived and worked on in the spirit that he had established. In this situation the chaplain alone in his unit was free in a unique way to be identified with individuals, irrespective of rank, and to help them articulate their hopes and fears. In long periods of inactivity when many became bored and depressed, this part of the job was vital.

When the division moved back into the central areas of Italy for reforming and re-equipping, we found ourselves near Lake Trasimeno. It was all superb countryside and the added interests and attractions of Tuscany and Umbria were most welcome: Assisi, Perugia, Arezzo, Monteverde, Siena and finally Florence were all on our slow and sometimes painful push forward. However, the morale of the army generally was very poor, and the beauty or culture of our new neighbourhood did not help there. Many soldiers had already been away from home for three or four years. They called themselves the forgotten army since General Montgomery went home to command the Second Front. Our Corps Commander, General Dick McCreery, did, however, come to spend a day with us and introduce us to the new situation. It made a momentary difference to meet someone so senior, and he did outline a future and help us to absorb new senior officers and new units in our enlarged division, including a Guards battalion. Fortunately the mountainous country did not present too many difficulties and quite soon Florence was in our hands. But as the winter drew on again we made only slow headway through the approaches to what was to be the final stand of the enemy on the River Po. Those were indeed tedious months for the men.

I was fortunate enough to have had a break from the regiment and indeed the brigade for some two weeks in July. The YMCA, working voluntarily behind the lines, had long been pressing for an episcopal visit, and in the event Father was the bishop who came. His coming was very opportune – there had been no episcopal care of the clergy for years. There had been no confirmations of men who had found their faith, and although our senior chaplains had done their best to help the regimental padres, their spiritual resources were at a very low ebb. The chaplains, in particular, had been isolated from the professional structure of the church, and it had rarely been possible to provide occasions for renewal or retreats where they could recharge their batteries. Officers and NCOs went off on courses, but there was little for chaplains except reliance on our own resourcefulness.

Father arrived by plane at Naples at the end of June and was met by the army commanders and the Chaplain General. Among those who could not be present to meet him was General Templer. We heard in due course of his somewhat bizarre plight: he had been hit on the back by a falling grand piano when the truck in front of his staff car had been blown up by a mine. The chance encounter when Father and I went to visit him in hospital led to friendship and shared concern which lasted until his death in 1984. The way he told the story, he had been hit not only by a grand piano but also by a bucket full of ice and bottles of champagne – 'all part,' he added, 'of the Grenadiers' normal equipment.' He was lucky to live to make a joke of it. Father ministered to him with prayer and laying on of hands – an immediate source of healing strength to which he testified long afterwards.

After several days around the base area holding conferences with chaplains, conducting quiet days, and taking large confirmation services, some of which had more than 250 troops as candidates, he went up to the front line. I went with him. On our way to the units he gave a number of open-air addresses. Meeting him in this context was a real joy. For years we had thought alike and worked together, and now there was the added pleasure of sharing to some measure in an opportunity to minister to a scattered congregation of nearly a million soldiers. We soon agreed how he should go about things, and the essential themes of his mission, and planned the best use of his time. The chaplains were clearly most appreciative of all his work, both public and private. Whenever he spoke he interpreted the faith within the present siutation or gave a picture of hopes and plans for better years ahead at home. There is no denying that he was superbly equipped for such a mission.

It was notable how welcome he was at the highest levels. He visited several divisional HQs and was always warmly received by the GOC. He had sufficient confidence to offer real personal help and encouragement to those in command. Field Marshal Alexander, Generals McCreery, Robertson and Whitfield were embarrassing in their appreciation. It was not that the generals and senior officers happened to be Christian; rather, they had clearly reached their important posts of leadership because of their Christian understanding of human nature and their personal commitment to God, his providence and his power. These qualities at the level of our commanders, though not necessarily explicit, helped to establish a confidence in them.

Returning from the forward areas around Florence, through Perugia, Assisi and Foligno, we reached Rome, where Father had a good talk with the Pope, leaving him fully aware of the contribution of the Church of England and the Protestant churches in the world-wide scene. Pressing on south, and pausing to look at the ruins of Monte Cassino, we stopped at Pozzuoli, in order to be able to stand on the site where St Paul landed in the first century – another moving moment. Then we were back in Naples. By invitation of the Military Command we were flown to Sicily for a few days rest and leave at Taormina. To find ourselves in one of Europe's most famous beauty spots was an unexpected pleasure. We talked, planned and prayed together. In particular we were able to compare the developing experience of the four of us in the ministry during these war years. As a diocesan bishop Father was clearly very pressed to maintain the hundreds of parishes in his care as well as to support his people over years of frustration; he would have much to tell the folk at home after visiting the troops in the Mediterranean theatre. Frank in the meantime had been appointed, after his return through Dunkirk and a short spell in Egypt, Commandant of the Chaplains' Training Centre at Tidworth, where he was well able to use his experience and abilities as a teacher. Sam was confined to New Zealand as a chaplain in the New Zealand Air Force. He was focussing his ministry in the training centres, and seeking to enable men to leave for service on the other side of the world was proving to be fulfilling, particularly since his marriage to Sybil Williams. I shared Father's hopes for the church and the supply of right-minded men for the ministry once the war was over. I was beginning to think about planning refresher courses for chaplains, and he helped me over that. Together we talked a great deal about the church at home and ministry to the men in Europe. Staying in a monastery which had been turned into a comfortable hotel, we spent three days on the slopes of Mount Etna, walking in the olive groves and bathing in the clear warm sea, both of us drawing and doing water-colours as we felt inclined. Then, all too soon, we had to part.

I returned to the division, but my time with it proved to be short. To my surprise, the adjutant of the First/Fourth Essex, John Kenrick, with whom I was to keep in contact over the years, sent for me. An order had come through requiring me to report to the Assistant Chaplain-General, Rear Army HQ, for consultation. With the help of my orderly I managed to get to Florence by jeep; there I met Francis Browne, a Sussex county cricketer and headmaster of St Andrews, Eastbourne, who at that time was senior chaplain to 56 London Division. He had received the same order. Together we found the Assistant Chaplain-General, Tim Hurley. Without delay he took us to General Sir Brian Robertson, Chief of Staff to Field Marshal Alexander, who told us what our visit was all about. Plans had to be made for the future. The Second Front was in full swing, and if we maintained our present rate of progress, the war would be over in nine months. After that there would be more then two million British servicemen and women in Western Europe. 'They can't be left standing around,' General Robertson said; 'they ought to be guided in their adjustment to peacetime occupations and to a sense of social responsibility in their future duties.' So would we please prepare to leave our divisions and accept the duty of establishing a 'moral leadership school' for the army in its present function, and in anticipation of its occupation of both Italy and Austria.

Robertson's timing, his powers of anticipation and his appreciation of the role of the church as we moved towards the peace were remarkable. He clearly saw how the war might be won through fighting but lost in occupation, unless the forces were ready for a quick change of role. He also stressed that the whole exercise was a priority for the chaplains. The interview was a memorable occasion; after it we even had a brief word with Field Marshal Alexander, who endorsed the scheme, again showing full awareness of the moral and social consequences of the impending victory.

We returned to find Tim Hurley ready to work at the logistics and requirements of a Chaplains' Centre and a Moral Leadership School for the Central Mediterranean forces and set to work to promote a new military unit. I could not have been more pleased; all this went far beyond my own modest plans and was still very much along the lines I had been hoping for.

We were allowed to choose the first centre and indicate what staff we would need for it. We chose Assisi, which seemed well fitted for the project, not only because of its remarkable atmosphere and associations with St Francis, but also because geographically it was very central. And so began the Moral Leadership Schools and Chaplains' Centres which were to take shape not only there but in Trieste, Hamburg, Jerusalem and eventually at Bagshot. These centres were as much the conception of the lay Christians as the clergy who would run them, a process which has been called for more and more in the life of the church. My respect for Brian Robertson has never wavered. He helped personally in the work, showing enormous insight into the needs of the community, which he maintained later as the first head of the Control Commission in Europe, as chairman of British Rail, and as an active peer of the realm.

The advance through northern Italy ran into difficulties over the next few months, so both Francis Browne and I returned to our units for some weeks that summer of 1944. Francis, in particular, felt that he should not leave his division for the moment, but I was asked to spend a month in Rome conducting experimental courses for chaplains. I found the seminary of the Waldensian Protestant Church in Piazza Cavour standing virtually empty, with only a number of elderly refugee pastors occupying the suitably small college and existing on very meagre rations. The army immediately took over the building and its occupants for a month, to their delight using the latter as civilian staff. It was there that we gathered four groups of some fifteen chaplains of all denominations, except the Roman Catholics, and through improvisation and self-help quickly devised a timetable of worship, Bible study, lectures and discussions on topics of need. The place also became a tourist centre since most of the chaplains not unnaturally wanted to see the Forum, places associated with early Christianity like the Catacombs and St Peter's, and the other sights. I found it a time to sit back and assess the needs of the chaplains and the impact of the church on the men. It is so seldom that clergy actually withdraw enough to consider the next objective in a parish or in a particular sphere of people's need. Here was a chance to do just that in four concentrated weeks of meeting chaplains and benefiting from their very varied experience of the years of war.

For me too, it was another place to bring home the New Testament: the scene of Paul's arrival, mission and imprisonment and the actual environment of the early Christians made the whole New Testament that much more intelligible.

Since I was temporarily answerable to the Town Major of the city, I went with the heads of the services to visit the Pope. He was very appreciative of the Anglican ministry but was momentarily taken aback by Peter Priest, the chaplain óf the Rome garrison. Peter introduced himself to His Holiness as the Vicar of Rome. 'Indeed,' said the Pope. 'I am the Vicar of Christ.'

Sunday 23 September 1944 was declared a national day of prayer. The situation was indeed critical, with the situation in Burma desperate and the Second Front at that time approaching Germany. Nor had we in Italy made the headway on which we had counted. I arrived back at my regiment for the day to meet with a warm welcome, but also a good deal of laughter and comment at my month in the fleshpots of Rome. Eventually we did move northwards into the final range of mountains north of Florence. The pincer tactics of pressing forward simultaneously on both east and west coasts forced the enemy to fall back on the centre. Over some two months, during which our brigade was strengthened by the Kings Dragoon Guards, we slogged away with our patrols pressing slowly up to Sarsina and Mercato on the watershed of the Appennines. At this stage there was increasing opportunity to establish creative 'Padre's Hours' with the troops largely on a voluntary basis. Here again I was to experience valuable help from the professional soldiers. Dennis Beckett, a company commander who was later to become a general, helped me with them. The men would in fact ask for him rather than for me in this context – a sobering reminder of the importance of lay ministry.

However, there was still the business of the leadership centres and chaplains' courses to get on with, and for that I would have to break with the division. I left the brigade and the Essex Regiment with real regret; the whole division had derived a reputation for fulfilling orders in battle throughout the long campaigns in North Africa and Italy: they were a splendid body of men. They had lost many of their number, wounded or killed. After a further week of consultation at Army HQ and the selection of our staff, it was time to say goodbye, with farewell services and amusing parties. By then it was mid-November and we could see over the hills: the plain of the Po was being cleared, Ravenna was within reach, and with luck the units that had been through so much since the early days in North Africa would not be severely punished again.

Throughout those last weeks with the division, in and out of the line and with preparatory visits to Assisi, my mind was on preparations for the course for chaplains, officers and men, and on finding qualified teaching colleagues as staff members and NCOs for administration. Francis Browne, who was to be the first commandant of the inaugural centre, and I, worked in the closest collaboration. He was a splendid schoolmaster, a first-class soldier and a very good priest. I left the line on 12 November and we received the first intake of chaplains on 7 December. By then we had brought in Willy Neil of the Church of Scotland, a teacher with real imagination, and later to become a well-known author and editor of a very widely read one-volume commentary on the Bible; also Bill Leader and Chris Jarvis, both of whom could relate to people. Captain Fred Graham became our administrative officer, to be followed later by Mike Fidgin (both were later ordained into the Anglican ministry); one corporal and five soldiers were posted as our staff. We had taken care in selecting people, but it was amazing how quickly we became a team that worked fast and effectively together.

For other staff we employed Italians, and we made use of local hotels for accommodation. Then, as always, Assisi was full of monks and nuns who were particularly pleased to be taken on to the military strength at a time when there was an acute shortage of food – a recurring theme. We were soon able to take good mixed groups of officers and men, first of all in the Minerva and then in the larger Albergo Subasio. Since we were next door to the great basilica and monastery of St Francis and were helped by the remarkable atmosphere of Assisi, we soon profited from the spirit of the place and were better able to introduce men from all walks of life to a fresh appreciation of the situation, a more objective view of society and an understanding of the role of the churches and their members in the pattern of life that we expected once hostilities ceased.

The variety of my experience – the years of university work with SCM, the lessons learned from the Signals Training Centre and the months of being with a regiment in the line – proved to be invaluable. Francis Browne and I shared the teaching and group discussions between us according to our interests and abilities; Chris Jarvis became our PR man and was in charge of cultural outings. The men came in groups of about twenty at a time over a two-week period. It was a useful exercise to have to reduce to military-type notes what it meant to be a Christian. We did in fact equip those who took part in our courses with short summaries covering the purpose of the Bible, the implications of the Gospel story, the passion and resurrection of Christ, and the meaning of Pentecost, for ordinary people. We were also bold enough to issue short guides to marriage, family life and the approach to work as seen by a Christian. To be able to prepare and issue such leaflets with no library and no outside help demonstrated the latent ability of chaplains in the three services at the time.

We were visited by generals, admirals, commanding officers – everyone who wanted to find out what the padres were up to. The Chaplains Department, the Educational Corps and units located in the vicinity gave us unconditional support and the supplies we needed. We were in business as a chaplaincy service, providing residential courses for officers and men with a new objective. We also became an agency and sorting house for those who wanted advice about entering the church's ministry at home, and thus became a kind of pre-selection centre. We also found ourselves taking in chaplains whose nerve had broken, and who had been mentally overwhelmed by the situation in which they served. A psychiatric centre actually settled down next door to us; perhaps we needed it as well.

By mid-summer, when some two hundred men had already been through the school, peace came at last. Our role was then even more urgent, and the pressure from units to send men to us rapidly

Assisi April 1945

increased. At that time I had some leave in Venice, where I met a number of COs and others who were well informed about where our forces would be deployed in the future. Troops were clearly concentrating in northern Italy and Austria, and Assisi was already proving to be too far away. The Chaplain's Department and Army HQ lost no time and I was instructed to close down our centre at Assisi and find a suitable location for a larger school in the region of Trieste. At the same time I was appointed Deputy Assistant Chaplain-General and Commandant of the centre. A peacetime civilian and temporary soldier, I felt very strange wearing the rank of a Lieutenant Colonel. We found a seaside resort, Lignano, midway between Venice and Trieste, where we commandeered a large hotel which became the Central Mediterranean Army Leadership School. Once again we were in business.

The feel of the resort in the north of Italy, the possibility of home leave, and the general buoyancy of the army, which was now in occupation, made the atmosphere very different from that which we had experienced in Assisi. We all missed St Francis quite dreadfully, and I missed Francis Browne. For just on a year we ran ten-day courses, with only forty-eight hour breaks between them. There were four of us chaplains, and with the help of regimental officers and NCOs stationed in the area we trained up the lay staff of the leadership school. A variety of demands soon led us to prepare special courses for those who were to remain in the regular army; for those young enough to be new to military service; for those who wanted guidance on careers after demobilization – and short two-day gatherings for senior officers of all three services who wanted some detailed information in order to be better able to send the right people. Again it is important to stress that centres and courses like ours were possible only because the lay military commanders were aware of the situation, adaptable and ready to improvise in the face of need – and they had a basically Christian conviction about the future.

Wherever they developed, the Chaplains' Centres set a new standard in teaching and consultation with the laity of the church. They established a mutual understanding between the denominations when old rivalries all too frequently seemed to prevail. The foundations of the ecumenical movement as it came to affect ordinary clergy and the growth of lay responsibility in many a congregation were laid in those years of military occupation. This was due not just to chaplains but also to lay men and women among the leadership of the forces who were concerned that those serving under them should understand the application of the gospel and the role of the church in a rapidly changing world.

After an absence from England of almost two years, over Christmas 1945 I was granted home leave. What reuniting days they were! To be with Henrietta and see Rachel now running around, when I had left her an infant in arms, to relax at Lichfield or Park Hall, and pick up the threads of life at home, was totally renewing.

I returned to the Adriatic for a final nine months over which the centre and its courses remained busy, useful and enjoyable. But our personal future had to be decided. The authorities pressed me to stay on and become a regular chaplain, but in those two weeks over Christmas Henrietta and I had had time to decide that our abilities and convictions would be best suited to the ordinary pastoral and teaching ministry of the church in a parish, either at home or overseas. I would be sorry to leave the Royal Army Chaplains Department, but very glad to return to the more normal life of the church.

= [5] =

South Wigston

While still on the Adriatic coast I received an invitation from the Bishop of Leicester, a friend of Father, to become Vicar of South Wigston. Neither Henrietta nor I had ever heard of the place. Simultaneously Leslie Hunter, Bishop of Sheffield, whom I had known since SCM days, suggested that I should go to a heavily industrialized parish. At a distance the choice was almost a blind one, and I did not get many replies to my questions. But here was a very important decision. Would we be able to accept a parish without seeing it together? I was ready to trust Father, with Henrietta, over formalizing an appointment. After years away from either of our homes Sheffield seemed a long way off while Leicester was within easy reach and the Bishop, Guy Vernon-Smith, knew what sort of sphere I should tackle. He and Father agreed that the parish of South Wigston on the southern outskirts of Leicester provided enough people (some 8,000), some tough industrial areas including the railway workshop and the LMS housing for drivers, guards and linesmen, a sizable shoe factory, and more than sufficient church members to form the nucleus for further development. Henrietta and her mother went to look at the vicarage and cabled saying that I should turn the offer down: the house was too forbidding. However, after further enquiries and a kindly correspondence with the Bishop we independently agreed that there were compensating features, and that since I had never been a curate this was a good parish to make a start. It was a shot in the dark, but it proved right and also indicated, as I was also to find later, that other people's choices of places of work for me were based on better judgment than my own might have been.

Those of us who had a profession to which we could return after the war were the lucky ones. So many of our friends had education to complete under severe restrictions, or the difficulties of finding employment. This was not so for us: after my demobilization we immediately prepared to go to South Wigston.

The very week I returned to England our elder son Robert was born, and we were able to enjoy nearly two months leave shared between my parents at Lichfield and Henrietta's parents at Park Hall. After a happy autumn of total relaxation we were ready to collect ourselves, our family, furniture and requirements and move into our first parish and a permanent home. I was thirty-two, Henrietta twenty-nine, Rachel three and Robert eight weeks.

The house was a good solid late-Victorian building without pretensions but with plenty of space. It stood by a crossroads in South Wigston, on the edge of the city of Leicester, and was in no sense isolated. Terraced houses largely occupied by railwaymen or workers from the boot and shoe factory backed on to our garden; the WCs with clanking chains at the end of their yards formed our boundary on one side, and a pork butcher who did his pig slaughtering at eight o'clock on a Sunday morning was on the other. We soon settled down, and became closely identified with our parishioners from the moment we arrived.

Tommy Toon, a railway guard, was the vicar's warden, and Jack Goodwin, the local grocer, was his colleague. They soon took us in hand and made sure that everything would go on in the church just as it had for years previously. As my predecessor had been hard-working and well-loved in the parish, there did not in fact seem any urgent need to make immediate changes. But as in countless situations where a new vicar takes over, there was no official hand-over: no introduction to the church officers, no lists of regular communicants, and no notes about the worship or cultural activities in the area. So we started from scratch. How much the church misses by inadequate handing-over from one incumbent to another! When so much information could well be used and developed, the new vicar at that time was, as he often still is, expected to find his own way and make his own contacts. As a church, Anglicans could well take a lesson from the Methodists in this respect.

Mrs Toon, the warden's wife, was a large woman in every sense: her size was matched by her generous attitude to life, and her sheer bulk embodied a readiness to meet any need in the church. The Mothers' Union was her particular sphere, but other things centred upon her too, including the Mothers' Meeting, another group of

women who by accident or intent were not sufficiently churchy or classy to be in the Mothers' Union. Henrietta became in all probability the youngest local member of the MU, and we did our best for both organizations, on which so much else depended.

The continuity of the parish undoubtedly owed much to successive vicars, but the real work was sustained by lay men and women in the parochial organizations. The Parochial Church Council, the choir, the Sunday School teachers, the leaders of the Scouts, Guides and Cubs, were all indispensable. It was clearly vitally important for me to be able to recognize their contribution and to enable these men and women to be the outreaching arm of the church, shunning the roles of Mr Know-all Incumbent and the Jack-of-all-Trades Vicar, which were all too ready at hand as temptations to fall for.

However, thanks to South Wigston we learnt the lesson of lay leadership and lay participation in the life of the congregation twenty

The Family at Lichfield, Christmas 1946

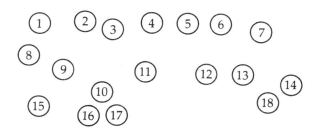

1 Reynolds Stone *m.* Janet
2 Sam
3 Sybil Woods *m.* Sam
4 'Budge' Firth *m.* Priscilla
5 Priscilla
6 George Pike *m.* Gabrielle
7 Gabrielle
8 Frank
9 Jean Woods *m.* Frank
10 Janet
11 Mother
12 Father
13 RWW
14 Henrietta
15–17 Edward, Humphrey & Phillida Stone
18 Rachel

years before its essential character and the need for it began to grip the average parish. It would have been easy to be overbearing towards the choirmaster or the Sunday School teachers, but their experience was greater than mine. I learned the lesson sufficiently early in the parish ministry not to introduce changes by my suggestion, but to enable them to be made, or seem to be made, at the suggestion of the laity.

For example, behind the altar in our crude red-brick church was a painted reredos of a garish and ill-designed scene from the gospel. When the first Lent came round, we all agreed that it might be appropriate to cover the reredos with a blue curtain. When Easter arrived and it should have been time to take it down, the laity requested that the Lenten hangings should become the norm. So by accident we had begun to beautify our church. And how it needed beautifying! Dedicated to St Thomas, the church had been built in 1890. Its structure was reminiscent of the rounded girders of large railway stations. Its red brick and careful pointing had turned dark in colour, both inside and out. The designer had had a field day in laying patterned tiles over the aisles and the choir and forming a dado on the walls. Having accidentally improved the sanctuary we soon set about other areas of the church including the formation of a useful and well-designed side chapel. Rows of chairs, seating some three hundred, were at least adaptable. The gas lighting popped and created rather a smell. The heating was just adequate because Cyril Smith, who did the stoking, knew how to treat the temperamental boiler. Just as an army moves on its stomach, Christian movement was, and still is, dependent on church heating.

Others were not as lucky as we were in that respect. One winter's morning we were visited by a pitiful delegation from the Primitive Methodists, whose boiler had burst. Although they had been officially united with the Wesleyan Methodists since 1931, they did not want to join with them, so might they come and use our accommodation? Of course, our laity were only too pleased to oblige, and my early ecumenical hopes received a momentary boost. Alas, the Primitive Methodist congregation was only a small one and the vestry was all they needed: it would be quite sufficient for them. They didn't in fact stay long, but when they went they still refused to be identified with other Methodists.

Such a building and so diverse a parish immediately began to raise all sorts of questions. What were we there for? What did God want of a congregation of believers? To be cosy and inward-looking? To be the meeting place of like-minded religious people? Or to be the body of people among whom, Sunday by Sunday, men and women might receive sufficient instruction, spiritual support and human friendship to be able to exercise Christian insight in a wider community?

The perennial worry of the parish priest is how to steer the right course between acceptance of the *status quo* and recognition of the necessity for change in order to keep up with new thinking, new ideas and new situations. Wherever we were sent, Henrietta and I found that the way forward lay in listening to lay men and women, rather than accepting ecclesiastical tradition, and thus discovering what people really hoped of their parson. In the tradition of my grandfather in Hereford and Nottingham, my father in Cambridge and Croydon, or like other members of the family, I found that our ministry had to be one which was neither moulded by tradition nor governed by partisan demands. We were meant to be ourselves – and we had very good precedents for being just that.

'We can't get them to go to church' was often the complaint of the good parish worker as he tried his hand at youth work or enlisting friends in the local factory. Going to church, filling up the pews, doing the jobs on Sunday was all too often seen as the beginnning and end of being a Christian. And this was understandable in a situation where the upkeep of the fabric and more recently to this has also been added the payment of the parish quota, was consistently the most urgent in hand. Nevertheless, it was soon apparent to the novice incumbent – for I was constantly aware that I had never been a curate – that making the Sunday services attractive in themselves and relevant to the local situation was one place to start if the church community was going to grow. It was not long before we established a Family Service rather than Mattins or a monthly Sung Eucharist, and I soon found that time was well spent in training the choir by myself and then helping the congregation to sing. How thankful I was that I could play the organ just enough to show what was wanted! Still, all that was no more than the support for preaching and teaching.

After the years spent at the Chaplains' Centre, training soldiers in faith and behaviour, I found myself planning courses of sermons and teaching evenings with real pleasure. Preaching matters in any church, but in South Wigston I was determined that it should become a real point of contact with the congregation. All too often the clergy are content for there to be no come-back from their preaching: for

there to be no reaction and no indication that the congregation has learned anything from it. No wonder the art of preaching has declined so seriously! Preaching and teaching only become central to the ministry when the preacher and perhaps selected members of the congregation not only discuss a sermon but begin to outline the themes about which the ordinary Christian wants more enlightenment. I soon found it much more profitable to preach on given subjects to which the people could respond. Now that the Alternative Service Book has provided thematic readings, collects and 'propers', Sunday by Sunday, there seems little excuse for the rather arbitrary preaching that has marked our church for years.

On one occasion at South Wigston I thought I owed the congregation a change of voice. So I asked the elderly Archdeacon of Leicester to preach at the Armistice Service. After the service he went to the back of the church to shake hands with the congregation as they went out. He was greeted with the comment that he had preached the same sermon thirty years earlier, in 1919, after the Great War. The congregation soon spots old hat!

Among my other duties was that of being chaplain to the barracks of Glen Parva, the home of the Leicestershire Regiment. There I found myself on familiar ground. With conscription still the order of the day a group of eighteen-year-olds would arrive once a month for their basic training and 'square bashing' at the barracks. The officers were certainly glad to have a chaplain, albeit very part time. Army regulations laid down that all new recruits must be met by the chaplain of their tradition – as is also stipulated for prisoners on admission to gaol. Here again the work probably did me and my approach to ministry more good than it did the men. Taking 'Padre's Hours' for them and getting to know young officers and men as they began to experience army life proved an interesting bridge between the war years and trying to enable the church to serve the next generation. To the concern of some I soon abandoned church parades, and made opportunities for informal worship and instruction. This was readily appreciated. However, my work there was restricted as the barracks were being run down. This was not only disappointing because of the contacts that I would lose but also a material consideration. When recruits were there I was paid the princely sum of £2 a week for my services: that was a real extra when my salary was £320 a year.

Other openings soon came up. I became a lecturer in history at evening classes in the local school. Such adult classes were under the

◁ *A parade passes the Church of St Thomas, South Wigston*

auspices of the Workers Educational Association. I was glad to be identified with a movement that had had so much help from William Temple in his younger days. I was hardly qualified as a result of my knowledge of history, but there was enough flexibility for me to be able to choose my subjects. So I taught the biblical era, early Christian expansion and the period of the Reformation. This meant that I had to read and prepare, which was salutary for me; the classes also gave me a wider range of local contacts. Moreover, if you enlisted more than twelve in a class, you could earn £1 for an evening's work! So it was that through my links with the barracks, my involvement in adult education, and by walking and bicycling round the parish, which in itself led to friendships, I got to know the area pretty intimately.

At the same time, on most days Henrietta pushed the pram with the children up the street of shops. By doing this, she gathered the first group of young wives in the area and they became a totally new ingredient in our congregational life. Bruce Eagle, the chemist, 'Sweety' Smith the newsagent and confectioner, Alf Rawlinson the pork butcher and Eric Holmes at the bicycle shop all had wives and families, and all began to care for the Christian way of things. Charlie Moor, who conducted the local brass band and ran a shop in which he sold all kinds of musical instruments, enlisted the young. Here were just a few of the parish who began genuinely to share the life of the church rather than being passive attenders. Not surprisingly we came to love South Wigston and to enjoy the ministry.

It would have been very easy for the parish to become totally absorbing, and in many ways this was what happened. But you could not stop there. There were further dimensions to the life of our people: their work in the hosiery factory, the boot and shoe industry, and the railway and engineering works. The church, which was seen as a club for a few like-minded citizens, only touched the run-of-the-mill population for 'hatches, matches and despatches' and seemed to have no place otherwise. However, I discovered that Albert Eaton and George Jager, newly appointed clergy in the inner city, shared my concern for pastoral care and Christian values in the factories and workshops, so together we began to make our contribution to industrial mission, which was beginning at that time.

The Industrial Christian Fellowship, which had started up before the war, sponsored the visits of clergy to works canteens and encouraged discussion groups on Christian values in industrial life. It never attracted much interest in Leicester and it was fairly obvious in those years immediately after the war that while frontal attack through lunch-time services or special preachers in works canteens might have been possible for outstanding preachers like Dick Sheppard twenty years earlier, it was not going to stem the tide of secular and material pressures on the so-called working classes.

It was at about that time that Leslie Hunter, who had become Bishop of Sheffield in the early war years, was now developing the whole concept of industrial mission. He was kind enough to remain in close touch and from Leicester I watched the progress in Sheffield. In the first instance Leslie had written to the workers' committee of a large steel company proposing, with the approval of management, some talks on Christianity and society. After a long discussion the proposal was turned down on the grounds that the church had hitherto given no sort of help and had not even shown interest in the long effort to improve the material conditions of the working classes. Leslie admitted the justice of the criticism and concluded that it would take a long time before workers were persuaded to think differently of organized religion. Not surprisingly he distrusted the report *Towards the Conversion of England* which appeared in 1946 and the activities associated with it, which were largely designed to get people 'into church'. Leslie saw that that was not the first priority. While evangelism was needed, it had to be different, because of the new situation in which the church was finding itself.

Though conditions of labour, employment and housing immediately after the war left much to be desired, there was a sense of expectation, and rightly so, throughout the country, not least in Wigston and in Leicester city. Social security and some form of health service had been outlined by Beveridge; government grants were freely available for new housing and factory building; television was soon to capture its place in every home, creating a new concept of common knowledge and common recreation. Furthermore, the unexpected landslide in the 1945 election and the era of Clement Attlee and Labour leadership which followed was a sure sign of the way in which the nation thought that it ought to be moving. And just as in previous years all the energies of the average family in our parish, as elsewhere, had been absorbed in the war, so now they were fully absorbed in other directions: the concern for better schooling under the Education Act of R.A.Butler; increasingly full employment; and the demands of the productive and service industries.

Once again the church as such seemed to have little to say, and clergy were being trained as if nothing had happened. We had failed to catch in any way the heart and mind of working men and women since the first industrial revolution. Would we finally lose them in the new day of electronics and mass production? Aware of all these issues, a few of us in Leicester at that time thought it vitally important to establish a real relationship on the one hand with management, who were taking major decisions for the work-force, and on the other with those on the shop floor and their unions. During the war Father had been involved in pioneering work in this area at a great munitions factory in Staffordshire, a venture to which we shall have occasion to return in due course, so it was not unnatural that this should loom large in my concerns.

So it was that the Leicester Industrial Mission began to take shape. There were not many of us in it to begin with, and the venture progressed only as the Bishop, Guy Vernon-Smith, was able to direct resources of men and money in our direction – one very good reason for episcopacy! In the industrial scene, the British United, with John Lutyens in charge, the stocking factory of Donald Byford, Corah's Hosiery works and Bostik Adhesives were the first to open up in our direction and became constant in their support of industrial mission. Perhaps its most formidable advocate, however, was Bert Powell, a large man in both heart and body, the Regional Organizer of the Municipal and General Workers' Union. We were pleasantly surprised to find that he came from a Quaker background. His understanding and leadership in the local Trades Council guided clergy and laity alike. Without union support we would have been thought to be paternalistic and not really serious in sharing with the labour force the issues with which they were confronted, though Christian thinking on morality and society certainly had a good deal to offer in the situation. It was rewarding that, to the surprise of his colleagues, at the height of his trade union activity Bert became a member of our congregation.

There was a ready welcome in many of the larger factories and areas of work, but it soon became clear that the parish clergy who were ready to respond to these demanding situations were ill-equipped to do so. Then, as now, the maintenance of the church and parish had an almost iron grip on the activities of the ministry – as much in the Free Churches as in our own – and this is what shaped the clergy. In industry, by contrast, the requirement was not for services or for meeting the needs of the family, but for sustained contact, conversation and enquiry. Most of the clergy simply had no idea how to make a start with management or how to cope on the shop floor. Largely because of the lack of training in college or expectation in the congregation a specialist figure began to develop. This was the industrial chaplain, who made it his business to know and understand the conditions, restraints, apprenticeship and trade union membership that shaped the working life of the majority of men and women.

At the very time that I was finding myself becoming an amateur industrial chaplain, the Bishop asked me to be director of post-ordination training. As I met with successive groups of those who had been newly ordained, I learned something of the inadequacy of our training methods in the theological colleges. This inadequacy was particularly noticeable if one compared the professionalism of teachers as they graduated, or of doctors when they left medical school. Our clerical profession had adopted a hit or miss approach to society. When he reached ordination and put on a dog collar, all too often the new deacon had had no more than a critical introduction to the text of the Bible and had not been given help in interpreting it for the present day or using it devotionally. He had passed examinations in Christian doctrine, but had not been taught to communicate it; he had been shown what was conventionally done by clergy in caring for the sick or visiting hospitals – and not much more. During those years of rapid social change, with the advent of easily accessible contraception and all the new pressures on family life, exercised not least by the developing power of the mass media, not to mention the building of new towns and the resettlement of whole communities, the Anglican colleges actually abandoned courses in morality or Christian ethics. They said that there was a lack of experienced teachers! Last, but by no means least, there was little or no instruction in voice production or public speaking. All this led not only to ineffectiveness in the ministry but also to casualties – though on the other side there have always been those who in the event have proved resilient, adaptable and capable of learning as they went along.

Although I had an urgent sense of the need for the post-ordination group to get to grips with the social and industrial situation which dominated the lives of their parishioners as soon as possible, I also felt it necessary, because of the inadequacy of their training, to cram into their meetings much that should have been undertaken in college. Here again, without the sustained help of the Bishop, who had an open mind on doctrinal and social questions, and who was prepared to create a structure by which there was a partnership of the vicars in the diocese in guiding the newly ordained clergyman to take up his responsibilities, we would have made little headway either with in-service training or with the establishment of industrial mission. Two of those who came to me as curates, Michael Newman and Jim Thompson, thought through with me the needs of the new clergyman on the basis of their experience in their college years. Like several other curates over the years, they became invaluable colleagues in discerning our priorities, not only in the parish but also among their own generation of clergy.

It was perhaps because of the variety of our work and the way in which we examined and tried out methods of local parish ministry that Kenneth Carey, the then Principal of Westcott House, Cambridge, selected South Wigston to be the host to half a dozen ordination candidates for two weeks. In his letter to me the Principal said that he was very concerned that some of his men should have the experience of seeing parish life at first hand to prepare them for their own ministries. Would I show them as much as possible and introduce them to the various things that went on in the parish? They would be accompanied by his chaplain as their team manager. At that time, this was a surprising proposal, but we were delighted to be asked, and got ready to receive those whom the porter at Westcott House still called the 'young gentlemen'. It seemed best to arrange for them to have bed and breakfast in parishioners' homes; Henrietta provided lunch every day and evening meals when they were needed.

They arrived under the care of Harry Williams, the chaplain of Westcott House, with whom we were to establish a lasting friendship. There could have hardly been anyone better, with his clarity of mind in theological and social issues together with a remarkable ability to teach and lead. The party that Harry introduced included Paul Goddard, who more recently has been at Sherborne Abbey; Dennis Russell, whom I later found in Worcester diocese; Simon Phipps, a pioneer Industrial Mission Chaplain and now Bishop of Lincoln, and Bob Runcie, the present Archbishop of Canterbury. Given the little amount of parochial experience I had had, it seems strange that I should have had a hand in training a group like that! Everyone clearly had great personality and much ability; they were all well above the average ordination candidate, so it was no surprise that once they had arrived the group made the parish hum with activity during the two weeks they were around.

It took them only a matter of hours to size up the parish and plan how they would share in the worship, the youth club, the Sunday School, the Mothers' Union, the Scouts and wider activities. All the parish officers, including the vicar, were soon given nicknames, and all the activities, including visiting the sick, became a source of endless laughter and mimicry. My own efforts at preaching and guiding the situation, with a regular daily meeting, were treated, in the best of spirits, with equal hilarity. But friendships were made and in fact the parish benefited from it all more than the students: their imaginative contribution to the scene left us standing.

These eligible young men were, of course, the focus for the eyes of all the girls in the congregation. Far more of them than usual came to the monthly parish dance, where the mothers watched hopefully and their daughters often seemed quite overcome. After church on the Sunday, a father in the congregation asked if I would send along 'one of the young men' for tea that Sunday at his home in order 'to bring our Enid out'. We unanimously elected R.Runcie, who duly obliged. Harry Williams forecast what would happen: 'I know; next week back at Cambridge we shall get a telegram, saying, "Come at once, cannot get Enid in again".' Tongues did in fact continue to wag in the parish for many months.

We also met for prayer and serious discussion about our parish, and what it would mean to work for a long period in such a place; in the end, though, the two weeks did not finish with a service but with a variety show arranged by the 'young men'. The various turns put on by the visitors were opportunities to take off the personalities of the parish, including the vicar; they showed up our idiosyncrasies with more insight than we had been able to communicate to them. But then Simon Phipps had already made his reputation with the Footlights at Cambridge.

Living above the shop is both a convenience and a disadvantage for the average parson, but we found that it was absolutely essential, if at all possible, to live next to the church and in the middle of the parish. It is a pity that more professional people – teachers, doctors, social workers and others – do not live among those whom they serve. Our vicarage proved to be a very happy home. It was large enough to accommodate our growing family. We had arrived with Rachel and Robert, and Edward and Eleanor were both born at home during those years. The result of this was that the congregation became deeply interested in us all, and were very considerate over our family life. Nevertheless we did long for some escape route, both for holidays and for shorter breaks. One day, when Henrietta was in bed after giving birth to Edward, we saw an advertisement in the personal column of *The Times* for a disused cottage farmhouse on the north coast of Pembrokeshire. The opportunity to buy a cottage on the Prescelli hills overlooking the sea, with sandy beaches a mile down the road, seemed too good to be true. And almost miraculously, a letter came that week from the War Office, two years after my demobilization, containing my war gratuity. Although there was rationing, our friends at the garage opposite were able to supply extra petrol on the side, so there was a chance to go down to inspect it. Henrietta obviously could not come, so in our Morris Eight I hurried off to Wales with my sister-in-law Eleanor. The cottage was certainly very disused, with broken doors and windows, but its potential was great; there were three bedrooms, and its location, with views of the coast, was superb. Together with twenty-five acres of largely bracken-covered fields, even then it was so cheap as to be almost within my gratuity, which was £1000. I bought it over the counter of the local pub, with the publican acting as estate agent, and hurried home to convey the news. All of a sudden we were the proud owners of our own house, with some fields and the freedom of a mountainside running up behind. Immediately every holiday became an occasion to do work on it, and for the children to benefit from the sea air and beaches. We rapidly came to love it. 'Penlan' has been a place of relaxation, walking, fishing, sailing, riding, water-colour painting and good company for the family now for almost forty years. How lucky we were to get such a place so early, and so well before the rush of holiday homes!

Henrietta and I have no doubt that our first parish brought us more than we dared hope for. Those four years at Leicester were formative for the rest of our ministry. We were fortunate in the parish, the opportunities and the diocese; and we also benefited from the ready advice of Father, who was only a few miles away at Lichfield. He exercised a wide ministry for many parishes in his conferences at Swanwick for church councillors and lay officers, in direct succession to the Life and Liberty movement. We took our own people to them. He was a member of the House of Lords, the Bishops' Meeting and, of course, Church Assembly, and would pass on to me much of what was going on in them. He returned from London always refreshed. Once it was with a broad smile, as Geoffrey Fisher, the headmaster

Archbishop, had rebuked him for not wearing gaiters at Lambeth. Father had a quick answer for his bossy archbishop. Meanwhile Frank had the principal parish of Huddersfield, to which Simon Phipps went as curate as a result of the time he had spent with us. Samuel, on demobilization from being a chaplain in the New Zealand Royal Air Force, came home to a parish first in Southport and then in Hatfield, in each place in charge of a large and interesting commmunity. All four of us were ready to compare notes and exchange experiences; each of us was in the strong liberal tradition, both ecclesiastically and politically, and this made our life and our jobs a vigorous partnership, and the ministry a shared pleasure.

However, all this was not to last for much longer. We had already refused to go to a job in Cairo, but Harry Baines whom we had known when he was Vicar of Rugby, and who by now was Bishop of Singapore, had asked one of his colleagues, going home on leave to the United Kingdom, to press me strongly to become Archdeacon of Singapore and Vicar of St Andrew's Cathedral. It was in the autumn of 1950 and at first this personal invitation did not interest Henrietta and me at all. In the first place, while I had indeed signed the pledge of the Student Volunteer Missionary Union to serve God overseas, if circumstances permitted, at the back of my mind I had always had the notion that if this happened it would be to the Middle East that we would go, because of my previous connections there. The job sounded daunting but the more we thought about it the more interesting it became. First there was the cathedral and the care and building up of its multi-racial congregation. There were also daughter churches on the island, whose congregations spoke Chinese or Indian dialects, which would be responsible to me. There were mission schools and hospitals not only on Singapore Island but in Malaya and Indonesia. Travelling would be extensive but interesting and I would have a firm base at Singapore where the administration was comparatively good. But there were our parents and the children to think of. As we asked for advice, our minds began to change in favour of going. We were deeply aware of the growing importance of the younger churches, and if we were to serve overseas, it was going to be now or never. Here was an opportunity that we had not looked for but which had been offered to us, and those who knew both me and the nature of the work in Singapore thought that there was the right place for my ministry. So in the end the decision seemed both inevitable and God-given. To Singapore we would go, family and all.

=== [6] ===

In the Far East

As I was standing outside the house while were we packing up at South Wigston, one of the mothers from the street came up and asked a favour. 'My boy, 'e's serving in Korea; will you keep an eye on him, vicar?' Distances in the Far East were, of course, a closed book to the parish; all those who went as far as Singapore were thought to be easily in touch.

Saying good-bye to any parish is curiously agonizing. Clergy tend to use the word 'fellowship' in a devalued kind of way to denote fairly superficial gatherings and social relationships. We found that when it came to bidding farewell to those to whom we had tried to convey the gospel and for whom we had tried to let something of the goodness of God come through, the word was true in it fullest, authentic sense: something very deep had been established among us all. Real friendships had replaced any superficial 'fellowship'. And indeed, as I look back after forty years, I find that in fact it is the early friendships which have proved to be the most lasting.

We began packing up in March 1951. Our move was made much easier by the fact that we had our parents' homes of Park Hall and the Palace at Lichfield on to which to off-load our goods and chattels. At Park Hall the two weeks with Henrietta's parents were during daffodil time with the whole place bursting into springtime blossom. For all of us there were the garden, the farm, the wood, the lake and the many activities of the estate to enjoy. They had all become a source of great interest to me. At Lichfield, with its busy round of cares and duties attached to the cathedral and the diocese, we had a chance to spend a fortnight with my parents over and after Easter. We had always shared in their interests so it was natural for Edward, Lord High Almoner to King George VI, to take us, together with Rachel

On RMS Chusan en route to Singapore, May 1951

and Robert, then aged seven and four respectively, to Westminster Abbey for the Royal Maundy Service that April. There we were presented to the King and Queen, who wished us well for our time in Singapore. With that, and with the combined efforts of both the Church Missionary Society and the Society for the Propagation of the Gospel (for this was a joint appointment), as we left the church in England we were certainly surrounded by prayer and good wishes. In saying farewell at Lichfield it was impossible not to realize how frail Mother had become and how dependent she and Father were on each other. She was insistent that her prayers had been fulfilled by our going off as missionaries: another generation of the Barclay family was finding its vocation. We bade them good-bye almost as St Paul in the Acts of the Apostles left the quayside at Miletus.

Air travel was still at a premium, so all six of us were driven from Park Hall, with a great deal of baggage, to Southampton. We were fortunate to sail in one of the great passenger liners of the P & O, RMS Chusan, an experience which is sadly almost completely unavailable to today's travellers; it allowed the East to grow on one stage by stage.

[91]

A little over three weeks on such a voyage was also an admirable introduction both to the tropics and to living overseas. As we steamed our leisurely way eastwards, round Gibraltar, along the Mediterranean and across the hot and steamy Indian Ocean, making a number of stops on the way, there was time to get adjusted to different climates, traditions and ways of life, and there was time to think. The four children also became adaptable in a way which might not have been achieved otherwise. So all in all those weeks on RMS Chusan were a real bonus. Our times ashore at Port Said, Bombay, Colombo and Penang, our first contact with Malaya, where we enjoyed a day on the sandy beaches, all proved fascinating in one way or another, until at last, after cruising down the coast with views of Malacca, where Francis Xavier made the base from which he hoped to convert the Chinese in the sixteenth century – that mission which was both a remarkable start and a tragic failure – we turned into the Indonesian archipelago and docked at the quayside in Singapore.

Our expectations had had plenty of time to build up. We had imagined situations ranging from that of the isolated missionary under a palm tree to that of the ever-pressed parson in a large city. It all proved very different. The immediate welcome as we landed that Saturday from Harry Baines, the Bishop, and from both Europeans and Chinese, was kind and reassuring. I could not wait to start asking questions, and as on many occasions, I was glad to be tall enough to be able to look over the sea of faces that stared at us on the quay. We were driven off to our new home, Cathedral House, which proved a pleasant surprise. It was airy, and the breeze blew right through it. Of course there was no air-conditioning, but the verandahs were cool and spacious, and there was a good garden in which the children soon made themselves at home; it was not long before the boys were building a railway line for their Hornby toy trains. 'Cooky' and his wife were all set to look after us. How incredible it was to be greeted by three domestic servants! We soon learned that we couldn't do without them, but this did not quite seem to match the concept of the missionary. We were shown the bedrooms and were surprised to find no glass in the windows; only stretched steel netting. It all seemed embarrassingly sparse. As we went to sleep we could hear conversations in the road or a cough in the next house, a few yards away. But it was a fine house, and located as close to the city centre as any residence could be.

We had passed by the cathedral, dedicated to St Andrew, on our way. It too looked fine: a large white stucco, Victorian Gothic church with a western tower and spire, standing with real dignity on the waterfront of the bustling city. We went to church rather dutifully the next day, sitting in a pew like any other visitors, and we wondered what it would all be like and why we had come.

We soon came down to earth, as you have to with a family. At first it was an anti-climax. Perhaps we had expected the life of the church overseas to be refreshingly stimulating and vibrant, an improvement on the situation at home. But this did not seem to be the case. I realized just how difficult it must be for any vicar to be landed on a strange church. The liturgy was formal and intrusive, and in the prayers and the address we were subjected to what was at that time an annual appeal for money. Any sense of worship was pushed aside as we were forcibly made aware of the dire financial straits of the parish and indeed of the diocese. We were also quickly warned about the crisis over ministry there. There had been no official vicar of the cathedral and parish for more than twelve months: my predecessor's marriage had broken down and he had left unexpectedly, and any assistant priests were occupied in one way or another in schools or with the military.

In this situation I found an invaluable helper and companion in Chiu Ban It, who was and has remained a remarkable priest. Trained as a barrister and called to the London bar, he felt his real work lay in the ordained ministry. After some months at Westcott House and in a much appreciated curacy at Bournville in Birmingham he returned to his part-Chinese and mixed racial community in Penang and then to Singapore. When we arrived he not only had the cathedral in hand but formed an essential link between the Chinese and European communities. Along with the Bishop, Harry Baines, and his wife, 'Bunny Chiu', as he was affectionately called, welcomed us to share in and develop the work of the church.

Singapore at first sight was a seething cauldron of peoples, races and traditions. Within it was a strong foundation of Christian worship and witness which had been laid by successive generations of clergy and laity in the colonial and commercial services ever since Stamford Raffles had established the colony in 1822. The completion of the cathedral forty years later and the arrival of American and British missions to the Chinese ensured a strong Christian presence. We found a congregation in the cathedral of some two hundred regular communicants. They were a responsive group largely of educated,

English-speaking Chinese, Indian, European and American families. Within the parish and located not far from the cathedral at the heart of the city there were groups of Tamils from South India, Malayalis from Travancore, Cantonese, Hokien and Fuchow speaking Christians from South China, all building up their own church life and all enjoying a working relationship to one another and to us at the centre. Most of them had come with a strong Anglican heritage from South India, South China and Europe. They were a loyal and trustworthy people, very conscious of their traditions and producing from their midst a competent and dedicated ministry. My main base for worship and pastoral care remained the cathedral, where there was considerable potential for the many activities of the mission. However, for someone like myself, with a good deal of self-confidence, it was puzzling to find so many groups of Christians on the island who knew what they were doing but did not move forward because they were looking for further leadership. What could be done? I thought and prayed a good deal about them and came to realize that in the first instance my contribution must be to listen to them. To Matthew George, a senior civil servant; Cheong Hock Hai, a chief inspector of education; and Yip Tung Shan, the head of a large commercial concern, all of them ready to help and advise in the enormously complicated social, political and racial community of that parish, I still owe a debt of gratitude.

Still under British administration in 1951, Singapore Island was a self-contained colony attached to the Federation of Malay States. In ecclesiastical terms, for a century and a half it had been constituted an Anglican parish which had been formed largely with the Europeans in mind, who by that year numbered some 10,000. By the time of my arrival, nearly a million Chinese and Indians had settled as traders, manufacturers, rubber planters and in commercial enterprises of all sorts. The Indian community had arrived largely as labourers at the turn of the century; they soon also settled down in the role of civil servants and established themselves in the medical and teaching professions. They became, however, increasingly nervous about Chinese dominance and tended to turn to the British for protection. As a result of the war the strong European commercial community had come to be matched by an overwhelming military, naval and air-force presence, which tended to emphasize the special status of the British, American, Dutch, French and others involved in the general melée of the rapidly expanding commercial situation.

◁ *Singapore River*

Under direct colonial rule the whole of Singapore was officially my parish, and I was inducted into the living just as any parson might have been at home. In the presence of the Governor, the Chief Justice, and a large crowd I was commissioned to take on numerous duties about which I knew virtually nothing.

One undoubted benefit that I found in assuming my responsibilities was that I was entering into the heritage of a solid missionary policy which went back well into the last century. All over the area over which my responsibilities as Archdeacon took me, whether in Singapore or up in Malaya, or further afield in Thailand, Borneo or Hong Kong, the church was genuinely local and largely self-supporting. To inspire me I had the example of Leonard Wilson, later to become Dean of Manchester and Bishop of Birmingham, a strong churchman with wide sympathies whose work was abruptly ended by the Japanese, after which he spent many years as a prisoner of war in the notorious Changi Gaol. With him in prison was Graham White, a priest and pastor of legendary goodness who died there at the hands of the Japanese. I found that he was venerated almost as a saint. Then there had also been Sorby Adams, an educationist of real ability who had set up grammar schools and made arrangements for teacher training. Alongside him had been Nora Inge, who with Jessie Kilgour had made the church aware of the need to extend schooling to girls as well as boys, and who had shown the importance of Christian teaching in the home as the centre of the church's life. Not only did these people give the church a great reputation in the captivity years, but they also left a fund of good will and professional expertise.

Over the years the British missionary societies had given superb education and social leadershp, not only in South-East Asia, but also world-wide – a fact which is not always recognized. I found it worth while to read up and learn about the racial and cultural situation in which I found myself. I realized that experience at home was not enough. Both I and the family discovered that the problems posed by such a new and varied ministry were indeed a challenge to our resourcefulness.

Either the Bishop or I acted as chairman on each of the governing bodies of the schools and the mission hospitals. But were we right in being so dependent on our institutions? They certainly provided a steady flow of people for the professions and the civil service, but did they provide for the care of the community or the ministry of the church? Writing home in October 1951, I commented:

When I set out, I didn't expect to find myself with the detailed responsibility of administering and guiding the vernacular churches and schools and hospitals, etc., in Singapore and further afield. I enjoy it all, and yet the institutional life of a young church like this is difficult. The schools produce practically no converts – perhaps that's not what they are for? But we pour effort, personnel and money into schooling for 300 or 400 children in this parish alone – something which could easily absorb one's whole time. The most exciting work here is the purely Chinese. In various dialects in three or four centres we are making real headway in building up a Christian community. In one place I have rented, in my own name, a shop-house – a large room backed by two small ones – in which we are starting a mission and clinic to one of our new housing estates where 20-30,000 Chinese and Indians are being settled. It is like an American resettlement area in which the Government is miles behind in providing schools or social centres.

There is widespread recognition that in the colonial days the partnership of state government and mission was beneficial. It laid the foundation of education through almost the whole of black Africa, and led to the creation of remarkable universities and colleges in India. The result in Singapore had been beneficial to the state, but less so to the grass roots of the churches. So my pressing concern in those years was to enable our schools, hostels and hospitals to become seed-beds of Christian ministry in its widest terms. The unconditional gift of medical or educational care made by the Christian churches had been a remarkable contribution from believing Christians in the West. But now that the indigenous church was entering into a period when the emphasis had to be on self-help and self-support, the wisdom of demanding a good deal of financial support from outside for its large-scale institutions had become questionable, to say the least. The Government was ready and able to maintain the schools and hospitals which the church had founded so they would still continue. Was it not time for the church to put them in other hands?

Despite the readiness of some local people to accept responsibility for development, as I look back I can see clearly how our Christian institutions across the world had been founded in such a way that when we came to hand them over to the indigenous church we were also in danger of abandoning them. Fortunately, in Singapore, Malaya and Borneo a new partnership of local and expatriate leadership easily developed.

My own contribution to ministry in Singapore was not so much in the schools and similar organizations as in helping to develop small local congregations in the ever-widening urban sprawl. Here the local clergy were keen to respond. The cathedral had absorbed too much of the local resources, particularly those of the new Chinese converts.

One day I had an unusual request. I was summoned to a prayer meeting by Pastor Guok Kuo Mo (we later made him a canon). He had arrived from China with his family shortly before the Second World War. He had built up a bus company which almost rivalled the municipal one, so he was well-to-do; and he had an enormous family. However, he was also a very traditional Chinese – teetotal, with a very simple life-style – and he was a deeply committed Christian. Just as the Japanese were overrunning the city, Leonard Wilson ordained him both deacon and priest on the same day so that he might lead his people in the crisis.

To my surprise, this prayer meeting was to take place in Chinatown on the footpath that divided the stream of cars and buses from the busy and bulging shop fronts, where an auction for a small parcel of land was to take place. A church was much needed in this area, but could the Christian community afford the site? Would the Archdeacon both help and pray? Might the Christians be outbidded? To the astonishment of the crowd we did indeed kneel on that footpath and on the roadway, and there we stayed until the hammer came down in our favour. The Church of the True Light stands today in that crowded area, with a medical clinic on the ground floor, an infants school on the second, a community centre on the third, the church or worship centre on the fourth and the parsonage as a penthouse on the fifth. It was fun designing such a church in order to make the most of a restricted site, and it became one of our most happy developments. Incidentally, rather to the dismay of the architects the congregation insisted that a tank should be let into the church on the fourth floor, in order to provide for baptism by total immersion. That is still recognized as a proper procedure in Anglicanism if required, and for those new Christians it was important.

In due course the Canontese, the Foochow and the Hokien speaking Christians all began to approach me and it became my work to provide them with advice and resources. The Indians were much slower on the uptake and very aware of their antecedents. However, one priest, Abraham Daniels, a Tamil, with Sylvia his Chinese wife, living in a shop-house with the front as a church centre, saw the future of his area as a mixed community of Christians. His new church, dedicated to Our Saviour, had walls of glass so that the populace outside could watch Christian worship just as they were able to see the goings-on at local Hindu or Buddhist shrines.

It was not always easy to help the congregations who spoke regional dialects. Linguistically they were often as bad at understanding one another as I was at understanding them. They would scribble Chinese characters on the palms of their hands to get a point across; the written word was the great uniting factor. Our name in Chinese was the character for Woo in Mandarin, pronounced Tau in Hokien, Ng in Foochow and something else in Cantonese. It is no small wonder that under the strict regime that was to follow, classical Chinese, known as Mandarin, increasingly tended to become obligatory. At our weekly staff meetings, however, we were obliged to make English our medium if we were going to work and pray together. This we did, most effectively running the Island as one great parish with ten or twelve clergy accepting the leadership of the cathedral at the heart of the city. This was a team ministry in the real sense of the word, worked out and established twenty years before this approach was considered a good option for the church at home. Personalities had to be respected and any excessive leadership by us British priests was soon resented. Whereas at home the ministry was predominantly individual in character, the church overseas learned in good time that groups of priests were infinitely more effective than isolated ministries.

However, political trouble was only just under the surface of the colonial adminstration. The Communists, greatly aided by the New China with its promises of freedom and plenty, recruited many able Chinese and engaged the attention of several of the more thoughtful of the local community. Harry Lee Kuan Yew, later to become such an able and dominant Prime Minister of the independent state, was in fact held in gaol by the colonial powers for quite some months after the first wave of riots in Singapore City. He had demanded both independence and a socialist state. However, his power of leadership matured rapidly, and from his very radical beginnings he became one of the most remarkable leaders in Asia. Although there is now virtually one-party government, Singapore has flourished to an extraordinary degree in considerable freedom.

Up country things were much more unsettled. Sir Henry Gurney, the Governor in Kuala Lumpur, was murdered in April 1951, just before we arrived. The army was fully deployed in a totally inconclusive jungle war, and it was unwise for Europeans to travel without an armed escort. Harry Baines once reprimanded me for driving unescorted back from Malacca to Singapore, and in the city we became used to the riot squads, and we admired the way in which the British police, in their smart khaki shorts, would control unruly crowds. Even at home we were not without our worries, particularly when one of our Chinese pastors decided that his safety depended on remaining with us in Cathedral House for several days.

Living in the security of Cathedral House, which was next door to Government House, was comparatively easy. But the curfew which came to be imposed was a plain nuisance. One curfew was ordered which allowed only two hours of movement a day and one on Sunday. We made representations to the Government that they should allow for Christian worship, because we felt that a principle was at stake. The authorities responded by lifting the curfew in a controlled way for an additional hour or two on Sunday, but I proved to have made a mistake, and the congregation did not bless me. On the first Sunday only a few ventured out and most preferred to stay at home. The danger of the situation was evident enough: and the very next Sunday one of our regular servers, a devoted Christian, was shot dead while he was on point duty as a special constable.

Writing in the cathedral magazine in January 1952 I included a summary of the Government proposals for the rehousing of the Chinese, who had, after the Japanese occupation, pinned their hopes on Communism and were being supported by mainland China. These new developments were to include huge new housing estates on Singapore Island with attendant industrial incentives and 'new villages', as they were called, up-country. The new communities were not easy to handle socially or politically, particularly in Johore and Negri Sembilam, where the villagers lived enclosed within barbed-wire fences. It made me wonder what our faith, linked irrevocably to capitalist finance and social democracy, could do to help them. And if the church was to have any significance for the pattern of life in the future, we needed to break away from the concept of a money-making few to a more egalitarian society. Christian schools and hospitals had paved the way for an educated and healthy society; was it not now time for the British, and in particular the Christians, to help the

In the Far East

indigenous population replace colonial rule with a democratic, self-governing and self-educating society? Many members of the British colonial service were both ready and equipped to give the necessary lead and confidence. I felt that the socialism of Clement Attlee and Hugh Gaitskell would have a good deal to give, since at this point in the mission of the churches there was little articulation of any social gospel.

A new and hopeful direction to the emergency was provided from a civil angle with the arrival of General Templer, whom I had known since the time when he was a divisional commander in Italy. Our expectations of clear leadership and rapid decisions were not disappointed. In Malcolm Macdonald, Commissioner General, a 'supremo' appointed by the government at home to be senior to governors and service commanders, we had another friend who exercised a consistently quiet and helpful influence. His many activities included helping indigenous political leadership, establishing local government, working on education and enlarging medical services. He and Gerald Templer together were indispensable personalities in enabling Malaya, Singapore and Borneo to face the Communist challenge with a social and cultural programme which held the communities together at this time. Malcolm, whom we came to know well, a man with a broad-minded civilian approach, and Gerald, a man with a splendidly human approach to military and social problems, both took Harry Baines and me into their confidence. As Commissioner General and Governor of Malaya respectively, they understood the rights of the Malays and the aspirations of the Chinese; they also saw most clearly the role of the churches and voluntary organizations as being complementary to the military measures. Together with some fine colonial civil servants they saved the day in Malaysia for the foreseeable future. It was a real sadness that so soon after the emergency was officially ended the fashion of dividing communities and segregating races overtook Malaya. Palestine had already been carved up, and India and Pakistan were used as precedents, but to divide Chinese Singapore politically and economically from the Malay mainland was surely an error.

One outcome of the triumph of Communism in China was the expulsion of experienced Chinese-speaking missionaries from the country: it was our good fortune that they were then available to work in Malaya. At first we were cautious about them: would they associate with our 'church'-orientated Christian community? Would they introduce too narrow an interpretation of the gospel? Would they even despise our ways, which were small and amateur when compared to the Christian movement in China?

They arrived: Canon and Mrs Carpenter, the Williamsons, Sverre Holth and several others, among them two remarkable women, May Griggs and Molly Rudd. Few who met them will ever forget these two – so different and yet so equally representative of the dedicated Anglican missionary of the nineteenth and twentieth centuries. When she arrived, May explained how she was aware of the anxieties in the minds of Chinese farmers and village folk in the face of the pressure from the Communists that they expected. She spoke their language like a native, and was ready to penetrate the Malayan jungle areas and search out the men, their wives and children. After a few weeks she decided to settle in one of the most vehemently anti-British new villages, two square miles of huts surrounded by barbed wire. Those confined there soon recognized her as their friend and adviser. She came to organize a school, a church, social life and even the development of local industries – all as part of the Christian way of life. She gave herself to those people and brought peace to a whole area of Malaya. When Gerald Templer had been as Governor to see Yong Peng, this 'new village' in Johore where Communist Chinese had been rounded up and enclosed, he told us how impressed he had been with what our missionaries were doing. He commented that May Griggs was worth more than a division of British troops. But alas there was only one May, and many new villages. How could we initiate leadership in them?

Years later, when May died, I went to take her funeral, in a village church in Kent. Only a few friends were present but at the back of that village church I saw Gerald Templer, sitting alone. By then he was a Field Marshal and Chief of the General Staff, but he told me that he felt he had to be there. For a moment we recalled the Malayan Emergency and the work of the China missionaries up country: their contribution to the future stability of the place remains great, but it is unrecorded.

It would be untrue to say that our lives were lived against the continuing background of the Emergency. Our colleagues in the churches of Malaya suffered that most, and they were subject to far more difficult pressures than we were in Singapore. There the

[102]

cathedral developed in a way that would seem almost strange to the hardened churchgoer in Europe. Chinese, Indians and British soon responded to some solid preaching, good music and congregational participation, and we came to expect three or four hundred communicants every Sunday. I found it wise to have a standing baptism group for Chinese, British or Indian adults who wanted to be baptized and confirmed. They attended the worship; they also came each week for discussion and instruction, and every six months or so the Sunday service was punctuated by the moment when the catechumens (for that is what they were) were welcomed at the big open west door and led inside to the font for their baptism and to the altar for their confirmation. It was always a moving occasion, and to this day I have lists of those for whom we needed to pray as they renounced their wholly secular or official Buddhist past and accepted Jesus.

To meet the opportunity for rapid and thorough expansion of the church in those years, clearly the most urgent need was for a real local ministry. Overseas priests could not be recruited or sustained, and indeed to follow that course would have been wrong anyway. The Methodists supported from the USA had already made a start in developing a local ministry, and they proved ready partners. Funds collected for theological training in China, the Nanking Foundation, were made available for overseas Chinese, and in those early years we were given the expert help of John Fleming, later to become Professor of Theology at St Andrews. Incidentally, but in a way which proved very important, he brought the Church of Scotland into our enterprise.

A potentially good base for theological teaching was strengthened by the arrival with May Griggs of other highly capable Chinese missionaries. Sverre Holth was an ordained Anglican from Norway; he could teach fluently in Chinese and he became the pastoral head of our new college. And there was that other great woman, Molly Rudd – known to our children as Ruddy Moll; she was a very close friend and lunched with us, as did Brian Barker, Rachel Wharton and other European staff, at Cathedral House every Sunday for nearly four years. Just as some missionaries had established the community service of the churches in Malaya, my colleagues at the cathedral, and above all Molly Rudd, enabled a whole new concept of theological and pastoral training to be developed in Singapore.

The place where Molly Rudd exercised her gifts had, though, first to be developed. I had never made any pretence that I could teach theology, but I was concerned that we should make it a priority to

provide adequate theological training in Singapore. I did not want the result of this training to be a series of academic young men and women; rather, our future ministers should learn how to meet people, how to teach and listen to enquiries, and how to preach. Harry Baines, Chiu Ban It (who afterwards became a bishop) and I, together with our new colleagues from China, and with substantial help from the Methodists, set up Trinity College, Singapore, to serve all the Protestant churches there. The list of the courses it offered included Old Testament, New Testament, church history, religious education, theology, ethics, practice in preaching, kindergarten methods, public speaking, music, languages (Tamil, English and Chinese), and Bible study. There were hostels for men and women and we taught regular students (those with School Certificate or equivalent Chinese qualifications over a three-year course) to earn a licentiate in theology, a diploma in music, or a certificate in kindergarten methods; there were also special courses at which students with lower educational qualifications could improve their effectiveness as lay workers, and evening courses for those in full-time work. Here Molly Rudd enabled a whole new concept of theological and pastoral training. She was resourceful enough to get young Chinese scholars to start writing theology for their generation and to enable the clergy to make better use of their propensity for art and calligraphy. A woman of heavy build, who always walked with a stick, she came to endear herself to the Chinese church and Chinese culture.

It was not until I had consolidated the worship and activities at the cathedral and further afield in Singapore that I undertook journeys and visits to the parishes, schools and missions up country in Malaya, or in Indonesia. Harry Baines usually did most of this work, but with the Emergency causing so much anxiety I found myself fairly regularly in Kuala Lumpur, Ipoh, Penang and Malacca. On one such journey I was visiting John and Helen Litton; John was a senior colonial officer who was eventually ordained and became a vicar in the Winchester diocese. At that time he was in Taiping, where he was in charge of a Rehabilitation Centre for Communists who had been captured or who had surrendered. He was doing a marvellous job and his personal Christianity made a tremendous impression on those with whom he dealt. But as I wrote in my journal:

We are not allowed to introduce Christianity openly for fear of offence. It is all so contradictory. Our administration both in Malaya

◁ *With the church and congregation at Yong Peng New Village, 1952* and Singapore, because they are never allowed to be open in their loyalty to any religion, can never, I believe, win the people. This neutral attitude to all religion – a sop to the Malay Muslims – means that our cause against Communism has little cutting edge.

By contrast it so happened that when staying with Sir Gerald Templer a week later, I met the man who was in charge of the Rehabilitation Camp in Kenya set up in the context of the Mau Mau troubles. There they were openly and avowedly Christian in their teaching, and even had chaplains in the camps. The time of independence in Africa became an era of confidence for the church. It made me wonder why it was that confidence in the Christian gospel among civil servants and traders has all too often been dissipated by a self-conscious respect for other religions.

Early on at the cathedral we realized that some form of community centre was needed for the growing activities of the congregation and to accommodate the teaching mission of the time. When we arrived, there was no real memorial to the Commonwealth servicemen who had served, suffered and died in the defence of Singapore and people felt that to be an omission. It was not that we needed to recall the Japanese war, but there was a real wish that something should stand at the heart of the city to commemorate the bravery and sacrifices of regiments, ships, air squadrons and the civilians who joined up in what were the desperate days of 1941/42. So we planned a Memorial Hall, as a substantial north transept to the cathedral. Lay men and women were soon busy with the task of realizing the project. Jock Morrison, the local head of the Hong Kong and Shanghai Bank, took on the money raising; Tom Cotterell, Chief Executive of Singapore Cold Storage, became cathedral treasurer; Gee Vincent, the local brewer and cold drinks king, led the musical and cultural side, and the Chinese rallied in a big way. I found myself left with time to build up the spiritual life of the various congregations and classes. Building operations were rapid: whole structures and new roads seemed to come into being overnight, and in no time the Memorial Hall was ready. The Hall with its ancillary rooms, offices and library was opened on 12 September 1952. At the opening, the Governor, Sir John Nicoll, took the chair, the Commissioner General, Malcolm Macdonald, performed the ceremony, and General Templer spoke.

More important than new buildings was the personal care of new

Christians and frequently inexperienced missionaries and ministers. Henrietta took over much of this side of the work, helping each expatriate member of staff and families to adjust to the local situation. She further developed both the Church Women's Association and the Mothers Union, both of which organizations were adapted to this developing Christian society and so enabled Chinese, Indian and British women to meet and enjoy one another's company through their many activities.

Mrs Ho, educated at the Methodist mission school, had twelve children. She came to be a believer and loved and read her Bible, but her husband would not allow her to be baptized. What could we do? The Mothers' Union was our first line of help: she joined their branch and it was most welcoming. Eventually we were allowed to baptize the children but not the mother, but nevertheless we sustained her faith. In another pew, another family was in the cathedral Sunday by Sunday. The father was invariably accompanied by both his wives, the older and senior wife having chosen the younger and junior wife according to Chinese custom. They were all believers and all confirmed, but could the Christian discipline accommodate a family like that? Harry Baines ruled that the husband could not receive communion without putting one wife aside. But to break that household was impossible: so Mr Tau remained in his seat while both wives and their children came to the altar. This is a pastoral issue that still challenges the younger churches of Africa and Asia. For his sake and for family unity in believing, before he died I did in fact give them all communion.

Half way through our first tour, which was of three years, we were beginning to get our second wind. At that stage the RAF chaplains asked whether there could be a mission on their stations, not only in Singapore but also in Hong Kong. They wondered whether Father might be prepared to leave the diocese of Lichfield for a while and come out to conduct the venture. It was just the sort of thing he was good at, and we completed the arrangements for him to come out in November 1952. However, he would be alone, since Mother felt that such a journey was more than she could manage. At home there were many agonizing discussions about how Edward and Clemence would fare in separation, since they were both well into their seventies. They both felt that God was calling Edward to the mission, and Mother was determined not to stand in the way. But the prospect of the loneliness was terrifying: they had been married nearly fifty years.

Father was at a bishops' meeting in London when he was suddenly called out with the news that Mother was seriously ill. She had been staying with her sister Christina. When he arrived, he found that she was just about to be taken to hospital. He hoped and believed that she knew that he had come and recognized him, but in the event she died in the ambulance, with him at her side. He cabled us: 'She gently fell asleep yesterday. Jesus Lives. Dear Love.' Henrietta and I were bereft by the loss of my Mother who had been such a support to both of us, even at a distance. But in her death she had completed her life work for the family and for the church; she left Father able to go off on his own. He was due to be with us a week later, and he had every excuse to change his plans, but with considerable courage he set off on his way. Not surprisingly, he arrived quite exhausted after a flight which had been involved in many long delays, and grieving over Mother's death. Nevertheless, his pleasure at being with our family soon helped to bring him back to his old self. He carried on with his visits to the RAF, gave some extremely apt addresses, and established himself among them extraordinarily quickly. The chaplains and many others greatly appreciated the way in which he had kept to his plans, and both in Singapore and in Hong Kong he bore remarkable testimony to the need to see mission and conversion as the real role of the church.

We went together to Hong Kong, where Father had a full schedule of addresses and meetings. Our time there was altogether happy, and we felt that it was in God's providence that Clemence was now in his hands. But things deteriorated on our return flight. We were in a Hastings transport plane; almost an hour out of Kai Tak airfield Father turned to me complaining of faintness and in a matter of moments he was unconscious. The pilot himself came to assess the situation and immediately lowered the altitude of the flight so that the old lumbering plane, with no pressurization, was flying just above the waves. Father came round, but he was clearly very ill. The pilot decided to land at Saigon rather than Singapore, and there the British embassy took over. However, Father was unwilling to remain in so remote a spot, and although our ambassador was kindness itself, we took to the air again and flew on to Singapore, almost touching the waves of the China Sea. Father's one wish was to be nursed at Cathedral House by 'Wifey', as he called Henrietta. His days were clearly numbered, but Keys Smith, the mission doctor, tended him with such care that he proved well enough to preach on Christmas

In the garden with Father at Cathedral House, Singapore, December 1952

Day in the Cathedral. We talked and prayed together before he embarked for his last flight home – travelling by air against the advice of the doctors. He died some ten days after reaching Lichfield, with the rest of the family around him. I knew that we would not meet again, but the immediacy of his going was a shock. He left notes on his table for a sermon on 'Render an account of my stewardship'. It was an account which he gave direct to his Maker, and for that we could only be thankful.

To have had Father with us and the children for the last four weeks of his life was an unexpected and unforgettable experience. Our home, with tree houses in the garden and toy trains running round the verandah, gave plenty of opportunities for Rachel, Robert and Edward to play with their grandfather. Eleanor, two and a half years old, was his special delight: he called her 'Twink', a nickname which has lasted ever since. Mary, who at that time was one year old, was his youngest grandchild. In that expatriate society of Singapore it was noticeable to us how serious was the absence of grandparents, uncles and aunts: families became independent and segregated without the congenial and honest inter-communication that is really possible only within the family circle. How lucky we were in having seen and known there the one who had set so much of a pattern for all his children, and particularly us three boys. And now his ministry was our ministry.

Before air travel became so easy, it was a natural pattern for those overseas to leave their work and environment for six months every three years. To get right away was not always simple, but we found that by the time we were due to return to England for a while in 1954 the life of the cathedral parish was being well served by a large group of dedicated lay men and women who were ready to take charge. At the same time, I had to lose my closest colleague, Chiu Ban It, since he had been appointed Vicar of Kuala Lumpur.

We had carefully arranged ten days at Zermatt with my brother Sam. His ministry had taken a different shape from mine, but we remained very close and had planned the holiday for recreation and reunion. The walks in the high Alps and all the pleasures of Switzerland in summer left us wishing all the more that Frank could be with us. However, he had been made Bishop of Middleton in the diocese of Manchester since we had left for Singapore and could not leave his episcopal work just then. Those days were followed by weeks at Park Hall and then in Wales at Penlan, which we had so carefully retained. The whole summer was a time of refreshment and reassessment. Thanks to the care and foresight of Kenneth Wilson, Henrietta's father, we were also able to take possession of Hill Orchard, a pleasant house with a lovely garden on the west side of the Malvern hills overlooking Colwall. This meant that we had a real base and a home from which we could organize schooling and life in England for part of the family. It was never easy to take the decision to educate the children privately in England. Schools in Singapore were adequate, but the climate was not conducive to steady development. At home Rachel, by now eleven, was able to go to the Alice Ottley School in Worcester and thence to St Mary's, Calne. Robert went to prep school at Cothill near Oxford under the care of George Pike who married my sister Gabrielle, from where he was later to go on to Winchester, and the three youngest, after some time in the kindergarten at Colwall, were ready to start up their schooling back in Singapore. Henrietta remained to keep the children together for several months after I returned to Singapore in January 1955. We were then set for another period in the Far East, but with children commuting backwards and forwards. That was not altogether satisfactory, but it was the best arrangement we could make and it did not involve grandparents or relations having to assume responsibility at home. In all our plans for the children's education we were fortunate in having the help and advice of three heads: Betty Gibbins at Calne, Sir Desmond Lee at Winchester, and George Pike at Cothill; we could return to the Far East knowing that these schools would educate the children on our return to England, which was a considerable consolation. Their help to a travelling archdeacon was very real. I found myself flying back alone. It was January 6, the Feast of the Epiphany.

I had spent Epiphany 1939 in India, 1941 in the Birmingham Blitz, 1943 at Assisi and 1948 at a missionary conference. For me it has always been a day on which I have tried to see what the mission of Christ was all about. Is the day meant to be a comfortable reminder of the gifts of the Three Wise Men with all the symbolism of gold, incense and myrrh? Surely there is more. Is it not rather a day in which to focus on the offering of many to the living God? Ever since I had visited the Church of the Epiphany in Delhi, I had come to see something of what we mean by the light that was to illuminate the non-Christian world of the East. The Kings saw the light and responded to it, and that gave the church its real motivation to enable light to shine in darkness. What Epiphany made me think about was far wider than any concern for the maintenance or prolongation of the institutional church; that would look after itself. The Feast of the Epiphany was a reminder that the church was primarily for the benefit of those outside it rather than for those within it – the theme frequently pursued by William Temple – and that led into the very heart and foundation of ministry and mission.

We had spent the night in a hotel at Hatfield, near Sam, and the next morning I flew off from what was still then a shanty-town of tin huts and temporary buildings at Heathrow. My sense of loneliness and isolation was relieved by the interests of the journey, which at that time took much longer and involved a number of stops. There was Amsterdam, with two hours of talk about some Dutch help in our diocese; Düsseldorf, Rome, Cairo and Karachi, each with time to

[111]

look around. Air travel was indeed leisurely! At Delhi two mornings later we were warned that there were dust storms ahead which had ditched an earlier Comet: the pilot would have to take an alternative route. As the sun was rising, our own Comet flew away from the plains and made a diversion right over the top of Mount Everest, and in perfectly clear early morning light we were able to look down on the top of the world. From the momentarily sublime view of God's creation we dropped down to the dust and human degradations of Calcutta and Bangkok. Singapore was welcoming, but the house was very empty.

Nevertheless, work rapidly became all-absorbing, and now with some years' experience of the Far East behind me I was able to identify priorities.

The staffing of the mission was my responsibility, and while in Europe I had spent quite some time in finding men and women with specialist abilities who would join us in Singapore for specific purposes. Time was not on our side; Europeans were increasingly handing over to Asians, and it was particularly necessary that the same thing should happen in the ministry. Brian Barker came from Manchester, willingly released by Billy Greer, who had a good eye for the right man in the right job. Brian took charge of the young peoples' work, baptism classes and much else that built up the Chinese congregations. Rachel Wharton came out and brought to women's and children's work a quality of leadership and care that was remembered for years. Michael Halford, now an archdeacon in Western Australia, got to grips with students and professional families spread out over a rapidly expanding city.

Lester Phankuch joined us from New Zealand. As a good evangelical he did not really approve of vestments or 'Catholic' practices. When he celebrated, we put him in a cope and called it an eiderdown. On his birthday the rest of the boys arranged that a Chinese ice-cream vendor should ring bells outside the east window during the celebration of the eucharist. The congregation almost collapsed with laughter!

Many ideas for the ministry and for the congregations were welded together in our meetings. We had come from very different backgrounds. Rachel Wharton was a trained lay worker from the Midlands; Brian Barker had served his curacy in Manchester, and Jeremy Sampson already had good experience in Newcastle and up-country in Malaya. There were also contributions from the Indian and Chinese staff. We always met for prayer, breakfast and planning at seven o'clock on Tuesday mornings and again for a totally relaxed and often hilarious curry lunch on Sunday.

The building up of the congregations of the cathedral into large groups at 7, 8, 9.30 and 10.45 each Sunday morning, together with the development of daughter churches in the suburbs of Upper Serangoon and Changi, went ahead almost too quickly as so many whole families and individual young people came forward for membership and baptism.

Under the influence of Sorby Adams, our Australian headmaster, St Andrew's School became a church with its own congregation and did in fact become a source of new Christians. In a similar way, through our girls schools and among the women in the city, Nora Inge, the Principal of St Margaret's Girls School, was also successful in this respect. Of all the changes in Asian society after the war with Japan the most marked was that to be found in the life of women and children. This change of attitude was largely due to the Christian schools. We were not looking for emancipation as such, but for freedom from the chains of ignorance and fear. Of course our schools enabled boys and girls to grow in wisdom, but there were also new relationships between parents and children, mother and child, women and the community. And all this did in fact begin to change the shape of non-Christian family life. Plural marriages became fewer, mixed marriages in which one part was Christian were entered into with more understanding; children were no longer chattels, and of course women increasingly took their place in society, commerce and the professions. Singapore, of all the large cities of Asia, seemed to develop a freedom, not just of trade, but of attitudes, and established social disciplines that were and still are quite unique. There are good grounds for claiming some credit for the mission schools in all these respects.

It was, however, the training of a local ministry which continued to be the most pressing demand on us. The Cantonese, the Mandarin and the Indian congregations looked to Trinity College, which we had founded, for their ministry. To help to meet something of their particular needs, the Episcopal Church in the USA gave us the services of a theological teacher, Kelly Clark, and his wife Priscilla. They arrived in 1956. Kelly was a man of great ability and stature and a competent sportsman, and with his experience of theological education in California he brought a new dimension of religious and pastoral training. He was attached to the cathedral, where he preached regularly, and under his guidance a hostel for Anglican students at the college was developed in such a way that it played a role within the ecumenical project. His arrival, and the real imagination and professionalism which he brought to his work, helped to make the training of a truly local ministry into a reality. And we British learned a lot from him, too. Having worked for four years in Singapore he went on to develop similar but much more substantial work in the Philippines, and then became Dean of Berkeley at the time when it was amalgamated with Yale Divinity School. His contribution to the critical era of establishing an indigenous priesthood was as much through his personal care as through competent theological teaching.

The pleasure of those years in Singapore was regularly enhanced by the visitors who passed through. There were many of them, since it was at a crossroads of international travel. Frank came to stay on his way to visit brother Sam in New Zealand; indeed it was while he was staying with us that he was invited by the Diocesan Board to become Archbishop of Melbourne. Dear old Ernest Moule, Archbishop of Sydney, got muddled and thought that I was the brother who was expected to go to Australia; it took some cabling to clear the confusion. A worse situation might have been created when Geoffrey Fisher simultaneously invited both myself and Freddy Temple, Dean of Hong Kong, to become Vicar of Croydon. He took a calculated risk that one of us would refuse, but he did not realize that Freddy was staying with us when his invitation arrived! We both refused. Bishops and Moderators, members of the family and many others, found Singapore a convenient place as a stop-over or as an introduction to the Far East. Benjamin Britten and Peter Pears were our guests when they came to give concerts in the city. I had hardly seen Ben since we were at school. We recalled our making music together, and Ben invited Edward, who was six years old at the time, to play a duet with him. Clergy and members of neighbouring churches in Borneo, Java, Saigon or Bangkok also came our way: Henrietta kept open house to dozens of visitors every year.

Harry and I continued to share the travelling over our enormous diocese. He kept a watchful eye on Indo-China (as it was then), and indeed he did much for the war-stricken areas of Vietnam. Some of my time was spent in Sumatra and Java. I had been quite unaware that the Dutch Reformed missions in Indonesia had established by far the largest Protestant church outside Europe there. The church in central Sumatra had a million or more members; it made us Anglicans feel very small. But over the years the university and theological school there, which were efficiently based on Continental European patterns, had decided that English was to replace Dutch over much of higher education. This presented me with the challenge to select and supply a theological library in English. The Society for the Promotion of Christian Knowledge came to our rescue. Fortunately Christoph Barth, son of the great theologian Karl Barth, was there at the time and was well able to develop the Christian contribution to the university. He had the Barth aura about him, and by his personal magnetism was able to play a vital role in that country in the crucial period when it was finding independence.

Although relations with other churches over such a vast area were important, a further purpose of our visiting the outer stations, as they were called, was to care for our British commercial community. Rubber plantations, mines and many other enterprises all employed European staff. These were my main concern when travelling in the area, but there were also diplomats and commercial managers scattered all over three vast islands of Indonesia. To visit them was an activity quite unlike anything else! Alcohol, marriage difficulties and links with the home country were the usual problems which kept coming up. In their isolation there was little for Europeans to do other than have another drink, play bridge, or listen to the BBC overseas news. To be offered gin and water in lieu of early morning tea at 6 a.m. shook me a bit! In one area of tin mining and rubber plantations they had called a 'church' committee to meet me. To ensure a good attendance it was agreed in advance that a whisky and soda would be served to all present every time the agenda moved forward. That was in northern Malaya. In central Java I could show no surprise at the presence in a planter's bungalow of children he had had by his women servants, or at the woman of the house, who was clearly of mixed races. The Eurasian community created in East Asia by Dutch traders of the centuries, like the Anglo-Indian community created by our forbears in that area, in many ways provided a liberalizing and bridge-building section of society. However, with increased nationalism these mixed-blooded communities were often rejected.

There were more than enough matrimonial problems in the out-stations and oil fields of Sumatra to engage one's time and resources,

[115]

but at the same time they provided an opening for a Christian explanation and a forgiving attitude. Being all things to all men was a necessity when travelling round isolated British communities: one had to be flexible not only in the passing of judgments but in being ready to meet almost any domestic situation if one was to win their confidence. In nearly every location, however, it was encouraging to find numbers of isolated families and individuals who did in fact keep up their faith, who made good use of our postal Sunday School arrangements, and who maintained a loving respect for the church, though absent from its services.

Returning to Cathedral House and the security of Henrietta, the family and our friends around the cathedral was always refreshing. But changing gear from the highly personal ministry needed when on outstation visits to administering the archdeaconry was usually quite a jerk!

Administrative work was not always just as might have been expected. Snap decisions had to be made over the expanding life of the mission. I made a practice of acquiring land that would probably be useful in five or ten years time. This led me to buy, in my own name, the site on which now stands St Margaret's Girls School, one of the largest and finest high schools for girls in Malaysia. By the same means I secured the land for the first Anglican Chinese High School, to meet the needs of the growing Mandarin-speaking community of Christians. It was possible to see future developments, though in the late 1950s, when I found myself with a few trusted advisers planning for the future, it never occurred to us that we were in fact making only just enough provision for a city that would contain two million people within twenty years. However, the ingenuity and industry of the Chinese meant that what the rather amateur missionaries had inaugurated was developed efficiently in a very short time.

Riots reared their ugly head again at the time that Singapore was moving towards its independence in 1956. A curfew was imposed and violence erupted in the streets. For the children, both riot squads and Chinese funerals provided equally good entertainment. During the months leading up to independence it had become a privilege to be able to share in the consultations producing the settlement that established Singapore as a self-governing state within the Commonwealth. Against a background of the highly materialistic and secular outlook of the Chinese the distinctive Christian requirement of democracy and equality of opportunity stood out fairly clearly, and within the membership of the Constitutional Commission there were Christians who saw here the basic requirements of a state. Things were more complicated in Malaya, where the Malays were demanding a Muslim state comparable to the one established in Pakistan. When I was invited to give evidence before the commission for independence sitting in Kuala Lumpur I had the interesting responsibility of trying to advise on the implications of establishing a religious state. For Christians, and indeed for the Chinese, such a proposal did not augur well. All too often the established church in England was quoted at me, but to try to transfer such an unwritten constitution into a Muslim multi-racial situation was clearly impossible. A few of us tried to persuade the representative of the Malay Rulers not to adopt a Muslim state constitution. We showed what serious ambiguities can arise from trying to apply the Koran and the leadership of Imams to a democratic and evolving society, and strongly advocated a constitution of the kind that had evolved in India. Within that kind of framework Chinese, Europeans and others would find real partnership. However, our advice was not accepted: as result it is not difficult to discern the very slow progress that Malaysia has made in comparison to its neighbour in the south. It was sad to see the two countries forcibly divided. Although Government, commerce and cultural ties were broken, the Christian community remained as one of the few uniting factors in South-East Asia.

Without any bloodshed or really hard feelings both Malaya and Singapore thus moved into independence within the Commonwealth, but also, alas, totally independently of each other. Singapore went forward, as might have been expected from its tremendous resources of Chinese initiative, ability and hard work, not to mention finance. Malaya appeared amputated from the start. North Borneo became a partner, but that did not make up for the European or Chinese expertise upon which the Malays are dependent. One can only hope that those countries in South-East Asia that are subject to totalitarian and corrupting pressures will find some form of economic and political community in order to preserve their inherited values and ensure not only commercial progress but social cohesion. The churches had a contribution to make with the existence of a strong sense of Christian community between the congregations in Singapore and those in Malaysia; furthermore, each needed the support of the other. Political pressures were too great and the two new states were also obliged to become two dioceses.

Personally, too, things were changing. By mid-1957, we had come to realize that we could not remain much longer as a family in the Far East, or in a tropical climate. So our plan was to return home in 1958, and I looked forward to a call from a parish. During those remaining months I concentrated my activities not so much on the structures of the church, its ministry and impact on society, as on what I came to call in my journal 'courage to be Christian'. It had become the done thing for educated Chinese to become Christians. It was admitted that the old Taoist-Buddhist hotchpotch of family loyalties had broken up, and these pragmatic people realized that they needed another religion. So how could they be guided into true religion, 'knowing Christ, the power of his resurrection and the fellowship of his sufferings'? How could we see that they did not just embrace baptism as fashionable and something that reflected even further the American or British way of life? As a result the most rewarding activity of that last year came from the Friday lunch-hour periods of prayer and meditation in the cathedral. I had always loved teaching the ways and means of reading and knowing the Bible, and so the classes grew, both for those coming forward in need of renewal and those coming forward for the first time. Moreover, Chinese, Indians and Europeans had to learn to trust one another. And if they could not do that in the Christian fellowship, where else could they?

On arrival seven years earlier I had tended to see the role of the archdeacon and vicar as being a matter of personal leadership and administration. For the first year or two this made it a lonely start, but then the whole venture became a happy partnership. Singapore is a unique place for inter-racial cooperation and the parish was also unique in holding together so many national and religious traditions. It was only possible to make a contribution to the social and political scene because a sense of inter-racial unity had been totally achieved in the church. Further progress in mission and evangelism was made possible by the continuing life of worship and prayer practised by the hundreds who had become our friends at the cathedral. It was a congregation the life of which I never found again nor have ever seen at home. The fresh approach to faith, the joy in believing and the buoyancy of commitment and stewardship was such that I and the other clergy were able to do the Lord's work without hindrance. In time they will be sending a mission and ministry to Europe.

= [7] =

Sheffield

Accepting a parish blind is always a risk. We had taken that risk once when I came out of the army. Surprisingly we did so again when I accepted the parish of Tankersley together with the archdeaconry of Sheffield. To accept such an appointment without seeing what it involved at first hand would have been a great risk had we not been able to trust Leslie Hunter, the Bishop, who had both an enormous understanding of the personal abilities of people and a ready grasp of where the clergy whom he knew could minister effectively. So we accepted the judgment of an old friend as to where we should start afresh back in England.

All too often a clergyman these days opts for an environment that he feels to be right when in fact the decision is conditioned by the professional hopes of his wife or the educational needs of their children. This is not a satisfactory state of affairs, as I found twenty years later when it was my turn to guide men. Other people's assessment is always better and more enduring than one's own: we would never have gone to Singapore or Sheffield had we assessed our own abilities or even wanted a say in the sort of place in which we envisaged our ministry.

Leslie Hunter was not everybody's cup of tea, but as a deeply committed Christian and a very able professional clergyman he probably developed the best-administered and the happiest diocese in England during and after the war years. He it was, more than any other man, who shaped my ministry and dominated my thinking about the role of the church in England during the post-war years. Public affairs were for Leslie Hunter a proper sphere of Christian obedience and ministry, but he was equally clear that the church must give fresh thought to its own administration and activities. He was very well versed in the form and content of public worship, and indeed in 1965 he produced a Diocesan Service Book for his clergy in order to improve the use of words, singing and participation in the parish churches. His radical pursuit of church reform and concern to meet the needs of society was undergirded by a strong but simple personal faith, which he shared with his friends; it was also rooted in his years on the staff of the Student Christian Movement.

Leslie Hunter collected around him a team of men and women who responded to his far-sighted leadership. Oliver Tomkins, later Bishop of Bristol and a colleague with me from SCM days; Alan Ecclestone, a remarkable parish priest with a deep and effective social consciousness; and Pamela Keily, who was able to develop drama and women's ministry in the diocese, were among them. By the time Henrietta and I arrived he had persevered in his efforts to relate the church to the wider community in South Yorkshire; he had won the confidence of both labour and civic leaders; and he was held in considerable respect by the management and unions in the steel industry. In this particular field he had working with him Ted Wickham, and together they had created the Sheffield Industrial Mission, recognized as a unique development among the churches in Western Europe. In order to enable both clergy and laity to become involved in wider issues he established two conference centres, Whirlow Grange and the Hollowford Youth Centre, where those in education, the social services, industry and other relevant areas could meet and discuss together the problems and ethics of working life.

I found his individuality attractive but not always easy. He did not suffer fools gladly and was renowned for his lack of small talk: he would be quite ready to sit in silence when confronted by difficult people or intractable problems. However, his interests and ability as I have described them did·serve as a 'job description' for what I would have to deal with as archdeacon. In my parish I could test out his methods; in the city I could follow up his contacts in industry: and I would share in his leadership of the church's mission. There was clearly more than enough to get on with, and the rectory at Tankersley proved a most happy and satisfactory home from which to get to work.

And after the separations of the Singapore years, when increasingly the children had been at boarding schools and had even been cared for by uncles and aunts for their holidays, Tankersley rectory indeed made a memorable home. Set in a piece of unspoilt country, with

Orgreave colliery, South Yorkshire

Hoyland Common to the East, Tankersley Main and Wharncliffe Silkstone pits to the north and with the suburbs of Sheffield just over the hill, it was ideal for us. At the top of the garden was the fifteenth-century parish church, isolated from the population, but in its quiet setting nevertheless serving the needs of the locality. A never-ceasing chain of buckets carrying coal from the pit to distant coke ovens went across the garden: a perpetual reminder of the coalfield on which we lived. With enough space for each of the five children to have a separate bedroom and with old coach houses alongside, the rectory wrapped itself round us as though to defy all efforts to separate our family again.

Tankersley parish was a mediaeval benefice attached to the estates of the Earl Fitzwilliam, whose enormous mansion, Wentworth Woodhouse, was a mile or two away over the hill. Our two pits provided the livelihoood of the whole neighbourhood. Around and beyond them, and separating them from Rockingham pit, a housing estate of about a thousand persons had grown up between the wars. The houses, though simple, all had gardens, with a shop and the pithead at the bottom of the hill and a small brick church with a tin roof at the top. The village with its church was known as Pilley, and formed the heart of an otherwise very strung-out parish. In spite of its lack of 'village green', and with a remote parish church not untypical of the South Yorkshire coalfield, I soon found how rewarding it was to be involved in a ministry to a mining community. This was a totally new experience, and one from which I was to learn a great deal. They were marvellous people.

From the day of our arrival in Yorkshire Henrietta and the family seemed able to enter into the venture. We had never experienced the warmth and friendliness of Yorkshire folk before, and we all were able to enjoy the place and our neighbours. However, although the children were away from home for much of the year, they did not lose touch with our people and the congregations in our two village churches, and at the same time they found a living religion of their own. Looking back, we cannot be too thankful for having had a real vicarage life just when the children were going through their formative years.

For the family as a whole this was the most rewarding of our appointments and it became an era in which we were all able to share in the worship, the social life and the general concerns of an enjoyable parish. It was never quite the same again in terms of a corporate family commitment to the church. For Henrietta it also presented opportunities for developing women's organizations, moral welfare and the care of unmarried mothers, together with an increasing partnership with clergy wives in the diocese, all of which she took up readily.

The rector's warden of the parish was Reg Guest. He had worked underground for nearly forty years but had recently been 'promoted' to a labouring job at the pithead. He well remembered times of abject poverty in his early years, and he had gone without food and warmth at the time of the General Strike, but he had never lost his vision as a

Christian. He recalled the days when the pit-owners would punish the misdemeanours of a collier – such a serious offence, for example, as being found with matches in his pocket – with compulsory attendance at church for three or more Sundays running. No wonder the established church and the role of the rector had become isolated from the working community! Nevertheless, the activities of the church and a sustained Methodist ministry, all located near the pits, had preserved the deep-seated Christian brotherhood of the working man, his wife, his children and his home – and that in housing which today would be regarded as wholly unacceptable.

Early in our time at Tankersley, Henrietta was away with the children over a Sunday. 'Will you come and share Sunday dinner with us?', said Reg Guest. I was both touched and delighted to go to their old colliery dwelling, one in a row close by the pit, a house which had no bathroom and a WC only across the back yard. Reg and I were invited to sit at the table in the kitchen while Mrs Guest waited on us. 'Wilt tha' have pudding, Rector,' announced the meal, and a large plate of Yorkshire pudding adequately laced with raspberry vinegar was put in front of me. It was delicious, and was followed by a helping of meat, potatoes, peas and gravy. Reg complained to his wife, 'Eh, missus, tha'st given Rector all clart but naw dinner.' I expressed my surprise and gingerly enquired what he meant. In fact he felt that there was too much fat and gristle and not enough lean meat in my helping, so it was all 'clout', the red cloth or handkerchief that wrapped the bread and cheese which he took to the pit each day. The total integrity of the Yorkshire miners, many of whom had deep religious convictions, was an element in the community on which the church was built, but it has now been dispersed and they are disillusioned.

Over the years the benefice had acquired great resources from coal royalties and valuable glebe. Under the patronage of the local Earl it had been a plum living. However, even before the law compelled such benefices to share their riches, Leslie Hunter saw to it that no vicar or even archdeacon should be paid more than a good diocesan average. He had forgotten about the resources of Tankersley until he was due to come on a March evening in 1958 for my institution in the parish church. He met me in the vestry with a strange greeting. 'Before we go any further, Robin,' he asked, 'would you sign this?' I asked what the document, by now laid out in front of me, contained, and discovered that my stipend was to be limited to the diocesan average and that the balance due to the benefice would be channelled into the bishop's discretionary account. I had to sign – otherwise there would have been no institution. That was clear. But in being firm Leslie was always caring. The very next day he was off to pay a personal visit to a parson's wife who had been taken ill, which involved him in a long drive.

Once established in that area of interesting coalfield around Barnsley and Hoyland Common from which our congregation was drawn, I entered into the wider responsibilities of the archdeaconry which soon began to open up. The job of an archdeacon was really what you made of it; it certainly involved the administrative nuts and bolts that held together the hundred and more parishes in and around Sheffield. It was Leslie Hunter's philosophy to share his episcopate with his assistant bishop, his two archdeacons (for many years Peter Bostock was at Doncaster), the provost of the cathedral and his diocesan lay staff. This may have been cumbersome when it came to making appointments, assessing men's abilities and their family commitments, but it ensured that the members of the leadership team knew one another's minds and the diocese knew which way it was going; it also gave the bishop confidence in delegating responsibility to staff who were trusted by the clergy. This left him free the better to cope with the constant demands of the central church and the House of Lords. As far as I was concerned, our staff meetings at Ranmoor Grange, the Bishop's house, set a pattern for both policy-making and administrative efficiency that was to see me through future spheres of work.

However, being an archdeacon was much more than adminis-tration. It was soon made plain to me that my primary commitment in that role was the individual mission of each parish and the corporate mission of the diocese to the population. I was expected to give useful information about the state of a parish to the bishop before he visited for a confirmation or institution. He was not always sympathetic to those with difficult ministries. On one Monday morning meeting with him I was curtly informed that it was not his custom to take a confirmation for a bare half-dozen children. He fully expected me to have taken such a barren parish in hand before it got in that kind of state. It was, however, my role to point out that he could hardly avoid going to this parish or any other that was at a low ebb for one reason or another, and then trying to provide some support for clergy working in very difficult conditions. Hence quite soon after I arrived

I found that I had to protect the man who had been got down by the lack of response to his ministry. I would visit his vicarage or volunteer to attend his church council, and indeed perhaps offer to help on a Sunday to enable him to take a holiday. This established links for me with many disconcerted parish priests. Perhaps more important was the need to help the clergy not to blame themselves overmuch for the indifference to religion in industrial society and to enable them to take a broader view, pointing out for how long the church had been ineffective in reaching the working population and how constricting was the society of the working man.

Over the years too many priests have become too busy in their efforts to maintain their congregations and their buildings to see their situation in the context of the long and slow process of adjusting to Christian values which has had to be followed as a result of the industrial revolution. My becoming identified with the weak parishes and helping their people to see the real issues was one of the most rewarding aspects of my archdeaconry.

In the late 1950s and early 1960s the diocese was in the vanguard of the stewardship movement. We were at the height of employing professional fund-raisers, who were hired by the individual parishes. Many sectors of the church were reluctant to accept the approach, but overall there can be no doubt that the impact of this American method of lay commitment not only produced cash for the hard-pressed parishes but also introduced a new concept of lay participation in the life of the church. I made it a point to attend stewardship dinners or the equivalent opening occasion in parishes which launched into the programme. However, I must admit to having had cold feet where our own parish was concerned: I found it embarrassing to announce our own personal pledge, which was a prerequisite of the fund-raising programme. But if the Rector did not declare his own position and the extent of his own giving, how could he expect his lay people to do the same thing? It was also plain justice that if lay people were to be stewards of their resources, then the diocese should undertake the same kind of self-examination and make estimates of the churches' resources in buildings, houses, land and other assets. Long before the days of pastoral reorganization under a synodical measure Leslie Hunter called for assessments of potential in the parishes, and with his encouragement certain parishes and their churches were totally reorganized. St Mary's, Bramhall Lane, close to the Yorkshire cricket ground, was transformed with great care from being a gaunt 'Waterloo' Gothic cavern into a two-storey community centre, leaving a small worshipping area and much good accommodation for children's work, youth clubs, adult education and social occasions.

This was a project on a substantial scale not untypical of much of the work in which I was involved. It required a new constitution for a parish church inasmuch as the incumbent and his PCC agreed to share the financing and management of the building with the local authority. Local organizations, schools, social services and voluntary bodies could not be legally identified with the churches, however willing they might be, inasmuch as they did get grants from local and central sources. Could such an arrangement, involving education and social service grants, be made within the framework of a parish church? That was the problem to solve for those involved in the new project. Hard work on it by the lawyers and even harder work by the incumbent – in the case of St Mary's, Bramhall Lane, this was Stephen Burnett – paved the way for multi-purpose community churches in crowded areas of the city. It fell to us archdeacons in both Sheffield and Doncaster to initiate and carry through such schemes to enable the resources of an urban parish to serve the newly-housed local community better.

Sir Basil Spence, the architect of the new Coventry Cathedral, was hired by the diocese to design two new multi-purpose churches and several conversions. He was not easy to deal with, but on the whole he did respond to the needs of a parish by producing something completely new rather than improving traditional designs. At one time, when I had to supervise the building of some new churches in Sheffield itself to replace outmoded ones, I was able to draw on my experience in establishing new parishes in Singapore. Spence, however, did not take kindly to advice from others. As for example over his font. I pointed out that his design for the font in a new church was unsightly: it was like a dustbin and unsuitable for use at congregational services. He made his own position quite clear. 'Mr Archdeacon,' he wrote, 'I am not used to being corrected in matters of my own competence.' But I got my way – and we remained good friends.

More demanding, and in a sense more important than the general run of parochial care, was my chairmanship of the Sheffield Industrial Mission. Historically the mission had had its origin in the Second

World War, when Father invited Ted Wickham to undertake a chaplaincy to a huge ordnance factory in Staffordshire where there were some 20,000 workers living and working on one site. This experiment at Swynnerton had enormous repercussions, one dimension of which was the plan Leslie Hunter developed for the steel industry. He invited Ted Wickham to inaugurate a comparable mission in the Sheffield diocese, among the heavy steel and engineering industries of South Yorkshire. It was my privilege on reaching Sheffield to share in the leadership of this venture. Ted Wickham welcomed me and recalled the early antecedents and some of the most essential and distinctive theological insights of industrial mission. 'The work at the Royal Ordnance Factory,' he said to his chaplains, 'was the mainstream, even if there were other rivulets, and it was made possible through the vision of Bishop Edward Woods. Now we have his son Robin with us!' These chaplains were a competent group; each one was involved with one or more of the great steel foundries. They had won the confidence of Firth Brown, Hadfields, Steel Peech and Tozer, English Steel, Park Gate and Fox's out at Stocksbridge – names of firms which have now been swallowed up in the British Steel Corporation or have disappeared altogether through lack of demand. Within those large complexes and their management, designers and workers, the chaplains went to work on the shop floor, at trade union meetings, with works councils and in personal contact with directors, foremen and shop stewards.

Looking back on the agenda of Industrial Mission committees and through the papers of those who were interviewed with a view to joining the team it is possible to see a rough outline of the chaplain's role. A typical job description would include the following tasks:

1. To enable your work force to recover personal identity in response to the personality of industry.

2. To work for relationships in your steel works that lead to trust and care.

3. To be available for personal and family problems that do not reach the churches or professional agencies.

4. To bridge the gap between conflicting groups in a foundry and to expose the realities of class/management/shop-floor and ethnic differences.

5. To expose the hypocrisy of much industrial negotiation.

6. To develop avenues of communication in your working environment.

All this enabled a priest to enter a secular situation with a clear brief. The description had been vetted and agreed by both management and unions. Its clarity stood out in marked distinction from the role of the parish priest, who more often than not has to work out his own priorities and responsibilities. However, the set of guidelines posed quite a problem. Was this really a job for the ordained ministry? Was it not too far removed from the sacramental role of a priest? How was the programme to relate to the local vicar and his congregation? And perhaps most important was the question of how the continuity of such ministries, once inaugurated, could be maintained. As archdeacon I found myself grappling with these issues, and in view of the long-term policies of the church generally and our diocese in particular they needed to be answered if the mission was not to become a flash in the pan or at worst a breakaway movement from the mainstream life of the churches.

Undoubtedly Industrial Mission was a fresh line of approach which might begin to bridge the gulf that separated institutional religion from the minds of 'working' people. Most clergy are ordained with a greater sense of mission and challenge for conversion than they are usually credited with. It is only force of circumstances in a great many cases which substitutes for this a preoccupation with maintaining an eclectic congregation and their worship. Here indeed was a new programme primarily for conveying Christian insights to those who were ignorant of or shy about Christianity, which demanded a priestly spirituality and a strong motivation to communicate the gospel. It emphasized the need for patience and long-term encounters before the clergyman would be able to exercise his sacramental ministry, and at the same time it combined proclamation and teaching in the secular environment. Was this not perhaps the work of believing laity or social workers? Maybe in an ideal situation, but it was in fact the groundwork of any ministry, and too few clergy were able to benefit from it. In some ways it was close to what the service chaplains were trying to accomplish in the war.

How close a relationship could be established between an industrial chaplain and a local vicar and his congregation was almost entirely dependent on the open-mindedness of the clergy involved. These were fundamentally complementary ministries, but all too often this was not appreciated by one or the other: to bring them into some form of team venture was an essential but sometimes a long process. In the diocese we took care not to appoint those who would insist on a narrow or uniform type of ministry. It was a matter of weaving threads of different colour and strength into a pattern that demonstrated the wholeness of the churches' concern for the population. When it came to ensuring continuity, it was realized by the leader of the Mission and by ourselves that men accepting industrial work had to put promotion, or 'preferment', as the church regrettably names it, on one side. We also asked for a minimum commitment of six years if a man was to become identified with the management and work force of a major industrial unit or local works area.

One development illustrates very well the significance of the work of the Industrial Mission. One very large works, Steel Peech and Tozer, decided to dispense with a labour-intensive process of feeding the melting-shop and go over to electric arc furnaces, which needed far fewer men to look after them. This reduced the number employed on that one site from some 11,000 men to 7,000. This dramatic change was accomplished without any strike or expression of grievances. And it was largely due to the long-sustained presence and helpfulness of John Rogan and Michael Atkinson, the chaplains concerned. Both management and unions found confidence in their quiet work.

It was not more than a few years after I left, in the early 1960s, that the Mission collapsed – to the enormous regret of many in Sheffield and of others outside who had seen it as a model for the churches' ministry to industry. This is not the place for a detailed assessment of the causes nor an evaluation of the personalities and events that led to the venture proving to be only transitory. However, it must be said that the principal factor in the collapse was the appointment of a bishop in succession to Leslie Hunter who was unsympathetic to the deployment of the ministry as he found it in Sheffield. The system of Crown appointments must bear some of the blame. A sizeable group of clergy had a right to expect a continuity of policy, but Downing Street saw differently or was content to ignore the situation.

John Taylor, Principal of Wycliffe Hall, and not to be confused with John Taylor, Bishop of Winchester, or John Taylor, now Bishop of St Albans, came as bishop with a different perception as to what the ordained ministry was about, putting his entire trust in parochial and church orientated ministries. He arrived with a conviction that the mission needed to be sorted out, and did in fact dismiss two members of the staff, causing much distress to the men themselves and real sadness to lay men and women who had supported industrial mission at all levels. The doctrinaire attitude of this new bishop, when flexibility was needed, frustrated and scattered a remarkable move-ment of clergy and laity. In retrospect, however, it needs to be recalled that by the time we in the diocese came to realize his closed mind we also understood that he had been a sick man ever since the cerebral thrombosis which he suffered before his enthronement.

However, it must also be admitted that there were always the seeds of failure in the tension that existed between the parochial work of the diocese and the sector ministries. There were some chaplains who were hostile to parish organization – though that was not unusual at the time: it was all part of the radical reassesment of faith and churchmanship, of which John Robinson's *Honest to God* was a part, a reassessment that was disturbing traditional attitudes to religion. It is sad in retrospect to recall the differences of attitudes that led to the breakdown of that particular experiment in mission, and I personally was grieved that the demise of the mission came so hard on the heels of my leaving the diocese. A greater flexibility in the leadership exercised by the bishop might have saved the situation. Such flexibility is even more vital now than it was then, as we realize that fresh economic and social forces are at work in the deployment of the resources of every diocese.

At the same time as new connections were being established between the church and heavy industry, we were particularly concerned to see that the hospitals, the university and the new housing estates had comparable teams of well-equipped men and women to work within them. As the National Health Service took shape we hoped to enable the chaplains to undertake their work alongside the medical services in the hospitals with pastoral care and technical skills. The growing understanding of the spiritual in the sphere of healing was a moving development in those years.

In the diocese we made much use of Dr Frank Lake and his 'clinical theology' approach, by which the clergy could learn the elementary psychology of healing, pain-control and terminal illness, and so take up the healing ministry of Christ into their own experience. 'Cemetery Duty' was by no means irrelevant to this work. For years it had been the preserve of a small number of clergy who might repeat the burial service half a dozen times a day – and indeed have an additional source of income as a result. By order of Leslie Hunter, a rota of clergy was organized for cemetery and crematorium duty. This gave the local vicars another way of relating to bereaved families. A parochial street directory was prepared by the diocese so that an undertaker could not say that he did not know in what parish a house was to be found. Moreover, since the old burial office in the Book of Common Prayer was wholly unsuitable for the non-churchgoer, the Bishop himself wrote a new service and authorized it for public use. It was printed and distributed, and well received, twenty years before the Alternative Service Book appeared.

Dealing with such apparently minor issues came my way in those years. Yet they were not in fact as minor as all that. The problems involved were the cause of so much of the lack of the credibility of the church in the eyes of the public that they had to be tackled one by one if the clergy were to fulfil their real role and the laity to experience something of the spiritual traditions beneath the unprepossessing surface. In these respects it was never easy to monitor a parish or mission, or even a church school, but the archdeacon had to attempt something of the sort. An annual address to all the churchwardens at the time of their licensing was an opportunity over which I took much care, using it to deal with questions about congregational life to which the laity wanted some answer. The two of us archdeacons prepared the material together, showed it to the bishop and had it printed, so that the gap so often complained about between the thinking of the diocese and the practical needs of the parishes was at least diminished, if not bridged.

When it came to enabling and encouraging the clergy, whether parochial or secular-sector, in their work, the most pressing need was to help them to share their ministry with their laity. Here it was a matter not just of asking the men to be treasurers and the women to run coffee mornings but of encouraging men and women to be motivated by the gospel in their secular activities, seeing their work as a dedicated service 'penetrating into places and groups where the ordained minister cannot go, speaking and acting as the spirit guides', as we put it in one charge to churchwardens. That is easier said than done, but with gentle encouragement many a lay person began to share the ministry either at work or in the local community. At one of our Parochial Church Council meetings, when we got to the stage of Any Other Business, an engineer in my parish working at Newton Chambers, the chemical factory attached to the coalfield, got up and said rather solemnly that he and others would like to take on the care of those living at the pithead to enable the rector to get on with his real job of meeting and talking with people right outside the church.

When a PCC member had reached that point of initiative I felt that our local ministry had begun to take shape.

So it was that in the coalfield, the steel works and the diocese in general, with such laity around as John Peel and Graham Murray, both master cutlers in their time, and women like Pamela Keiley and Diana Whittacre, we were entering a new era of credibility for the churches. It was agreed that there should be a lay chairman for every diocesan committee and that he or she would be supported and helped by the assistant bishop or an archdeacon, a system which brought out the best in the laity concerned and in the senior clergy involved. It was quite inappropriate, therefore, as Leslie once reminded us, to use the analogy of shepherd and sheep for the congregation of believers. That imagery no longer provided the pattern of our professional ministry. Unlike other professions, ours was to become a ministry shared with non-professionals. The laity as they find their faith are not sheep to be guided or sheared; nor are they even to be trained as sheep dogs for the flock. They are the partners in any emerging Christian community.

I was not able to forget the impact of industrial, social and indeed wider mission that we had experienced. It made the church credible in an unchurched section of the population. It gave meaning to the church's often over-used word evangelism; it gave the clergy a sense of encounter with secular society which was often lacking in parishes, where they were over-committed to their congregations. It made me determined that, wherever I might be, I would not forget the wider mission of the church among those who carried the economic and industrial cares of the nation.

Early in 1962 I was encouraged to take a break, so I left home with Rachel, temporarily free on leaving school and before going to Trinity College, Dublin, for a visit to our old sphere of work in Singapore. The main reason for my going there was that it was the centenary of the founding of the church and cathedral on the island. We arrived on 24 January, the eve of the Feast of the Conversion of St Paul, and to our astonishment found about a hundred people at the airport to meet us. From the moment of our arrival we were welcomed in Chinese, Indian and European homes, revisiting many who were old friends and many who had been converted when we had been there. A great many questions were asked about what the church was doing in Sheffield. We soon settled in among so many of my old colleagues.

The centenary the next day was memorable. There again was that tall white cathedral down on the waterfront, with the skyscrapers of the commercial city and the teeming population of Chinatown close by. There were many hundreds of worshippers that day, mostly young people. I preached the sermon and did my best to recall for them the significance of the time when the great Daniel Wilson established a second cathedral in a see that then stretched from India to Japan. I reminded them of what had grown from that initiative. After a splendid evensong there was a feast, at which 1,650 church members sat down on the 'padang', the great lawn that surrounds the building. The Chinese are past masters at erecting temporary roofing and organizing such a dinner: chopsticks and ten courses for us all!

A week later the cathedral was once again a wonderful centre of thankfulness and friendship. Some 550 received communion at the parish eucharist, and in the evening the congregations speaking Cantonese, Hokein, Mandarin, Tamil and Malay all joined us in a most lively evensong. It is not easy to convey the thrill of meeting with so many new Christians and so many young people vigorously committed to the working out of their faith in days of constant change. Singapore by then had one and a half million people, and over fifty per cent were under eighteen years of age. The church there reflected this incredibly young community. It was a tonic to be back.

This was also a chance to visit my brothers in Australia and New Zealand so that we could catch up with one another's ministries and so share our varied spheres of work and experience. I found Frank, after six years as Archbishop of Melbourne, leading a tremendous programme of diocesan advance; in his province of Victoria he was appointing and guiding bishops over a wide area of Australia. The work was well suited to his ability and energy and I could see that he was much appreciated; he was in due course to become Primate of the church in Australia. He had always had considerable gifts of speaking and administration, and it was all proving a lasting and happy move. In New Zealand, Samuel was vicar of a large parish in Christ Church, as well as being archdeacon, and his wife Billy was giving him much support. The church in New Zealand had clearly taken them to its heart. To see the methods of both Frank and Sam in that part of the world gave me many fresh ideas and incentives: by comparison the church at home was stuffy and unresponsive to a new situation. The visit to Singapore, Australia and New Zealand with short stops in the USA on our way freshened up my plans for the work on hand in Sheffield.

It was good to be back at the rectory and in harness again with Leslie and the diocese. I never regretted having a parish in addition to the archdeaconry. It gave me a much closer relationship to the parochial clergy than I would have otherwise enjoyed and it supplied a sphere in which to test the methods and opportunities of congregational worship and some of the developments I have described. Both at Tankersley and at Pilley our little churches in the one parish began to thrive, and with the help of successive curates including John Nurser, now Chancellor of Lincoln, who ran youth clubs on the basis of leadership from behind, we made progress with the next generation.

It was an added bonus to have standing almost in our garden our beautiful mediaeval church, in which I was able to pray quietly every day. We had come to love the parish, the miners and their families. We came also to love Sheffield, its people, its churches and the countryside around. We were busy but we were also, as a family, wonderfully happy.

Henrietta was able not only to run the women's activities in the parish but also to give a hand in the care of clergy, their wives and their homes at a time when wives were increasingly leading their own lives, going out to work, and needing to find a new role in partnership with their vicar-husbands. She also shared in shaping fresh avenues of social work in our urban areas. What Henrietta was able to do in the diocese and parish was small compared with managing the house, the gardens and the schooling of the children; writing letters to those away or ferrying the two younger ones to their schools in Yorkshire was a priority on her time and energy. She would constantly be visiting for half-terms or other occasions which required long journeys by car, just when I could not get away because of Sunday or other duties. We bought a mini and became a two-car family.

I was looking forward to carrying on the same activities for several more years after the break, but one morning we had a more than routine telephone call. It was an invitation from the chaplain at Windsor for me to preach before the Queen on the weekend after Ascension Day, and for us to stay with him in the Great Park. Of course we accepted. The prospect of going to Windsor was a great thrill. The theme of the Sunday was the kingship of Christ, so with a well-prepared sermon, we set off to make the most of the occasion.

═ [8] ═

The Unexpected Deanery

Ascension Day and the Sunday afterwards are particularly restful and satisfying days in the Christian year. They also mark a turning point for the would-be Christian, in that following Christ moves from being personal allegiance and even local experience and activity to accepting the recognition of his kingship over the whole of life and the world. The potential extent of the kingdom is borne in upon one at Ascensiontide, and so it was when we left Tankersley for Windsor, in a state of pleasant relaxation and without any expectation. We returned realizing that our visit was probably to be a turning point and milestone in my life.

We reached the Great Park on the Saturday before the service at which I was to preach and found our bearings; Ted Ward, the resident chaplain, was kindness itself in making us feel at home. We were glad to meet the principal Private Secretary, Sir Michael Adeane, and Lady Adeane that evening, but hardly expected that our acquaintance would deepen. I preached on the Sunday morning, and many of those in the village church in the Park were very friendly. Since the Queen Mother had invited Henrietta and me to lunch, we walked with her to Royal Lodge. There we were further greeted by the Queen and Princess Margaret. The lunch party was an enjoyable occasion, with many reminiscences of the long friendship that Father had had with George V, George VI and Queen Elizabeth during his years at Croydon and Lichfield, and as Lord High Almoner. However, the main topic of the conversation was rather different: it was about the need for the church to discover avenues of renewal and to promote leadership for the rapidly changing circumstances of the day. The Royal Family seemed to know of and appreciate much of the work that I had begun in Singapore and Sheffield; Henrietta, too, was deeply involved in conversation about the role of the parson's wife. No mention was made of St George's Chapel at Windsor, and we never had an inkling of what the real purpose of the sermon and the lunch was all about. Perhaps we were slow, but Father had been a friend – and what a pleasure it was for us to meet the Queen and her family once again! After much spirited conversation we took our cue, and left.

We had planned to break our journey home almost immediately to see the Savill Gardens, since the azaleas and rhododendrons were in full splendour at that time of year, and had in fact told Ted Ward of our intentions. To our surprise no sooner had we stopped there than he reappeared. He had come after us with a remarkable message: we learned that he had been authorized to inform us, without further delay, that in all probability I would be receiving an invitation to be Dean of Windsor.

We immediately wondered whether that was the sort of job that I should do next. We did not see ourselves readily fitting into a very enclosed deanery or a sphere of work with no parochial or diocesan responsibility, and one that was potentially isolated from the mainstream of the church's life. We drove off very unsettled, and knowing nothing of the implications of the proposal. However, as it was by then only four o'clock, we thought that since we had time it might at least be helpful to see the famous chapel and its surroundings. But we found it closed to the public in preparation for evensong, so we were no further on in picturing the future. The long drive back to Sheffield was punctuated by periods of silence and much speculation.

Then the letters started arriving. I soon became aware that although it was the right of the Prime Minister to nominate to St George's, from Queen Victoria onwards the Sovereign had been personally involved in the choice of Deans of Windsor. Sir Michael Adeane wrote asking me if I would be prepared to accept the Deanery of Windsor; if I was, the Prime Minister would approach me officially. We were not able to make up our minds quickly. The nature of the job was undefined, and it was not easy to gain some reassurance by probing more deeply into the position. There seemed more than enough canons and minor canons to run a church which had no parish and no diocesan opportunities. Eric Hamilton, the previous Dean, had been an old friend of Father's, and indeed was formerly one of his suffragan bishops. Appointed during the war, he served George VI and Queen Elizabeth and their young family with quiet ability, but financial

difficulties over the Chapel and the independent attitude of the
canons, together with increasing ill health, had made his latter years
a burden. He died shortly after he had announced his pending
retirement, in 1961. We could not therefore go to him for advice, and
he had left little information about the Chapel at Windsor. Our friends
in the north fully expected us to pursue the urban mission of the
church. Was something like Windsor really our kind of job?

The Deanery of Windsor is a 'Royal Peculiar', a term which we
explored. Strictly speaking there are only two such institutions,
Westminster Abbey and St George's, Windsor. Each one is 'a collegiate
church with a self-governing community, extra-provincial and extra-
diocesan, coming directly under the personal jurisdiction of the
Queen who is the visitor'. Such a definition did not make us much
the wiser, except to show us that the appointment, though offered
by the Prime Minister, was the personal responsibility and interest of
the Sovereign. There were problems: while the canons had no place
in the selection of their Dean, they were all-powerful, as they soon
made clear to us in the rather reserved reception which they gave us
in our early visits. And it was also clear that I could not accept
the titular headship of a cathedral-like foundation without some
commitment to the local or wider mission of the church. There was
no sphere in the diocese of Oxford, within which Windsor lay, that
needed the leadership of the Dean of Windsor, and there were
adequate churches in the town – in fact there were too many of them.
There would be openings for the pastoral care of the two hundred or
so who lived in the Castle, but then the canons and minor canons
rightly saw this as their responsibility.

On the other hand there was the rather unexpected field of possibly
being able to be a real help to the growing family of the Queen and
Prince Philip; furthermore we had learned from our initial invitation
that Her Majesty was concerned that the resources of the Chapel and
the Foundation should be reviewed and redirected into avenues
which would be of service to the wider church. Clearly worship,
Christian adult education, and consultation on moral and social
issues, if imaginatively developed, could all make the foundation of
St George's Chapel more relevant to Windsor itself and to the
churches.

Here the canons were cautious in the face of any proposed change
or innovation. Yet if the ecclesiastical foundation associated directly
with the Crown became any more of a backwater it could discredit

the link between the state and the church. So it was not difficult for the Queen and her advisers to persuade me that new blood and new initiatives were a contribution I could bring. I was soon convinced that there was a real job, the conditions of which would shortly become evident.

Closely related to the immediate concerns of the Dean was, of course, the care, support and use of the great Chapel itself. There was much to attract and become proud of. St George's, one of the most splendid late Gothic edifices in Europe, is traditionally the place of worship of the Royal Family; it has also become the last resting place for many Sovereigns over the centuries. It maintained splendid daily services with superb music in the name of the Sovereign as part of the royal commitment to the established church; it was a magnificent centre and setting for the Most Noble Order of the Garter. It had a thriving choir school, closely linked with Eton College over the river. Moreover, any financial problems it might have were alleviated by the imposition of admission charges, which the Chapter had introduced to make sure that visitors who came to see the beauties and enjoy the historical associations of the Chapel brought in considerable revenue to support it.

However, there things seemed to stop. The place was also highly private and introspective. Michael Ramsey, the then Archbishop of Canterbury, although well-disposed, had real doubts about the possibility of doing anything with St George's, and Leslie Hunter thought that I would be wasting my time. 'Don't be a courtier,' said Billy Greer. But then Oliver Tomkins, Bishop of Bristol, who had been a friend and adviser ever since we had been together on the staff of SCM, clearly felt that this was a sphere of ministry well fitted to my qualifications. Clearly the Chapel itself was potentially a wonderful resource for worship, preaching and indeed developing a congregation of thinking people who supported the life and work of the establishment. With an endowment sufficient for three residentiary canons and two minor canons it should surely be possible to create a constructive team. And if Westminster Abbey, the sister foundation, with a similar constitution, had grown into a place of mission and involvement with the nation, should not the same also be the case with St George's?

It was all very difficult, and decisions were not made easier by the state of the Deanery that we had been invited to occupy. On first impressions it may have been splendid, but as a domestic proposition

[138]

it was desperate. In Tudor and Jacobean days it was all part of the royal residence. There were fourteen bedrooms and inadequate domestic arrangements: could they be improved, and if so, by whom? By the Chapter? But it had minimal funds. By the Crown? But it had no legal responsibilities. With whom should we deal?

Here our problems were answered to a considerable degree by the ready help of the members of the Royal Household – in marked contrast to the corporate attitude of the canons. We soon received good advice not only from Sir Michael Adeane but also from Sir Edward Ford, Sir Martin Charteris and Lord Tryon, the Keeper of the Privy Purse. With their encouragement a small block of the seventeenth-century addition to the Deanery was pulled down, new bathrooms were installed and the kitchen made adequate. Although the house still had twelve bedrooms together with historic reception rooms, it became a very pleasant place in which to live. Indeed it was the most lovely house, and thanks to Henrietta became a home the family will never forget.

Helpful though others were, the man who most readily shared the prospects and the opportunities that lay before St George's was Roger, Earl of Scarbrough and Lord Chamberlain. We had got to know him well in Yorkshire, where he was a good friend of the diocese of Sheffield, and now as Head of the Queen's Household he soon became a remarkable support and adviser. At his suggestion I produced a memorandum on the future of St George's for the personal consideration of the Queen. It included the following recommendation:

It is estimated that the most urgent need of the parochial clergy of the Church of England is not more pay or better housing but ways and means to obtain a contemporary understanding of theology and experience and at the same time an updating of pastoral and teaching methods. For soldiers, there is the Staff College; for commercial executives, there are courses in management and salesmanship: for teachers, refresher courses, etc., etc.; but the clergyman, once he is ordained, perhaps in his early twenties, is given little further help or opportunity of learning new methods and developments in his vocation. The use of the College of St George for training the ministry has been pursued at different times, and recently considered afresh. Our intention would not be pre-ordination training of older men, but bringing in incumbents, rural deans and specialist clergy to a period of refreshment and instruction.

Increasingly, the church is inviting and accepting the insights and understanding of the laity. The re-establishment of contact between the church and the estranged urban communities is dependent on the laity being able to think through the application of the faith to countless situations in the normal life of society. The Order of the Garter as the lay component in the Collegiate Church provides a precedent for developing courses and consultations for lay leaders in the nation.

I had still not made up my mind. And I felt strongly that before I could take any final decision about the job the authorities should agree on a wider role for the Chapel. Otherwise the severe warnings of the Archbishop and Leslie Hunter that I would not find fulfilment at Windsor might prove to be right.

There was, and still is, a remarkable harmony of mutual efficiency among the Household and Secretariat of the Queen. But when it came to my enquiring in some detail about the wider role of the Chapel I was politely informed by Michael Adeane that it was not for me to question the terms of a Crown appointment. That hardly helped me in my dilemma, but at this point Lord Scarbrough promised that he would speak personally to the Queen about my various uncertainties, and about the proposals surrounding the Foundation and my leadership of it. I heard no more until Ascot Week, when Lord Scarbrough told me he had found a good occasion to talk at length to the Queen and show her my memorandum. He conveyed to me a message of unqualified support and reassurance from Her Majesty in all the matters connected with my personal work, the use of the Chapel itself, the reshaping of the Deanery and the future establishment of a centre for clergy and lay training.

Towards the end of many meetings and consultations it was becoming clear that we should tackle the job. Taking the decision was made easier by the understanding of my brother Frank, who cabled from Melbourne, 'Unsought responsibility cannot be refused. Acceptance will surely reveal purposes at present hidden. Sympathy, love, laughter. Frank.' This message was followed on the same day by a note in his own hand from Sir Michael Adeane:

> If I can be of any help to you please let me know. I don't pretend to any deep knowledge of the work of the Dean and Chapter but Eric Hamilton – who incidentally mentioned your name on several occasions with much affection and regard – told me a certain amount

about what he hoped his successor might be able to do. There is certainly a great deal of scope, so I think that Eric's poor health prevented him from doing as much as he would have liked.

There is one other point I ought to mention. One often hears Windsor referred to as the sort of job from which no one ever emerges except to retirement or the grave. It so happens that this has been its history since the First War.

But I can assure you that this is not the Queen's policy nor is it that of the Archbishop of Canterbury. Her Majesty's hope, which she has mentioned to me several times, is that the Deanery should not be a terminus but an important wayside station.

Please forgive my unecclesiastical language, but I can think of no better way of explaining what is meant.

After more advice from John Hewitt, the Prime Minister's Appointments Secretary, and a talk with Harold Macmillan, the Prime Minister himself, who indicated the Royal Family's great concern for a strong ministry in the context of Windsor Castle, I received this letter:

> 10 Downing Street
> 11 July 1962
>
> My dear Archdeacon,
> I am glad to inform you that The Queen has been graciously pleased to approve your appointment as Dean of Her Majesty's Chapel Royal in the Castle of Windsor in succession to the late Right Reverend E.K.C.Hamilton. I understand that The Queen wishes you also to be the Register of the Knights of the Most Noble Order of the Garter.
> I would like to offer you my best wishes on your appointment to this important post.
> Yours sincerely,
> Harold Macmillan

Even so, had it not been for the generous and kind intervention of the Queen and Prince Philip, who welcomed us and hoped to see something new coming out of the appointment, we would not have been able to accept the situation. It was through their personal interest and support that a great many changes in the collegiate life and purposes of St George's came about.

Our final days at Tankersley were very happy. The congregation of miners and other who lived around the great pits where the

Wharncliffe Silkstone Seam was mined proved loyal and lasting friends. The archdeaconry was well supplied with clergy, for this was immediately before the days of shortage: nor was inflation a serious bother. The summer holiday at Penlan turned out to be a memorable occasion: all five children were with us, together with other friends. Rachel was starting her years at Trinity College, Dublin; Robert was now free to enjoy history, art and wider reading for his A levels at Winchester. With Edward, Eleanor and Mary also happily at school, Henrietta and I started on the move to the Deanery. Fortunately the M1 had just been opened, and the new era of rapid road journeys was with us.

The Chapter had proposed that I should be installed at a routine weekday evensong in November with little or no extra ceremonial nor any special invitations either to the Royal Family or our own friends. In the end things were very different. The service of installation took place on a snowy winter's evening on 10 December 1962. The Queen most generously broke with tradition and came in person, with the Queen Mother. She was readily content to sit in a special temporary seat since the Dean has to be installed in the Sovereign's Stall, where he invariably sits in her absence. By tradition, the Lord Chancellor, as Visitor of the College, had to be present, and he came in full regalia with the Clerk of the Crown. Many friends had driven from Sheffield, including a coachload from Tankersley who, I am sure, enjoyed the reception in the state apartments as much as the service. Rarely had we experienced the support of so many and so varied a circle. For my part I felt very clearly that God was speaking through the particular circumstances of Windsor and calling me to go to what would be a privileged and unique sphere of ministry. In my sermon on the threshold of becoming Dean I used the superb imagery of the call of Moses at the burning bush, the assurances given him by God in the face of an unknown future and the promise that God would be his guide in leading the people to a new freedom. Not that St George's was exactly in captivity – but it was certainly in need of liberation if it was going to meet the demands of this century.

My early months were properly taken up with the immediate care of the needs of this cathedral-like church. Edward IV had built it in the early 1470s. He was determined to do better and build bigger than his despised predecessor Henry IV, who had raised Eton College Chapel down in the valley below. Edward III had built the first chapel,

[142]

but now St George's Chapel was to be the scene of unbroken daily worship in a church that would reflect the faith of the Sovereign of the Order of the Garter and of the nation. It was also enjoined on the College that appropriate prayers and masses should be said for the kings, queens and knights who had departed this life. To this day the regular 'Obiit' services are in fact rather wonderful. And so the result of Edward VI's requirements and benefaction was a church in the pure perpendicular style, a final flowering of Gothic architecture with fantastic stone tracery of majestic proportions, all on a miniature scale which, with King's College Chapel at Cambridge, remains unmatched in Western Europe.

All was not well, however, with a building that rested thousands of tons of vaulting on slender columns and walls that were basically too light for their purpose. Two centuries after its building Sir Christopher Wren had added flying buttresses; other architects of the seventeenth and eighteenth century had placed the heavy 'King's Beasts' on the parapets as make-weights for the vault! Lutyens and others had supervised an exhaustive vault rebuilding in the 1920s, but the Chapel, even with hidden tie-rods, had a somewhat precarious roof. The great west window, itself the size of a tennis court and filled with splendid Tudor glass, was one of many where the leading leaked and required attention. The world-famous Quire with its carved oak stalls needed constant protection from woodworm.

To the financial expenditure called for by the many problems of the fabric was to be added the day-to-day cost of maintaining a professional ministry of priests, lay clerks, choristers, vergers, masons and others. Our task in all these respects was not made easier by Queen Victoria who, in 1872, required the Chapter to exchange their property of lands and estates for a permanent fixed annuity 'so that there might be no further anxiety in the maintenance of her Collegiate Church'. Such was the blind optimism of the Victorian era, where inflation had never been contemplated.

Cathedrals in the 1950s were encouraged to update their legal statutes; unfortunately not so the two Royal Peculiars of Westminster and Windsor. Of course events overtake outmoded constitutions in any organizations, and fortunately the Spirit is always at work guiding the church in one way or another. But I was to learn the hard way in my years at Windsor that ecclesiastical change comes slowly.

The development of any cathedral or great church has constantly been hampered by adherence to rules and traditions. I had been led by my parents and teachers to realize that the Spirit worked independently of them. To begin with it looked as if I would need a great deal of help from the Spirit. Bryan Bentley, the senior canon in the Chapter, who had been acting Dean, was a fund of detailed information, but not one for flouting, let alone changing, 'The Statutes': in the eyes of the Chapter I was to be bound by them. It was impressed on me that any variation of public worship or ecclesiastical practice would jeopardize the collegiate life, and in particular I was informed that the Dean was only *primus inter pares* in his relationship to the other canons. At the time this made me impatient. But partnership with the canons rapidly deepened and improved, and with the help of Jim Fisher and Robin Hawkins, and in the later stages of Bryan Bentley himself, we moulded ourselves into a team committed to a far wider programme than that envisaged by those who prepared the Statutes in 1340.

Finance and the care of the fabric became the particular responsibility of Canon Fisher and successive Chapter clerks, who took the burden of monetary matters off the Dean. In the same way the musical life of the place was directed and developed by Bryan Bentley, the Precentor, and by Dr Sydney Campbell. Dr Campbell arrived shortly before my appointment, from Canterbury Cathedral, in succession to many famous composers and organists of St George's, including Merbecke, Thomas Tallis, Sir Walford Davies and Sir William Harris. I found it an enormous pleasure and privilege to be supported in daily worship and tradition by a choir and organist of wide renown. The constant flow of very fine treble voices was largely due to the happy atmosphere and good academic standing of St George's School and Bill Cleave, its headmaster for over twenty years.

Music filled the Chapel so often and so much that it spoilt us. The choir improved over the years we were there. Sydney Campbell was a superb musician, competent composer and imaginative planner, but he was also highly temperamental. One evensong the choir were singing an eight-part Tudor anthem. He came down from the organ loft to conduct, a note was given and the choir started the unaccompanied work. However, as never before, the trebles went astray and the motet ground to a standstill. Sydney took his score and, to the astonishment of both choir and people, tore it up and threw the shreds at the boys. Total confusion was averted by the minor canon, who broke the silence with 'Let us pray'. Poor man, Sydney came to offer his resignation an hour later. However, I was able to calm him down and help him regain his confidence. Is there not always an emotional price to pay for good music?

The succession of choristers, lay clerks and assistant organists was watched over by Bryan Bentley on behalf of the rest of us. As we consolidated our members of the 'college' we increased the repertoire of music and became once again one of the great choirs of the country. The occasions on which we all went, choir included, to the private chapel inside the Queen's apartments were encouraging and happy times. In this respect Prince Philip provided invaluable assistance in helping us to establish organ and choral scholarships for shorter or longer periods, so that we always had young and hopeful musicians around as well as the professional choir. Later he was to commission Benjamin Britten to write a *Jubilate*, not for any special occasion but to be sure that our great composer of the day was composing for the church directly. Nevertheless, here, as in so many other matters, the buck stopped at the Dean. I was thankful that at home, at school and at Cambridge I had had a first-class grounding in classical music and in the appreciation of church music in particular. However, only twice in all my years there did I dare to play the Chapel organ – an enormous instrument with two consoles.

History has never been a strong point of mine: both my brothers took the History Tripos at Cambridge and had a good general knowledge of it, but I was largely ignorant of all but 1066 and all that. However, when it came to living and working in Windsor Castle there was no getting away from history: it confronted us at every turn. The first chapel built by Edward III could be entered from our drawing room, and that same superb early English royal church came to house the children and relatives of Queen Victoria. It became known, incorrectly, as the 'Albert Memorial Chapel' – in fact it spanned over five hundred years of the monarchy, almost within our home.

The great Chapel itself was always a reminder of the conflicts of the fifteenth century. Early in our days we became used to the visit of Eton scholars to lay lilies and roses on the tomb of their founder, Henry VI. He was originally buried at Chertsey, but Edward IV brought his body to St George's out of respect for his predecessor and perhaps as a penance for his treatment of him. The Princes murdered in the Tower have no memorial in St George's, but the building itself was erected largely to atone for the sins of the act. A daily mass for the soul of Edward IV was written into the Statutes at an early stage, and he clearly needed the mercy of the Almighty in view of his

treatment of friends and enemies alike during the Wars of the Roses.

Henry VII, who succeeded him, decided that Westminster was his own abiding love, and this became his resting place, but Henry VIII chose St George's Chapel in which to be buried. The Dean is reminded of him daily as he walks over the king's gravestone to his stall. Moreover, leading out of the study in the Deanery is the Aragon Chantry, which Henry VIII prepared for Catherine, his first and long-lived love, and it was there that she was permitted to attend popish masses even after the break with Rome.

The study at the Deanery also houses the table on which Charles I was laid after the hurried journey to Windsor on a snowy night immediately following his execution. Choirboys to this day swear that the stains on that Jacobean table are the king's blood. My predecessor had treated the great table with some reverence, allowing only photographs of the Royal Family to adorn it. Ted Ward commented on the winds of change when he first came to see me, and noticed that it now bore a drinks tray and flowers. From this enormous room in which I was to enjoy so many consultations and periods of work and reading, the body of Charles I was carried to the Chapel, there to be interred in the same grave alongside Henry VIII. There was no time for him to prepare his own tomb or special grave, and to this day the great black stone carries the names of those two very different monarchs.

The Dean's study is panelled throughout, with the coat of arms and names of the Garter Knights since James II. It was also through this same room that Queen Victoria regularly passed on her way along the roof walk prepared for her to the Aragon Chantry from which she watched the services in St George's after Prince Albert died. From there she watched with anxiety the wedding of Edward VII. Small wonder, then, that we found ourselves in the midst of history that was living; we came to love the Chapel and the house mixed up with it. As I sat and worked in that memorable room with its big window looking up to the Round Tower I was constantly aware of the church, the Crown and the state all being interlocked together.

The Dean is the only member of the Chapter who holds the personal appointment of Domestic Chaplain to the Queen. Not unnaturally, this leads to the common assumption that the Chapel is the church to which the Sovereign and the Royal Family regularly go when they are at Windsor. This is by no means the case: the Great Park church provides not only regular Sunday worship but also a steady and

◁ *Windsor Castle with St George's Chapel from the River Thames* familiar local congregation to which the Royal Family can easily and naturally relate. With Royal Lodge close to both the church and the Chaplain's house, Queen Elizabeth has been able to take a very close interest in the life and activities of the Great Park church. This was and remains a good arrangement, and it was made easier for me by the close friendship and ready partnership first of Ted Ward and then of Anthony Harbottle, successive Chaplains in the Park. It was always a pleasure to help out by preaching or taking services in this village church, which were in very distinct contrast to the formality of the worship in St George's Chapel.

In addition, the private chapel inside Windsor Castle is located behind the Waterloo Chamber and at the end of St George's Hall. It is octagonal, with galleries, heavily panelled and with poor 'religious' glass; the altar is rather small and the furniture in true Victorian style. All in all, it is rather dark and sombre, and not well suited to family worship; however, it was my duty to celebrate the eucharist there for the Queen, her family and her staff, at Christmas, Easter and on other high days in the church's year. Over the years the duty became something more: a very great privilege which increasingly deepened the relationship of the Royal Family at home in the Castle to the Dean. Reading the various records kept by previous Deans – Wellesley, Elliot and Randall Davidson in their ministry to Queen Victoria, and Dean Bailey, who served through most of George V's reign – I was made very conscious of this priestly and very personal contact with the Queen's family: it was a small but essential part to play in sustaining the faith and hopes of the head of our state and indeed of 'the Supreme Governor of the Church of England'. That it became so much more than that during our years at Windsor was due to the Queen's deeply felt faith in Christ, her unfailing concern for the religion and integrity of her people, and her day-to-day interest in the life and leadership of the church. At the same time, the enthusiastic interest of Prince Philip in both the faith and its applications acted as a spur in relating it not only to royal needs but also to the needs of the nation. Not many clergy these days have at the heart of their parish and congregation such a family that wants to believe aright and to understand commitment in today's world. Henrietta and I counted ourselves fortunate to have just such support.

For years I found preaching before the Queen difficult; and I came to expect critical – but always constructive – comments from Prince Philip afterwards. My notes would begin to take shape a week in advance, but time and again they were being rewritten on Saturday evening – a time we kept strictly for ourselves at home, no matter how many invitations were pressing us to go out. Sunday would come, and I would remember B.K.Cunningham, who taught me not to pray for myself before preaching but for the congregation. It did seem to me that it must be very hard for the Sovereign and her family to remain silent on so many matters and at the same time to carry considerable burdens on behalf of the people. So to preach was not in any way knowing better but a matter of sharing hopes and insights.

Of several occasions which stand out in our memory the birth of Prince Edward was a particularly happy one – for the Castle community and for the nation. To my surprise, I was asked to christen him. About a week before the baptism a message came from the Queen to say how pleased she would be if I were free to take the service, as the Archbishop of Canterbury would be out of the country. I went up to see her and we had a good talk about the hymns and arrangements; she told me how she would like it to be a very family affair. Overpowering and restless as Queen Victoria's chapel could be, filled with flowers and lovely gold plate, and with books and windows open, it came alive.

A gold font made for William IV was brought from London. It was like the one in the Tower of London, standing about four feet high, on a wooden base, with a large undecorated but very lovely bowl. With flowers all round it looked beautiful. At the christening the Queen, Prince Philip and the immediate family sat in front on one side and the godparents with more relatives and friends on the other. Henrietta was also included in the gathering. I introduced the service with a short explanation of its different parts and promises, we had two good hymns, and all went very happily. Princess George, Prince Philip's sister and one of the godparents, handed me the baby, who cried gently, but when I had him he was very good, happy and beaming. At the end I gave him back to his mother. It was a happy service.

The older children of Prince Philip and the Queen were very much of an age with our five. This enabled us as a family to be in close touch with Prince Charles and Princess Anne. Whether it was sharing go-carts in the Home Park or making music, Prince Charles with his 'cello and Mary with her violin, helped along by Dr Campbell, or through evenings and parties at Christmas time, our families came to know each other. When the time came for Prince Charles and Princess Anne to go to boarding school we shared many common concerns. It fell to me to go to Gordonstoun more than once for weekends with Charles and to Benenden to see Anne. Their parents were frequently not sufficiently free to go and take them out. The two weekends I had walking and talking with Prince Charles proved to be happy and useful occasions; this was the time shortly before his confirmation. Philip Whitfield, the school chaplain, gave us the facilities of the chaplain's house, as there was no privacy in Prince Charles's boarding house and it was not easy to be relaxed there. I was also lent a car and we got away from the constant public gaze. Back at home, in the holidays both Henrietta and I were able to talk leisurely about matters of faith and the future, first with Charles and a year or two later with Anne. The confirmation services were conducted, as only he could do it, with much meaning, by the Archbishop of Canterbury, Michael Ramsey.

There were indeed many occasions at Windsor which were marked with celebration and much enjoyment. There were also those situations where, as in any Christian community, we shared in one another's sadnesses. Early in our stay we were all bereaved by the death of Princess Marina, the widow of the Duke of Kent. Having tragically lost her husband in the War, she had lived the last twenty years exercising many royal duties and caring for her children. We had come to be quite familiar with Coppins, the Kent family home not far away. It was while on holiday in our cottage in Pembrokeshire, in August 1968, that we learned that the Princess was dangerously ill. I hurried to Kensington Palace to be with the family, but it was too late for her to be aware of my ministry. After a very beautiful service in St George's Chapel she was laid to rest next to her husband in the royal burial ground at Frogmore. There they lie, side by side, in this very lovely and quiet corner of the Home Park. Because the Queen's residence at Windsor was closed for the annual stay at Balmoral, the day was made the more memorable for Henrietta and me in that we were able to entertain the whole family, including the Duke of Windsor, in our home.

Compared with our time at Sheffield, where the archdeaconry and parish were totally time-consuming, Windsor provided a number of opportunities to pursue various aspects of the church's mission. It naturally proved much easier for me to take my place on the executive committee of the Church Missionary Society, which I found both interesting and challenging with its care for the church overseas. I had also been a member of the Council of the Churches Television Centre, on the invitation of Lord Rank. The Centre had been funded through the generosity of Lord Rank to assist all the churches in the growing use of the media, whether radio, television or the press, and provided a training and production centre for television and radio programmes. It proved invaluable and was an enormous financial saving to the churches; as it continues to be to this day, in partnership with the Roman Catholic Centre at Hatch End. In 1963 I took over the chairmanship from Lord Rank, and at the same time joined the Central Religious Advisory Council for Broadcasting. I felt that the contribution that I could make on these two bodies was not so much by originality of ideas in religious broadcasting as by seeing that the right people were enabled to use their gifts and get adequate training in the ways of the media. When I left Windsor, I handed over the chairmanship of the Centre to Bob Runcie, who at the time was Bishop of St Albans; by then it needed new leadership.

It was also interesting to join the Council of Haileybury College, and when Harold Wilson was in power he invited me to join the Public Schools Commission. This was a time-consuming but worthwhile assignment, and Windsor also proved host to much of the discussion; I shall be returning to it in the next chapter.

As I welded these and many other activities, particularly those associated with Church Assembly, on to the framework of my ministry at St George's, by 1964 it was becoming clear that in view of its historical traditions and resources the whole Foundation should be moving forward in undertaking a real share in the church's mission. We began to think and talk not only as a Chapter, but also in the wider context of the Order of the Garter, and of the fresh requirements of the churches for the latter part of this century.

═ [9] ═

Church and State in Miniature

The Most Noble Order of the Garter traditionally takes its name from the occasion when in 1348 Edward III recovered the garter of Joan, the Fair Maid of Kent, Countess of Salisbury, and placed it on his own knee with the words 'honi soit qui mal y pense' – 'dishonoured be he who thinks ill of it'. More likely is the origin which is partly outlined in the Black Book compiled in the days of Henry VIII, which remains in the care of the 'Register', who is always the Dean. In that account Richard I, while his forces were employed against Cyprus and Acre in the last crusade, was inspired through St George with renewed courage. His way of animating his weary soldiers was the device of tying about the legs of a chosen number of knights a leather thong or garter, thus reminding them of the honour of their enterprise, which had the aim of recovering the Holy Land for Christendom. This was supposed to have been in the mind of Edward III when he gave his own garter as a signal at the battle of Crecy, which fortunately he led to victory.

Whatever may have been the imagery that lay behind the founding of the Order, it was established to provide the King and his counsellors with a group of dedicated people. There were to be twenty-five knights and twenty-five canons, who were all to have their religious life clearly defined, the canons maintaining the sacred office of prayer and preaching and the knights united with the canons in heart but going about the affairs of state. Both knights and canons were to take promises of obedience to their Sovereign and to the various demands of Christian faith and conduct. For their part the canons were also to maintain a chapel, daily worship and the discipline of a collegiate church of knights and clerks in Windsor Castle, as a permanent base for the Order. For six hundred and more years the Sovereign has selected and encouraged a succession of knights not exceeding the statutory number. The canons, however, although also appointed by the Crown, gradually became reduced in number – at first because of their employment in offices of state. At the Reformation, when the status of the clergy declined, and in latter years, through domestic and financial economy, their numbers fell drastically. There remain only a Dean and three canons to fulfil the original statutes.

The partnership of Sovereign, knights and canons implied a Christian community managed not just by clergy or 'religious', which is what the church too frequently has become, but also by laity who knew their religion and who as a consequence exercised their responsibilities. To this day the Order of the Garter is fundamentally a religious Order, involving laity and clergy. On investiture every knight, kneeling before the Sovereign, still takes an oath of great solemnity, administered by the Dean. On being presented with the Blue Riband and the Star the knight is admonished to wear '... this Riband adorned with the image of the Blessed Martyr and Soldier of Christ, Saint George ... that thou mayest not only receive the praise of this transient combat but be crowned with the Palm of Eternal Victory'. And as he is robed with the mantle, 'Receive this robe of heavenly colour, the livery of this most Excellent Order... that being in this temporal warfare glorious thou mayest obtain eternal and triumphant joy.'

I always found it a most moving occasion when once a year, as Register of the Order, I assisted in investing the new knights, the donning of each item of their regalia being accompanied by a prayer. As I look back, I can picture such varied recipients as the Prince of Wales, Field Marshal Sir Gerald Templer, Clement Attlee on retiring from politics and Kim Cobbold, along with many others, kneeling for their investiture with prayer and becoming part of the 'cloistered' community of St George's Chapel.

Tradition has it that, when the early knights were unable through absence to observe the obligations of the Order for worship, they appointed deputies to be at prayer on their behalf. Thus, it is said, there came about the 'Poor Knights of Windsor' as a lay element in the Castle community, and committed to sharing the life of the Chapel with the clergy. Again tradition would seem not to be quite accurate. It appears that the 'Military Knights', as they are now known, took their origin from a decision of Henry VIII to care for such soldiers in need. There were also Naval Knights in the eighteeenth and nineteenth centuries, but their existence was short lived, as Queen Victoria dismissed them for their drunken habits!

Lay participation in the religious community was therefore ensured from the beginning: in that sense it was forward-looking in that it took lay people more seriously than in other mediaeval institutions; it was both more lay in leadership and more attached to life than the monastic communities which were largely brought to an end in the sixteenth century. The partnership also sowed the seeds through many generations of mutual understanding between the state and the church. Here were the two elements of the national community interlocked, not in antipathy, as became the situation in many areas of the continent, but in a common commitment to and vision of the future of the nation.

In Windsor Castle, then, there had in the providence of God grown up over the centuries a community of priests, clerks and knights who had together, under the Sovereign, borne witness to a common allegiance to Christ, shared common worship and prayed together for the welfare and salvation of all men. St George's had thus exemplified the conviction that in Christianity neither is the sacred to be divorced from the secular nor the clerical from the lay, but in the one body all the varied life of society should find unity and consecration. It has also upheld the ideal of a nation united not only in loyalty to the Crown but also in devotion to Christ. Consequently it was in keeping with the inheritance of the past that today there should be established a fresh opportunity for clergy and laity, Christians and non-Christians, and men and women of diverse skills and from diverse walks of life, to seek to rediscover what in our time has been so greatly obscured – the unity of truth and the unity of human society.

It is not difficult, particularly at St George's, to see and value the long tradition and grandeur of English religion. The church in our country has never been an elect few drawn out of secular society; it is a 'folk' church, the expression of the spiritual life of the whole of society permeating its institutions and its many avenues of life (as Owen Chadwick so clearly showed in his contribution to the 1964 Report of the Commission on Church and State). In the 1960s people were not prepared lightly to discard the idea of a national church; rather, the diffused inarticulate assent to Christianity to be found throughout the country was seen to be vitally important. It is still difficult to overestimate the value of this heritage, though in an increasingly plural and secular society the heritage is not easy to maintain. It is not only in the 'gathered flock' but in this continuing deposit of faith and goodwill and in the Christian vision of a political state governed by religious principles that the opportunity of the church is still to be found.

It has always seemed to me important that this common inheritance of Christian values should be articulated and presented to the public at certain points other than the Coronation and state occasions. At any time it is all too easy for the state, with a national Parliament, and the church to drift apart, particularly when the church is establishing a parliament of its own. Opinions differed, as they still do, as to whether or not it was a good thing to separate the church from the control of Parliament. In discussions of relationships between church and state some recognize that the hand of history can be a dead hand: they demand, further, that the church in the twentieth century should justify its own existence and in no way be dependent on even the sympathy of the Establishment. Others feel that the church should fade away and be replaced by better education, with the universities and intellectual and artistic institutions forming the basis of our society. Most are agreed that the nation would be the loser if church and state were formally separated as they are across the Channel. Given the existence of such rival views there is no doubt that a renewed theology of the state is needed. In the last century, Gladstone had an explicit Christian doctrine of the state, and F.D.Maurice saw the democracy of Great Britain as being closely allied to Christian values. In all walks of life it is still agreed that for all its possibilities for evil, demonstrated in local and international issues, the state is and remains an instrument of God, that God-given moral laws apply to it and that it has a duty to encourage the good and discourage the bad. At the lowest level of estimation it is still realized that the state has a curious dependence on true religion. And whatever else the churches may do or fail to do, they can exercise strong moral influences to which the state cannot be indifferent.

If, however, such a religious relationship was to be endorsed and enriched, I felt that above all the churches needed to recover a fresh understanding and acceptance of the role of the laity in formulating not only ethical standards but belief. It is the laity who can, far better than the clergy, identify and determine the Christian view in the economic, industrial and social areas of the nation's life. In these areas time is not on the Christian side and no longer can the churches sit back on tradition or enjoy differing approaches and alternative policies if there is to be any consensus on Christian values. The church can no longer be seen as the clergy, nor as the Archbishop making utterances; nor indeed are people to be seen as 'going into the church' only when they were ordained. Thankfully in the 1960s, as today, the church was emerging from a long period, indeed too long a period, in which for many churchpeople 'living the Christian life' meant upholding Sunday worship and a passive inactivity as Christians in local and central goverment. Religion had primarily become a matter of individuality or a social habit. The 1960s presented an opportunity not only to bring about a thaw but also to try to see why the churches had endured the freeze-up for so long. St George's seemed to fit this challenge perfectly. The opportunity offered at St George's would therefore provide the occasion not just to help people relate their faith and make it operative in the twentieth century, but also to enable the clergy to review their role, to measure up to new thinking and look at the future with a new degree of confidence.

Set as we were in a rich historical context, it was not difficult to be faithful to our own past. But such history as strikes one daily at Windsor, ranging from the Wars of the Roses, Henry VIII, and the Reformation, the turbulent days of the Stuarts and the over-comfortable eighteenth and nineteenth centuries to the present day, gave us a good daily lesson in humility and hope. Any new developments were not to be either too slick or too much allied to the establishment. If we worked hard enough we could reflect both the joy of the faith and the agony of the failures of our day, and somehow relate the two afresh.

In all this there was a ready and sure foundation for the development of the collegiate life of St George's. There was also substantial property and resources inside and outside the Castle walls. In the first place there was an endowment to maintain at least five senior or junior clergymen: that was a tremendous start! There were sufficient houses, many of them admittedly in need of modernization, for clergy, lay clerks, choir school, vergers, stone masons and the rest. Once rationalized, and with the opportunity of the Chapter Mews down below, there could easily be a 'House' in which twenty or thirty visitors could be comfortably accommodated. The Georgian residences of the two minor canons, if put together, could provide at least fifteen bedrooms, and neighbouring houses in the Canons' Cloister, including the Deanery, could provide further accommodation, all under one roof. In addition there was the library, a superb small mediaeval hall where books were kept but also where lectures and discussions could take place. St George's House needed to be a home, a centre of study and a part of the worshipping life of the church. All this was possible around St George's Chapel. More important was the fact that the Queen wanted to see her foundation develop into wider usefulness and fulfil a more distinct role. In this respect her wishes were confirmed and furthered by the increasing participation of Prince Philip over many months of consultation, and architectural and financial planning.

So it was that St George's House began to come into being. The Chapter was remarkably united, but not without painstaking discussion and after overcoming serious reservations. We had all been appointed on entirely different terms. Bryan Bentley and Robin Hawkins, the one a first-rate thinker and scholar, the other a splendid pastor and counsellor, continued to be basically in charge of the ongoing life of the Chapel with its music and worship, and care for both the local and the huge visiting population. The Chapter designated Jim Fisher to see to the administration of our new venture – a task for which he proved a most willing helper. He became the executive canon, supervising very large rebuilding operations and also the Secretary to the Trust that was to be established as part of, and within the terms of, the Noble Order and the College. I could not have seen the changes between 1963 and 1966 through without Jim Fisher's constant and detailed direction. I tended to be the one with the ideas; he monitored them and made it possible to fulfil them.

The generation of the Knights of the Garter in the 1960s still included outstanding figures from the military and political spheres of the Second World War and the years of rapid social change that followed. The Marquess of Salisbury, affectionately known as 'Bobbity', and Roger Lumley, the Earl of Scarbrough, together with 'Alex', the Field Marshal, had between them an accumulation of wisdom that was difficult to match. They formed themselves into a little advisory body and when they were joined by Prince Philip I realized just how fortunate I was with my immediate colleagues. With the addition of Viscount Slim, the Governor of the Castle, and Derick, Lord Amory, a very wise politician, the first trustees came into being. To begin with they certainly found it strange to be closely identified with an ecclesiastical establishment, but I could make it quite clear that the

Chapel had departed from its original foundation with prominent lay participation and had become too 'churchy'; these Knights were bringing the foundation back towards searching for new ways forward in Christian enterprise in the secular state.

It was a time, as it still is, when the world and society were changing with increasing speed. The environment in which the churches operated was being reshaped by science and technology and social 'engineering', all factors which in themselves opened up exciting yet sometimes frightening possibilities for the community in general. These forces, particularly in the field of automation, the mass media and expanding industrial activity, created new stresses and perplexities and imposed new choices to which the relevance of Christianity was no longer obvious, and to which inherited moral values often did not seem to apply. It was certainly true that the moral and ethical choices with which thinking people were confronted did not lend themselves to treatment in the pulpit: they were not issues upon which sermons could offer a final answer. The church's methods and structure for communicating the faith and 'Christian' values needed a totally fresh look. The role of the clergy as communicators of truth and behavioural standards was at sixes and sevens. The teaching of ethics had been practically abandoned in the seminaries for the ministry. But, as I have said earlier, the reason given was depressing: there were not enough men with experience to teach it!

Clearly the clergy who found themselves attached to St George's Chapel could not take on unaided the preparation, teaching, administration and personal care which would be called for by the succession of consultations and courses which we hoped to provide as our contribution towards doing something to improve the situation. Nor could we contribute any direct experience of industry or technology, which would be bound to figure in our gatherings. We therefore took the decision that our staff should include three fairly senior and experienced lay people. A warden was the first requirement, one who would be not only administratively in charge of the whole operation but would also be able to contribute from his own experience of the secular world and from his Christian commitment within it. In our long search we were fortunate in due course to have the help of Lord Mountbatten, then Chief of Defence Staff and a Knight of the Garter. He learned about our venture and was concerned to make it a success. He even helped us to draft the job description. To our surprise, when this was done he told us that he had an Admiral who, because of cuts following the financial pressures on the services, had to accept early retirement. After returning home and relinquishing his appointment, Rear Admiral Davies came to be interviewed along with one or two others from the academic world. The Canons and I were immediately taken by his wide social insights, his committed churchmanship and his clear administrative ability. We were agreed that he was our man, and after a meeting with him Prince Philip confirmed our views. Anthony, and Peggy his wife, with their family, joined us as soon as their house was ready. Over some seven years he prepared and carried through lay and clerical courses with a quiet efficiency and knowledgeable leadership. His naval approach to punctuality, dress and manners generally became a byword in the rather military atmosphere of the Castle. Over the years I have had many good curates and colleagues in the ministry. But my partnership with Anthony was as happy a one as I ever enjoyed.

Secondly there was the necessity of having a domestic bursar, a housekeeper and staff manager who would supervise the day-to-day running of a hostel. Again she would need to share our vision and relate happily to domestic staff if we were to retain them. Margaret, commonly called 'Ba', Morgan joined us when the House was being finally decorated and furnished. Not only did she prove a bursar of competence, but her welcoming way with those who came as strangers to the House and Castle soon made them feel at home. It was a tremendous asset to have her creating such a relaxed atmosphere. I was determined from the start that St George's House would not be either a retreat house or a formal institution. Nor, however, did we wish to establish a hotel. It was certainly to be comfortable, but not commercially so. Under our first bursar, who was able to recruit trained domestic and kitchen staff, we maintained regular prayers and even a confirmation class for the new employees.

The field of industry and commerce presented a complicated picture when we began to probe the opportunities for consultations on distinctly Christian leadership and management that rested on moral and ethical standards. Our third lay staff appointment needed to be a Director of Studies, one who could command respect in this area, but also could relate the industrial and urban state of the nation to those on clergycourses. We enjoyed the help of John Adair, then in charge of leadership training at Sandhurst. His proposals, particularly in the field of senior clergy training in leadership, were clearly important but new to the church. In this matter we were fortunate:

Kenneth Adams, at that time a Director of Hay's Wharf and deeply involved in the South London Industrial Mission, was prepared to consider leaving his secular appointment if a suitable opening occurred for him to serve the church directly. We were introduced, and after some hours of having outlined to him the general hopes of the house in the field of industry, trade relations and leadership training, all of which were very bold for a group of parsons, he clearly understood our purpose and shared my vision of what was wanted. His contribution over many years in outlining the creative opportunities in the industrial world has been widely appreciated. But more importantly his character and outlook fitted into our team of clergy and laity.

With our enlarged staff we clarified the purpose of St George's House and planned its inauguration. We hoped to gather leading men and women with a wide range of experience and knowledge in Government, Parliament and in the civil service; in industry, commerce and finance; in education and in medicine, for the discussion of whatever questions they regarded as being of religious and social importance. The various groups envisaged would contain those who represented Christian points of view and those who did not, since part of the purpose of the House was to look for creative interaction between Christian and secular-humanist thinking: it was by no means suggested that in these discussions Christian premises should be taken for granted – if that were to be a requirement we would not get the confidence of the non-believer. The House would be open to all who were seriously concerned to think about the problems of contemporary society and their own responsibilities within it. The impact of lay gatherings at St George's House is hard to evaluate, but they became known for their integrity and helpfulness. We were able to assess them some years later; I shall come back to this in due course.

Our second concern was to promote courses of study and training for the clergy of our churches in mid-career. At that time this had not been considered in any depth, except on a small scale within certain dioceses. We hoped primarily to provide occasions for those who took part to consider their ministry afresh in the light of social, cultural and theological developments. In addition we envisaged deepening their understanding of the continuing ferment of theological renewal in the church at large, as well as what was going on in the realms of science, education and industry. Sometimes this would be done on the severely practical basis of a discussion of parish administration, the place of team ministries, the deployment of money and manpower or the workings of local government and the voluntary agencies as they impinged upon the lives of parishioners. At least one course a year was prepared for rural deans, and another for archdeacons, so that these matters could be dealt with at their level of responsibility. We felt, however, that administration was not the prime area of instruction and discussion: that could easily become very frustrating. So we planned to try to help the clergy to rethink their ministry on the deeper level of belief in an unbelieving day. We would help them to analyse acts of worship, or of communication by preaching or teaching, and we would try to present the challenge of contemporary theology, biblical scholarship, psychology and the social sciences. Secular points of view would be introduced in order to acquaint the clergy with current ideas and attitudes. I was convinced that Christians not only have much to offer but also much to receive from the secular world. So I hoped that the general and clerical consultations would proceed side by side and would encourage cross-fertilization of ideas. Members of the clergy were therefore to be invited to sit in on the lay consultations and vice versa.

In addition to all this, I became a trustee of the interesting and important institution known as St Catherine's Foundation at Cumberland Lodge. Father had played a part in its founding. Towards the end of the Second World War King George VI and Queen Elizabeth resolved to make Cumberland Lodge serve a wider purpose than that of an over-large country house. After consultation with Father they invited Amy Buller, a woman of great ability, to open a centre for Christian consultation there particularly to meet the needs of universities, medical schools, the Inns of Court and other spheres of professional training. The warden soon made headway and enjoyed visits from a succession of senior and junior academics that have given Cumberland Lodge its well-earned reputation. Sir Walter Moberley was probably the most influential of the early leaders; he was followed by many distinguished figures. Although there were constant financial and administrative difficulties, this centre in the Great Park under Amy Buller's leadership was not in any way to be seen as irrelevant to developments that might take place in the Castle; rather, it has continued to enable those who met there to assess both their discipline and themselves in the light of Christian thought. Its ethos, different from that of St George's House, is certainly one for which academic life is the richer.

Throughout the months of planning St George's House we established a good relationship with William Temple College at Rugby. This centre for short courses, research and consultations had been developed by Mollie Batten and Bishop Leslie Hunter as a means whereby the forward social and theological thinking of the great archbishop could be carried further. It certainly met a need, particularly for the churches in urban and industrial environments. We saw ourselves as a comp-lementary institution, junior in the field of in-service training and ready to learn a lot from them. We were glad of 'senior' friends and advisers. Charles (Lord) March, now at Goodwood, who had been on the staff at Rugby, joined our council and guided the early consultations on values in industrial practice. Oliver Tomkins, Bishop of Bristol, was in the forefront of the ecological debate and hoped for a wider constituency of interest. John Habgood, the present Archbishop of York, then Principal of The Queen's College, Birm-ingham, was ready to lead discussion not only on science and religion but also on medical ethics. The concern of Ian Ramsey, then Bishop of Durham, was how best the church could take up the opportunities of the mass media. On the political, social and industrial side we enjoyed sustained help from Sir Burke Trend, Secretary to the Cabinet, Lord Redcliffe-Maud, Bill van Straubenzee and several from both Houses and both sides of Parliament. It was a privilege to have their help, but they all too frequently made it quite plain that this was the first time that the churches had engaged their abilities directly in the cause of religion. What had always been left to the clergy in the past had become the sphere of the laity in the present.

My appointment at Windsor coincided with the final stages of involving the laity in the government of the Church of England, since it was realized that the Houses of Parliament could not properly be regarded as representative of the parishes. The movement concerned with this, which had been at work ever since the Enabling Act of 1919 and through some fifty years of the Church Assembly, resulted in the setting up of the General Synod, which had real legislative power. Though conceived and striven for by previous archbishops, it was eventually carried through under the care of Michael Ramsey and Donald Coggan. To obtain the beginning of freedom for the church from the House of Commons was no mean achievement.

In such a situation we could not proceed without an ecumenical basis to our work: this did not fit too easily into such an Anglican foundation, but we soon had the advice and backing of Methodists, Roman Catholics and the British Council of Churches. In some ways we were breaking new ground for the churches in the United Kingdom by providing Anglican resources for the needs of other denominations, but in a wider setting we were quite backward. The churches on the continent had made much more progress, and we felt that we should know much more about what they were doing.

So in February 1964 I took myself off on a tour of other similar institutions and learned a great deal. After a quick visit to Dunblane and long talks with Ian Fraser, who had initiated much new thinking in the Church of Scotland, I left for Taizé. There I was able to pick up connections quickly. Through Leslie Hunter I had come to know the Order while I was in Sheffield, at an early stage of its development. On that hillside in Burgundy some twenty Protestant, Catholic and Orthodox priests and laymen had set themselves apart to be a disciplined monastic order but in no way enclosed. With their basis of worship they engaged themselves and an ever-widening circle of men and women, young and old, in working out the strategy of mission in Europe, South America and elsewhere. It remains an astonishing twentieth-century monastic movement. Taizé came to mean much to me. I made several visits to the place and, indeed was to return there a decade later as the Archbishop of Canterbuy's representative at its silver jubilee celebrations, sharing basic accommodation with five cardinals, and joining a eucharist of 20,000 people. I learned a great deal from Roger Schutz, the remarkable Prior of this ecumenical, monastic and yet open community. There, in the heart of secularized Europe, people were discovering not only a personal faith but ways and means of disseminating it within and outside the institutional churches.

I travelled on across the Jura, driven by a Taizé monk in a most dilapidated car over some very hilly roads to Geneva and on to Bossey, there to see the methods of discussion and communication developed by the World Council of Churches. All that Visser't Hooft, the General Secretary of the World Council, was directing through the various departments was invigorating for one who felt a bit weighed down with our institutional ways. The departments of Faith and Order, of Mission and of Christian Aid were all seen as being essentially complementary to one another. At the Ecumenical Institute founded by Hendrik Kraemer as a lay training institution at Bossey, a few miles along the Lake from the Geneva Headquarters, the consultative staff, the library and the opportunities for planned discussion or seminars gave me ideas for St George's House. Could we do anything as able, but on a much smaller scale? In the meantime the churches of Switzerland and the churches of Alsace had both established centres of lay training and ministerial renewal. On Lake Zurich, and near Hagenau up in the hills not very far from Strasbourg, the Reformed Churches of the two countries had established, each in its own way, a 'Mount of Transfiguration' for church members who had clearly felt the burden of urban and industrial life. They were wonderfully refreshing places, and the Bible study for differing groups and differing needs was an object lesson to the British churches. Their setting, the one above the Lake and the other in the quiet hills of Alsace-Lorraine, made me long to return. But that was not to be.

I travelled on into Germany to find Bad Boll. Here was perhaps the most substantial of the European Church Houses. Through the inspiration of Hans Lilje, Bishop of Hanover, and under the guidance of Eberhard Müller, Bad Boll served a whole range of church training requirements. Through the inspiration of the World Student Christian Federation they had exercised a great influence on the rebuilding of their nation. At the centre that the Evangelical Church had established, courses were available for teachers, doctors, personnel managers, clergy, youth leaders and others, all tailor-made for those wishing to pursue Christian values in specific fields. It was generous of the bishop of a huge German diocese, which is what Hans Lilje had become, and the director of Bad Boll to meet together with me at their Institute. We had last been together in the years before the Second World War, when the Student Movement had been formative in the life of the churches of Central Europe. It was in Sophia that we had met, trying to help the youth movements of the churches in Eastern Europe in their struggle against the grip of Russian Communism in the East and German Nazism in the West. So it was humbling now to have a reunion and consultation with two leaders of the Christian community who had both resisted Hitler, both discerned the evils of various totalitarian claims, both been imprisoned for their faith, and both been close colleagues of Dietrich Bonhoeffer and had even communicated with him in prison, at great risk to their families. The great days of the SCM had certainly produced great men. In no way could we British match the consistency of these German pastors, but even now we could be enriched by their experience of collapse and renewal. Indeed at the meeting we soon found ourselves able to compare the different situations confronting our churches in Britain and in Germany.

One reason why we could never aim at any activity at Windsor as all-embracing as that which I found in Germany was that the whole budget of the German centre was funded from the revenue of the German church tax: there was no lack of staff or physical resources there. But the very thoroughness of the Protestant churches in tackling mission to the new unbelieving, multi-racial and technological society of Central Europe was revealing. I went off not only laden with reports and proposals but with a strong resolution to make our new venture at Windsor in some way relate to our European counterparts. I put a fir cone from the edge of the forest outside their Institute in my pocket before my flight home. The seed germinated, and the two trees, one at Windsor and the other at Penlan, now some thirty feet high, are a reminder that we are all branches of the one true vine.

Over many months those who were sharing in the venture of St George's House made it very clear to me that however many ideas might be floated, or fields of activity or training envisaged, the essential next step was to raise the necessary funds. On the basis of the plan worked out by Paul Paget, our principal architect, and on the advice of financial friends, we were warned that not less than £350, 000 would be needed. This was a considerable sum in 1964. The figure was reached and was largely spent on the repair and rebuilding of the sixteenth-century Canons' Cloisters and other houses on Denton's Commons in order to enable a hostel for some thirty or forty visitors and staff to be incorporated into the houses and cloisters that clung to the north walks of the Castle. It was a costly venture to turn a conglomeration of sixteenth-, seventeenth- and eighteenth-century housing into real collegiate accommodation. Within this substantial figure was a sum of £75,000 designed to provide a modicum of capital to augment the income that would come from the fees charged to clergy and others to pay for the running expenses of the House, extra money which would be necessary in the early years. That my own salary and those of the participating canons were to be maintained by the Chapel itself made the whole proposition possible, and rightly enlarged the field of activity of St George's out of all recognition.

We were fortunate as we went to the country for this help. In the first place, not only was the economic life of the country moving into a boom period, but inflation had not yet raised its ugly head. Moreover, as I mentioned earlier, at this time the church had become newly aware of stewardship of money and resources and of the need for giving by the laity. Professional fund raisers were in fashion and had proved very effective in their service of parishes and Christian causes. Michael Hooker and his colleague Captain John Brown RN saw us successfully through our appeal.

However, alongside this special mention must be made of the direct and sustained help that we received from Prince Philip: he had already committed himself to many important projects, not least of which was the Duke of Edinburgh's Award Scheme. But in addition he understood the project of St George's House and consequently gave it his unconditional support. Anyone who had this exceptional backing could indeed consider himself fortunate.

Much inevitably fell on myself and my immediate trustees who were Knights of the Garter. Without their willing and prolonged help, and in the wider commercial field that of John Thompson, chairman of Barclays Bank, of Tony Keswick of Jardine Matheson, and several others, we would never have reached our target. As it was, we received several five-figure gifts from individuals or trusts who immediately caught on to the vision of the church engaging itself afresh with society. Lord Iveagh, Max Rayne, Lord Dulverton, Sir Edward Lewis and Humphrey Whitbread, together with the main banks and international companies, quickly took us forward. I personally or one of the active Knights of the Garter visited every potential donor. £250,000 was given or promised in a matter of four months. A further £100,000 was given by individuals with a real sense of dedication to our cause. It was humbling to be the recipients of such trust and generosity.

During the course of our structural and financial planning the Church Commissioners began to take a cautious interest. Ever since Queen Victoria had replaced the properties for which they had responsibility on our behalf with a fixed annuity, they had been wholly passive in our direction. Encouragement had been given to cathedrals and to Westminster Abbey to rewrite their Statutes and streamline their staff; not so to St George's. We did in fact approach Lord Silso, head of the Church Commissioners, for some advice, but that is all we received. He offered no material help, nor did he give any undertaking that the central church might help our royal foundation in the way in which it helped others. We were regarded as superfluous to need. Needless to say this became a cause of considerable estrangement. I tried to point out that the opportunity for lay involvement in the life of the church and also the in-service training of the ministry were not causes that would attract on-going public support, but should properly be carried by endowment resources. However, we made no headway. To this day one does get the impression that the central funds of the church are still too much geared to the maintenance of the parishes, which basically ought to become able to maintain themselves. It is the outreach and fresh ventures of the Church of England that so often need the pump-priming assistance of the central funds. One of the more difficult aspects of our development was the task of conveying to our lay clientele the unresponsive attitude of the Church Commissioners. Nevertheless, one way or another the money came in, and all of us on the Foundation received it with an enormous sense of gratitude. A major district central heating was installed for the whole of our end of the Castle; some twenty houses, including those clinging to the walls, were reconstructed, and St George's House itself emerged from what used to be the homes of the two minor canons. The Queen kindly took a close interest and with Henrietta and others advised on interior needs. The work was completed by the end of the summer of 1966.

It was on Sunday 23 October that St George's House was officially opened by Her Majesty. For the occasion and over the weekend we gathered a diverse and distinguished group of people at the House for its first proper consultation on The Role of the Church in Society Today. This very first consultation over the weekend of the opening of St George's House was an essential part of its inauguration. Lord Scarbrough came for the whole period and kept us informed, among other matters, of developments at Aberfan; it was that week when the houses and school of the South Wales mining village were buried by the slide of a slag heap with tragic loss of life.

On the Saturday, after evensong, we made a start using the library for the first time. The discussion was illuminating. Lord Caccia, Provost of Eton, led off. The point of his remarks was that the moral tone of the nation was, by default, dependent on the church. Who else could be responsible? The Prime Minister? No. The Commons? No. The Civil Service? No. Schools? Possibly. Lord Salisbury called the church to fresh thinking, as if he were addressing the House of Lords! A vigorous discussion ensued between those with very different experience and attitudes. When we resumed after dinner I invited Prince Philip to speak on 'What does the Nation expect of the Churches?' He spoke, quite brilliantly, for forty minutes and we had a far-ranging and productive debate conducted by laymen, which would have set an example for any ecclesiastical gathering. I was bold enough to chair the occasion fairly firmly and wrote a summary for them all on the blackboard. I was much complimented for holding such a group, thirty-five strong, in hand! At 11.p.m. that Saturday night we adjourned; I had a beer with Prince Philip, John Redcliffe-Maud, Gerald Templer and the Admiral and then walked to Engine Court with HRH, getting back to bed by 12.30. I was very gratified, but too tired to sleep before another long day.

The Sunday celebrations which marked the opening of St George's House by the Queen were full of pleasure and surprises. I celebrated holy communion, at which some twelve Knights of the Garter received communion in their own chapel along with many others – these days a unique gathering. My journal takes up the story:

> At eleven o'clock sharp met the Queen with Prince Philip, Michael Adeane and Lady Margaret Hay in attendance, on the steps of the Great West Door. As I led her up the Nave, packed to the doors, with the Military Knights on duty and the organ playing, the Choir broke into 'Vivat Regina': the whole setting was superb. Bryan Bentley as Canon in Residence introduced the service in a short but extraordinary explanatory word. He confessed his early misgivings and non-cooperation in the development of the collegiate life; he pointed out that a turbulent priest had been brought in as Dean; but then, to our astonishment, before the Queen and a large congregation thanked God for the new venture and for my leader-ship. It was a brave and frank statement that healed many wounds and now confirmed many hopes. The service that followed was one of common dedication of the resources of St George's for the increase of faith and Christian behaviour in our nation. Donald Coggan, Archbishop of York, was our preacher.

I then took the Queen in procession via the Quire and the Dean's Cloister round to the door of St George's House. It was a great moment. She named it, and knocked. We entered, and after that everything was easy and informal. I presented Henrietta, the staff, architects, builders and engineers. The Queen seemed very pleased with the House, which we soon left to walk down a lane of people to the library where she met some hundred and thirty people who had had a share in the work – many of them substantial donors. It was a lovely day, strong clouds and rich autumn colours, and I felt deeply thankful. How, though, I wondered, can the wider church capitalize on such a fresh beginning?

Soon after the opening of St George's House I realized that if we were to make progress with the secular side of mission then general consultations should concentrate on matters connected with business and professional ethics, and with relations between people in large organizations. Many consultations had the immediate aim of bridging the gaps between differing groups such as young and old in their attitudes, unions and managers, scientists and theologians, clergy and town planners, in the hope of defining areas of agreement and disagreement and perhaps finding some decidedly Christian values on which to build. In this way we hoped to involve both clergy and laity in each other's problems and so develop understanding and cooperation in our society that was becoming so segmented. As a gesture of support, the Rolls-Royce company in Derby indicated that they would second to us a manager who would advise us on the issues confronting the decision-takers in industry, and at the same time give some help to clergy, too, as they came to terms with industrialized society. David Ballantine was with us for nearly a year, and helped us through with several courses and consultations. His salary and expenses were found by his parent company, an arrangement which demonstrated a new form of partnership between industry and church. This gift from the company of his services and salary reflected the buoyant economic situation and the liberal attitudes of the day over manpower, and it proved a remarkable experiment for a theological institution. It was the laymen who came to us on loan who shook up our thinking and gave themselves to the in-service training and mid-career needs of the clergy.

We found that we needed to sharpen up our ideas and methods if we were to provide instructional or training courses particularly for clergy, who were accepting, or likely to accept, senior appointments. I therefore took myself off to the Staff College at Camberley for the inside of a week. It was good of the Commandant and the authorities of the place to permit a parson to sit in for a few days at a course in full flow: there I was able to see both the methodology of the Army in leadership training and the opportunities they clearly made for men to train one another. It was always clear, however, that it would not suit the ethos of the churches if we set ourselves up as a 'staff college'. Despite this, without using the terminology but making good use of the methods, we were able to plan a long series of mid-service clergy courses. We were able to borrow the planning and lecturing abilities of John Adair to a considerable extent in the inaugural long five-week courses for clergy: under the general management of Jim Fisher he set a pattern of instruction for the future. Together they created training methods that the bishops increasingly respected and to which they readily sent their more able junior clergy. Some four hundred men and a few women ministers have now been through St George's House on a four- to five-week course, and a great many of them have acknowledged its value for their ministry. Many have now accepted wider responsibility with a greater sense of preparedness.

Jim Fisher was the continuing link in running these courses: they took a good deal of planning and preparation. The selection of men in partnership with their bishops was very important at the start. Their personal areas of interest or research were encouraged by Jim, who followed their progress personally through this new initiative in ministerial training. It was no use having thirty men either arbitrarily chosen, or casually arriving, as had all too often been the case in other areas of clerical consultation. Once men had been selected they were given certain books to read and certain written papers to prepare. This advance preparation for a defined period of staff training meant that once they arrived we were able to make a rapid start and begin study and consultation within hours. When he was able, Michael Ramsey came for an evening of a clergy course. We found that it was an unprofitable use of his time to ask him to lecture on a given subject; the men were asked by groups to prepare questions to which they would like the Archbishop to reply. These were occasions when his erudite theology and wit came splendidly into play and they proved to be a productive use of his time, We also succeeded in mounting shorter and longer courses for the forty-year-old clergyman with a real prospect of being promoted to rural dean, whether in town or country; for the more senior man in his fifties who needed to find a second wind; and for those appointed to bishoprics. There was room, and I thought it important, to make time in all these groupings to talk through their ministry with individual priests. Often one needed to help them harness their abilities and concerns to those in other professions and so to work alongside secular experts in the world of social welfare. This personal ministry at St George's House was highly rewarding: the parson needs individual encouragement and advice, as it is all too often a lonely job, and this cannot be left to overburdened bishops. I was always made newly aware, as men came and went, of just how many good and dedicated men there were about the country.

Largely because there is no unified system of appointments within the Church of England, little attention had been given to men selected for bishoprics, introducing them to skills, methods and social information which would enable them effectively to hold the wider responsibility of a diocese. It went without saying that a course for aspiring bishops, archdeacons, Methodist chairmen of districts and moderators would not fit into the procedures of the church in the way that was quite natural for men in the Armed Forces who seek promotion, yet at the same time there was a need then as now for some sort of career structure if really good men were to be attracted into the ministry. At the same time those already committed to the arduous work of priesthood in an age of seriously declining numbers needed to be given help to develop their potential if they were to lead whole dioceses and relate to the wider national scene. We also found all too frequently that ministers in the churches, some of them holding senior appointments, tended to work in almost entire ignorance of and sometimes with complete disregard for the skilled help towards their work that could be readily provided by their local politicians, their local Education Authority or the social services.

Inevitably some thought it was a presumptuous move on the part of one who had no episcopal experience to be responsible for courses to help in the further training of bishops. When bishops, Methodist district chairmen and Presbyterian moderators were beginning to think and plan together, we inaugurated the course for those invited to senior appointments in the churches. It was a bold but tricky undertaking. We resolved to gather those appointed at least once a year while they were still fresh to their new job. The experience of staff colleges was available, but that was not the image we wished to convey. Nor was it a matter of imparting the nuts and bolts of diocesan administration, but rather of identifying the expectations that surrounded episcopacy and similar status. On the principle that people train one another I soon became clear that to pool knowledge and resources for the man who was to assume the leadership of several hundred clergy in any one area was valuable. And because our church, and to a lesser extent the other denominations, enjoyed a real respect in the life of the nation – in clear distinction to many churches in other parts of the world – the Bishops' Course provided an opportunity to meet the state. Through the good offices of Sir Burke Trend, and the willing cooperation of Edward Heath, we were able nearly always to have a Cabinet Minister with us for at least one long evening on each of these 'bishops' courses'. We were also able to bring top management in industry and commerce to the aid of top management in the churches. Such occasions proved their worth in those early years of St George's House; I am glad that they have developed and diversified in the 1970s and 1980s.

It did seem to those of us who were running the courses that one major reason why clergy become disheartened is that they set before themselves unlimited and unattainable goals, and thus deprive themselves of the normal satisfaction of human beings in achieving limited successes. This we tried to do something about. Many clergy just needed to have a cool look at parochial problems, and to make a prudent assessment of what steps each could take in his situation that might have a reasonable prospect of success. Moreover, all needed to have their faith and prayer life strengthened, and we did not neglect that either. I particularly enjoyed doing the Bible studies on successive courses, since in this way one could relate the superb historical and symbolic experiences of the Old and New Testaments to contemporary needs. After some years we were able to appoint Stephen Verney to a canonry. His Bible readings, devotional and practical talks greatly enriched any contribution the staff could make.

Without the help of many who must go unnamed here, but in particular David Say, Billy Greer, David Halsey, Simon Phipps and David Jenkins, later to be Bishops of Rochester, Manchester, Carlisle, Lincoln and Durham respectively, and the sustained help of Max Warren, Canon of Westminster, Cleverley Ford, Head of the College of Preachers, and Michael Mann, then Director of the Missions to Seamen, and in addition to them many laymen, including Sir Ronald Harris, Lord Amory, Sir John Partridge, Lord Redcliffe-Maud, John Garnett of the Industrial Society and John Gratwick, at work in management training, we could not have got off the ground in this new field of clergy training and lay participation in the ministry.

Because of the pressure of numbers of ministers from the various churches who wanted to come to St George's we also tried to work out the short courses mentioned earlier, lasting the inside of a week, for clergy who, mostly in their fifties, had lost their nerve in the face of the rapidity of twentieth-century change or had become despondent through lack of reponse. It became a real challenge to develop ways of assisting such men back into effective work. I approached diocesan bishops about this problem and learned of local courses designed to help, but in this area it was far easier to see the difficulties than to find the answers. Nor was it always easy to get people to come. The most discouraged clergy were the ones least likely to come to a refresher course, and in any case some would need psychiatric help rather than information or encouragement. We also realized that, if St George's House became known for helping the failures, an invitation to a course would be treated as an insult! With these and other problems I felt that for the time being we must regard remedial work as a by-product of courses which would have other aims.

As the Noble Order was founded in days of unrest, in the 1960s we were also aware of the passing political and violent situations to hand. The Vietnam war, Israeli expansion, the murder of President Kennedy in the United States, Common Market developments in Europe and much else gave us a realistic if sometimes grim background to our work. They made us the more determined to enable the insights of the Christian gospel to be more available to those professional and governmental groupings that were interested. The knights and clerks of Edward III's Foundation were beginning to meet again, but in twentieth-century idiom.

═ [10] ═

On Being a Royal Peculiar

It took a full five years to get the wider usage of St George's Chapel and its collegiate Foundation into some shape. The Chapel itself, with its daily worship and constant welcoming of thousands of tourists, was now well in hand. Even the head verger was reconciled to new services and increased activities. The canons and staff of St George's House were now a team that was pulling together. The consultations and clergy courses soon proved to be serving their planned purposes and in a way became self-propagating. In the summer of 1967 we had a particularly good holiday, mostly at Penlan, with the family enjoying good sailing around Fishguard Harbour, but also on Islay, with most pleasant and informal grouse shooting. We returned refreshed and ready for the autumn and winter.

In the meantime Rachel was at work in London teaching illiterate adults in Camberwell, developing the literacy schemes which were then adopted in London as a whole. Robert was enjoying Cambridge and Edward, having left Winchester, was in Pakistan with the CMS, expecting to go up to Trinity in a year's time. So I found myself establishing fresh links with Harry Williams, the Dean, and R.A. Butler, the Master – although I did not find it easy preaching in my old college. These contacts immediately proved useful, for this was about the time when plans needed to be made for the further education of the Prince of Wales. It was shortly before Christmas 1966 that a dinner party was arranged at Buckingham Palace for the purpose of advising the Queen and Prince Philip on the next step for the heir to the throne. Harold Wilson, the Prime Minister, Michael Ramsey, Archbishop of Canterbury, Lord Mountbatten, still Chief of the Defence Staff, Sir Edward Wilson, Chairman of the Committee of Vice-Chancellors, Sir Michael Adeane, the constitutional adviser, and I were invited. We were amused to learn that Queen Victoria had given a similar party when she was uncertain as to how to occupy her son, who was to become Edward VII.

At the table Harold Wilson tended to dominate the conversation, which was mostly about Vietnam and its consequences – at that time a grave issue. Once dinner was over, however, we began to talk in more detail. It was soon agreed that at this stage a university would be more appropriate than service training; it would best develop the Prince's considerable abilities and give him the breadth of experience that he needed. But where, and at which college? Oxbridge? A Canadian college such as McGill? A red-brick university? Mountbatten was all too ready to pull Harold Wilson's leg on this issue, forgetting that he was a fellow of his Oxford college. It was not difficult to recommend that when Prince Charles's years at Gordonstoun were completed he should go to Cambridge or Oxford, perhaps spending a term or a year somewhere in the Commonwealth. We broke up soon after midnight; Rachel was waiting in the quadrangle to drive me home. It had been a memorable little gathering and the decision for the Prince to go to Cambridge was given coverage in the press the very next day.

It was realized, however, that steps would need to be taken for the admission of the Prince to a college the following October. Time was short. It was with some surprise and a good deal of interest that I found myself asked to make enquiries and prepare an assessment of six colleges at Cambridge, outlining the arrangements that each would make were the heir to the throne to be admitted. Henrietta came with me. We spent a week in Cambridge, deliberately not staying in a college. I found interviewing heads of colleges and senior tutors very instructive. There were clearly benefits and disadvantages in each of the colleges, larger and smaller. I received advice from R.A. Butler (Trinity), Sir Henry Willinck (Magdalene), Professor Owen Chadwick (Selwyn), Sir Frank Lee (Corpus Christi), Edmund Leach (King's) and Sir John Cockcroft (Churchill). So I was able to summarize their academic proposals and indicate the arrangements for accommodation and security. I returned home with a full memorandum.

It was not difficult to arrive at a recommendation of Trinity College, though I had to admit the personal bias of having been there myself. 'RAB' Butler was not only very far-sighted over national issues but he was the best-fitted head of a college to undertake the supervision of a degree course and the informal opportunities that college life would bring. The partnership of RAB, Harry Williams the Dean, and Denis Marion, the Prince's tutor, worked admirably and created an environment that led to many good friendships and experiences. By the time October came and Prince Charles went up, Robert was in his last year and Edward was starting as a freshman; they were both well-placed for introducing Prince Charles to undergraduate ways and to college life. It was not always easy for them, but their protégé could not have been more willing or receptive. The following years, with a period at Aberystwyth, proved to be a constructive conclusion to his formal education.

It was a summer's day in 1969 when Caernarvon Castle became the scene of the Investiture of the Prince of Wales. Hundreds found their way there that day. Henrietta and I, together with Edward, were kindly included in the large circle of friends invited. We had numbered seats both on the special trains and in the castle, along with the Household, the Government and numerous others. We had been to the seaside for the day with the Mothers' Union from Wigston to Skegness; we had been with the parish from Sheffield to Blackpool, and had the funniest and happiest memories of those outings. But this was the seaside outing to end all outings! The platform at Euston at seven o'clock in the morning – we had got up at five! – looked like the queue for a fashionable wedding at St Margaret's; and as we surveyed the crowd we could see members of the Government and assorted MPs, peers of the realm, actors, musicians – in fact it was a cross-section of *Who's Who*. We wondered if we could keep our end up. In a matter of minutes we discovered our reservations and the train started. We were in good company: the Adeanes, Harry Williams and Burke Trend were among our travelling companions. After breakfast the trainload took on the atmosphere of a party. Lunch followed, with more refreshment by courtesy of BR!

On arrival at Caernarvon top hats and Ascot wear seemed out of place in the buses that took us to the town. We then walked through the decorated streets to that splendid castle to find excellent arrangements for seating; music was coming from bands and choirs, and the great crowd was already full of the occasion. The procession of mayors, county councillors, clergy and representative organizations arrived, followed by cheers heralding the Queen, who took her seat under a canopy. The Prince, wearing a simple uniform, was led in to be presented, and led away again to return for the Investiture by his mother. His excellent speech was delivered with a youthful and attractive clarity and confidence. In many ways he had already effected a social revolution in Wales by sheer dedication to the people, together with a creditable ability to understand and speak their language. Unfortunately the service led by an ecumenical group that immediately followed lacked the crispness and vigour of the rest of the ceremony. The Welsh church was too wordy at that stage.

Edward, who by then had joined other close friends of the Prince from Cambridge, left immediately to be taken to the Royal Yacht anchored off Holyhead for an evening and night of celebration. We and our colleagues, though, could not even loiter to see the castle or the ensuing fun and games. We had our train to catch. The party with which we returned included Jim and Mrs Callaghan, George Thomas (at that time Secretary of State for Wales) and Tom and Lady Denning. We were relieved and thankful that all had gone to plan with no bombs and no interruption. Accompanied by the Chief of BR, the Chief Engineer and top security officials, we arrived back at Euston at ten p.m. sharp. A memorable day.

That same year I was asked on behalf of the Queen to make some lasting memorial for King George VI and to prepare an appropriate place in which the earthly remains of Kings and Queens could rest. There was no easy solution. There is not a crypt under St George's and the eighteenth-century vaults under the east end were quite inadequate, so some new building was needed. To do any such thing would require the widest consultation and consent, not least because of the nature of the architecture of the Chapel, which had to be respected, and its structural weaknesses. It was agreed that the Table Tombs of both Edward VII, hard up against the high altar, and George V, occupying an area that broke the symmetry of the nave, were not examples to be repeated. For a time the building of any addition to the main chapel seemed architecturally too difficult. However, eventually there seemed no alternative but to build an additional chantry which would form a suitable burial place for the House of Windsor and which would not interfere with the interior simplicity nor vandalize the exterior. Who should design and who should monitor such a project?

Paul Paget and Lord Mottistone were our consulting architects and they produced a drawing which included piercing the north wall of the nave and adding a small rectangular chantry. All concerned were worried at the neo-Gothic design, in particular Lord Crawford, then Chairman of the Fine Arts Commission, who felt that the concept was unsuitable for the purpose. After much drafting and designing their plan was abandoned. I had always had great respect for the artistic ability of George Pace, so with permission I approached him. He had the unique ability to 'feel' Gothic design and relate a twentieth-century motif to a mediaeval building. After wandering round the Chapel for a whole day making little drawings and notes, he and I hit upon the idea of filling up the angle created by the north choir aisle and the Rutland Chapel. His eventual design for the King George VI Chantry was approved by the Queen, the Queen Mother, the Fine Arts Comission, the RIBA and many others who took a lively interest in the project. John Piper was brought in to design and make the windows, contractors were selected, and George Pace and I supervised every detail of the masonry, vaults, roofing and interior design. The first structural addition to St George's Chapel since 1475 was completed. It looked a bit brash to start with, but by now it has mellowed and settled into place with matching dignity.

It was a cold day at the end of March 1969 when the whole of the Royal Family, members of the Government and a large circle of friends came to St George's for the dedication of the new chantry and for the final laying to rest of King George VI. It was a moving occasion. The coffin was raised by means of the old eighteenth-century lift during the morning and rested in that historic Quire, just to the east of the tomb of Henry VIII and Charles I, draped in the King's actual standard of 1952. The service itself in the afternoon, with the whole family, close friends and members of the Cabinet in the stalls, began with some carefully chosen hymns, prayers and words from the gospel: the music was unmatched in quiet beauty. We then moved in procession westward, under the organ gallery, and round to the North Quire Aisle where the new vault and its chapel was ready. Standing beside the chantry with the family, I used the words from our burial service, adding the lines chosen by the King in his famous broadcast of 1939:

I said to the man who stood at the gate of the year: 'Give me a light that I may tread safely into the unknown.' And he replied, 'Go out into the darkness and put your hand into the hand of God. That shall be to you better than light and safer than a known way.'

[178]

He had taken these words from a poem called 'The Desert' by a quite unknown poet, Minnie Haskins, but they moved a nation, and they are fittingly now engraved on the wrought iron gates that lead into the new chantry above the new and permanent vault. The occasion, nearly twenty years after the death of the King, came and passed with simple dignity. I did not find it easy that day to recite the words in so emotional a setting, but all agreed that we had accomplished a fitting memorial to a king who was deeply religious and held in great love by the nation.

It was in the variety of duties and occupations that I found life as Dean of Windsor most rewarding. The Chapel itself with its processions of services and occasions provided enough in many respects, but once St George's House had got under way it proved to be a meeting place for more than we had anticipated and for me it led to other things. Much of the time of both the Chapter and the staff was rightly spent in providing facilities organized by bodies independent of St George's House or even of the churches. We were invited in on occasions to attend their lectures and discussions and learned much that contributed directly or indirectly to our own purposes. Amongst those in which I took a larger or smaller part were the meetings of the Royal Commission on the future of Public Schools, of which I was in fact appointed a member. This led not only to most informative discussion covering a wide field of educational issues but also to my visiting Public and Direct Grant Schools, sometimes preaching but always with an eye to discovering the potential of the private sector in education. Together with Ralph Alison, headmaster of Brentwood School, I wrote the minority report of the Commission, published by HMSO in 1968, strongly recommending the Labour adminstration of the day to retain the grant-aided status of many of our best grammar schools. Their failure to do this led to a serious loss of local involvement in many an old educational foundation. I also went to meetings of the Duke of Edinburgh's Award Scheme advisory body, with which I also became closely associated. It was just such groups which validated the concept of the Chapel providing wider service than just itself.

One of our first sustained consultations consisted of the early meetings of the Anglican-Roman Catholic International Commission. We were particularly glad to welcome ARCIC, as it came to be known. We were not invited to attend its meetings, but enjoyed the participation of the delegates in the ongoing worship of the Chapel.

The newspapers warned us that Ian Paisley had stated his intention of presenting a 'no Popery' declaration to the Commission, and sure enough he arrived with a delegation one morning. He was stopped by the police at the Castle gates, because demonstrations are not allowed within the Castle itself. The warden was summoned and listened to his statement, which was rational rather than rhetorical, and took the written version to the chairman of the Commission. Whatever his views, Mr Paisley had an impressive way of stating them. In the meantime I had established a precedent which would only be accepted in a Royal Free Chapel, of allowing visiting Roman Catholics to celebrate Mass in the Catherine of Aragon Chantry overlooking the Quire in St George's Chapel, the very place in which Henry VIII had permitted his Queen to attend her 'Catholic Mass' after the break with Rome had taken place. This privilege was much appreciated, especially as the Commission were to study the doctrine of the eucharist. Much of their time was spent on this issue, and we were told by an Anglican present that the agreed wording produced by a Roman theologian was almost word for word what Archbishop Cranmer had proposed some four hundred years earlier!

The visits of the Executive Committee of the World Council of Churches were very different but equally rewarding. They made extensive use of us in 1967. Franklin Fry, the Chairman from the USA, Visser't Hooft, the 'Father' of the Council, and Eugene Carson Blake, the General Secretary, three men with enormous knowledge of Christianity in Europe and throughout the world, were joined by representatives from all the continents. At the invitation of the Queen I was able to take the group up to meet Her Majesty. She kindly received them before lunch on their first day with us, and spent nearly an hour speaking individually to everyone. At that time the World Council was under various pressures, caused by the Vietnam war and its call to the USA to bring it to an end. It was experiencing the first opposition to its policy of assisting national and sometimes guerrilla groups, who asked for the aid of the churches in various parts of Africa, The Programme to Combat Racism which caused alarm in some quarters of the churches was not launched until a year or two later. The WCC was also recognized as a principal factor in keeping up links between the West and Eastern Europe, as well as speaking for the harrassed churches of Latin America. We at St George's were allowed to share in some of their deliberations, and –

probably more importantly – were able to supply the environment of prayer and worship on which all such movements must rely.

Within the context of the Ecumenical Movement St George's House also took on the role of host to the Anglican-Methodist Unity Commission. Largely on the initiative of Geoffrey Fisher, it was the first time that two main-line churches coming with differing historic and cultural backgrounds sat down to work out a united ministry, a common programme of mission and an agreed sharing of resources. From the beginning these conversations were watched with interest by churches throughout the world, including the Roman Catholic Church. I not only agreed that we should accommodate the Commission but accepted the invitation of the Archbishops to be the Secretary of that long and detailed series of negotiations. Eric Baker, the Secretary of the Methodist Conference, was to be my opposite number; Robert Stopford, Bishop of London, and Harold Roberts, past Methodist President, were the joint chairmen. Meetings lasted over seven years, interim statements were prepared, essays were circulated for comment, and at Windsor the two churches grew into an astonishing readiness to unite. Our 'half-time' statement published in 1968 contained an outline of mutually accepted biblical and Christian doctrine and general proposals for sacramental and ministerial understanding, together with a suggested timetable for drawing 'vicars', local ministers and their congregations together. We faced up to the reconciliation of two national administrations and the expectation of a wider but still established national church. It was a far-sighted statement. I well remember Eric Kemp, now Bishop of Chichester, explaining how he as an Anglo-Catholic could accept the proposals for reconciliation, how Leslie Davison, a much respected Methodist leader, found it hard to abandon the concept of lay adminstration of holy communion, but was ready to do so; and how Rupert Davies envisaged a much stronger stand in the field of religious education in state schools, with Harry Carpenter, Bishop of Oxford, always with dry but pertinent observations derived from his academic and episcopal experience. It was Geoffrey Ainger who introduced our work one day by giving us a Bible study on Moses' insistence that at the time of the Exodus the Israelites should carry the bones of Joseph with them. How would we carry the past, whether as Anglicans with a Catholic tradition and Hooker on the one hand, or Methodists with the spirituality of John Wesley on the other, into an enlarged and enlightened church?

The long-continued undertaking of writing accurate minutes of our meetings, and of supervising sub-committees and working parties on differing aspects of the two churches, was carried through by Peter Morgan: twenty years younger than the rest of us, as administrative secretary he kept us both up to date in paperwork and aware of decisions taken, an important aspect of any enquiry. We decided on having 'club colours' so that all our publications and statements for both churches would be easily recognized. The interim report was well received in 1968, discussed up and down the country in Anglican dioceses and Methodist districts, and returned to us by the appropriate legislative bodies with an indication that we were on the right lines. There followed three years of detailed work and careful drafting of theological and ecclesiological issues that could well have led to a situation in which the stalemate of separate churches would have been broken.

It was finally agreed that a period of some ten years would be necessary to acclimatize the two churches to each other before visible and structural unity would ensue. We therefore produced not only a proposed form by which the two ministries would be reconciled to each other as soon as possible, but also a new Ordinal, the service by which bishops, priests and deacons in both churches would be admitted into a uniting church. These detailed proposals accompanied by draft liturgical services were a superb piece of composition: the most thorough since 1549 or 1662. We took care to carry Catholic opinion with us, since we realized that ultimate reunion with Rome was a long-term ambition, and knew that their recognition of ministry was vital. We realized that the language used in our liturgical proposal was important, and in this respect were more thorough than the authors of the Alternative Service Book of 1980. We engaged the help of Professor Ratcliff, who at that time was regarded as the best prose writer for our purposes to be found. Owen Chadwick was not yet available! Ratcliff's introduction to the Ordinal and his rewriting of the charge of those being ordained presbyters remains a masterpiece of writing. Fortunately it has largely been incorporated into the relevant sections of the ASB.

Two stages were suggested in the recommendations. To use the analogy of marriage, the first stage was to be seen as walking out and engagement, and the second stage as the actual marriage. The competence and the thoroughness of the scheme met with wide approval. Even leading Roman Catholics saw in the proposals a

[182]

blueprint for wider union. I found myself watching the press and counting up those in favour and those against. Not surprisingly Anglo-Catholic strongholds were equivocal: they were determined to enable our church in the first instance to move towards Rome and in no way to jeopardize any relationships with Catholicism and Orthodoxy. It was an unrealistic attitude, as neither Rome nor Constantinople appeared interested in our national religious situation. The great bulk of the rank and file of both churches were in favour and were hoping for a completely new look for British Christianity. Thirty-eight out of forty-one dioceses voted in favour, and in every diocese the combined vote of clergy and laity favoured the implementation of the scheme. However, the General Synod of the church was and remains ill-equipped to take major decisions; it lost its nerve and disappointed the church in general.

Of the two great debates on this issue in the Church of England that of 1969 was the more powerful and poignant. It was memorable for two things. The first was the implacable hostility of certain extreme Anglo-Catholics and of certain Evangelicals. The Catholics fought the scheme basically because they believed that it sold the priesthood short and that the Service of Reconciliation compromised and undermined the Preface to the 1662 Ordinal. Those Evangelicals who opposed the scheme did so for the opposite reason. They declared that they were compelled to read the Service of Reconciliation as a quasi-ordination of Methodist ministers. Strangely – though not for the first time in church history – the extremists then came together and the extraordinary alliance of Bishop Graham Leonard and Dr Eric Mascall on the Catholic side with the Revd Colin Buchanan and Dr Jim Packer as Evangelicals achieved its objective by wrecking a splendid scheme.

The second feature which made the 1969 debate so memorable was a powerful and moving speech by Archbishop Michael Ramsey. Always very honest, in his thinking he was open to the concept of new graces and new ministries to meet a new situation in England. He found a degree of ambiguity acceptable, and he reminded us that, while our church already contained irreconcilable views of ministry and priesthood, we nevertheless had one body of ordained men. It was the greatest moment of his leadership.

But it was to no avail, for minds had been made up and ears and hearts were closed. Of the two convocations 68% voted for the vital resolutions, which was short of the requisite 75%. Many of us had believed that the scheme would be approved by the necessary majority, but by the time the whole issue came round for the second time, three years later, in 1972, the situation had hardened. We were resigned to defeat and indeed were already beginning to think of other possible ways forward. The issue that brought distrust would seem to most people to have been a minor one. The Service of Reconciliation for Anglican and Methodist ministers by which they would share each others' powers and responsibilities did contain certain ambiguities on the nature and bestowal of priesthood, but then there were plenty of precedents of ambiguity over intention in the Anglican settlements which followed the Reformation in the sixteenth and seventeenth centuries. Here was part of a new Reformation. What I felt mattered most was that God alone knew what was needed in calling men and women to minister and that he would give the grace for its working.

For their part the Methodists were ready to take episcopacy into their system, so that the two churches could grow together in structure. The new Ordinal was praised on every side, and intercommunion and shared worship in each other's churches was on the way anyhow. Always an optimist, I had concluded that common sense would win the day; and indeed another dozen clergy with courage at that stage would have changed the face of the national church, to its enormous benefit. But it was not to be, and the proposals went down in deference to a minority in the Church of England.

Throughout my ministry I never felt more despondent about our church. Nor did I feel any better for being invited to put the situation to the people in the nine o'clock news. When I got to the studio at Broadcasting House, having prepared a short and balanced statement on the decision, to my surprise I found Bishop Graham Leonard and Canon John Stott, the alliance of Catholic and Evangelical, also present. They accused me on the air of promoting a dishonest scheme and preparing a package deal of ecclesiastical joinery. It was nothing of the sort, and I knew that opinion in the churches and the nation was behind it. But the news on the BBC was not the moment for argument or for the discourtesy which my opponents demonstrated. Fortunately the newscaster recovered the occasion by saying how much everyone regretted that the two churches had abandoned their reconciliation. A dinner party followed for those of us who had promoted the scheme, in which we were joined by Henrietta and a few friends, at the St Ermin's Hotel, the home of lost causes for both Parliament and Synod. Both in 1968 and in 1972 I received a flood of sympathetic letters encouraging the majority of our churches not to surrender.

Correspondence with the retired Archbishop of Canterbury, Lord Fisher, both during and after the Conversations, was difficult and disappointing. He had been a good administrative leader of the church, but he did not take kindly to anything that would endanger the dignity of the establishment. He felt that our generation was selling the church down the river in order to preserve it in the face of secular pressure. He was particularly annoyed that his advice to go for much less, a federation without structural unity, was not heeded, and wrote finally to me in July 1972:

> My dear Robin,
> I am glad that you do not want me to discuss issues which I raised. I do not want to discuss them with you. But it is vitally necessary for the health of the Church of England that I should be put in touch with someone who can speak with authority from the side of the General Synod, preferably not as Bishop but someone (perhaps one clergy and one layman) with an adequate knowledge of theology and church doctrine. The Archbishop of Canterbury refuses to listen to anything that I say to him. The Standing Committee of the General Synod (Chairman, the Archbishop) has refused my request to be heard by it. I launched the idea of Full Communion in 1946 with general approval. I have seen it pushed off course by some Anglicans and some Methodists. Quite rightly our General Synod has twice rejected the scheme which was not a scheme of unity at all but a scheme for a particular method of setting up Full Communion. All these things, I am sure you will agree, ought to be discussed with me. Can you persuade the Archbishop to appoint someone to discuss these matters with me?
> Yours ever,
> Fisher of Lambeth

So it was that one of the major preoccupations of St George's House came to an abrupt end when the churches abandoned further consultation for a time. It was felt then, as now, that the parishes and local churches would have to find their own way, even if it meant a certain amount of chaos and confusion in the ecclesiastical situation.

It was not only in ecclesiastical circles that we covered a wider field of consultation than I could ever have expected; in addition it was the care of industrial and educational movements and concerns which found their home with us and made their own programmes. I welcomed them at St George's House on the clear understanding that the Christian input should be allowed to influence their programme. It was not always easy to speak to their particular situation: it meant that one of us on the staff needed to learn the background of such a consultation: one of the canons, the warden, Kenneth Adams or myself. Even if their concern was technical, scientific or sociological, it was our role to be able to relate Christian insights to the matter on hand. Whereas it had been taken for granted over the years that the church would preach or teach in an authoritarian fashion, we were now learning at Windsor that in a pluralistic society the Christian has to sit down and listen before he or she can make a real contribution to an otherwise secular concern. Is not this a valid approach to evangelism? Indeed, is it not what Jesus did when he sat among the doctors of his day listening? Increasingly it became clear to us that the cohesion of our society, if it was to be in any sense Christian, was dependent on the interaction of religion and society, of faith and expectation and of church and state, in the environment of mutual trust and shared hopes. In practice the attendance of unchurched laity at evensong in the Quire of the Chapel proved to be the most Christianizing influence.

Most consultations and conferences included one or more entertaining or unusual characters, varying from an aged American descendant of a Knight of the Garter and thus a friend of St George's Chapel, who set his bedding alight, to the Marquess of Salisbury, who arrived in a small and ancient Morris labelled 'Hands off Rhodesia'. Simon Phipps, then an industrial chaplain, was summarizing a consultation on 'Relations between People at Work' in straightforward language when he used the word 'eschatology'. Vic Feather, at that time General Secretary of the TUC, who was attending the consultation, but possibly relaxing that evening from the burdens of his normal work, came to with a jerk, banged his desk with Kruschchevian ferocity, and said, 'Wot the 'ell's eschatology?' Simon Phipps was most apologetic about his theological language. This was one of many occasions when we had to learn the lesson of using lay terminology.

The *Daily Mirror*, beset with problems of wages and restrictive union practice, brought management and labour together under our neutral roof for many annual consultations which became the particular care of Kenneth Adams and myself. It was a unique experience to become so intimately involved with the running and internal relations of such a large organization, producing a daily paper and printing half the glossy magazines of Fleet Street. The readiness of 'Pick' (Sir Edward Pickering), the chairman, or Percy Roberts, his successor, to engage the church in their industrial relations was in many ways an encouragement to this venture. Certain other companies followed suit, largely owing to the experience and expertise of Kenneth Adams. They also found that within the atmosphere of religious and social integrity they could get to grips with their divisions more effectively than in a London hotel or centre of arbitration.

Anthony Davies, 'the Admiral', insisted that we prepare an annual report to the Council of the House. He was right in suggesting this and it proved salutary for me and the canons to review progress in some detail once a year, an occupation that might well benefit other cathedrals or parish churches! These reports, together with the summaries of the consultations, contain a great deal of what was accomplished once our Christian centre had been established. They do not indicate, however, the marvellous cooperation we received from individuals in planning and speaking. Some of these distinguished people, who thought it worth while to give us their time, advice and help, and whose names I readily recollect, including several who served on the Council, were our two Field Marshals Alexander and Slim; politicians Lord Watkinson, Lord Redcliffe-Maud and Lord Eccles; and industrialists Sir Fred Catherwood, John Garnett, Sir Leon Bagrit and John Gratwick, to mention but a few who agreed to be 'on call'. Amongst many helpful clergy who did the same were George Reindorp, Ian Ramsey, David Say, Sydney Evans, Eric James and Basil Moss.

But on matters of policy there is no doubt that our greatest outside influence was Prince Philip. His regular attendance and advice at council meetings and also at many other occasions and on informal visits gave the House a credibility and consistency of purpose which it might well have lost in its early stages. More than once he also addressed clergy courses, giving a talk on the role of the parson in changing circumstances with detailed and theologically competent thinking, laced with tales of his own experiences in the church and outside it. His talks on the purpose of staff training and on the meaning of leadership within church and state were not only factual and detailed but also full of sympathy and understanding for the churches in their search for fresh avenues of mission. At his suggestion we took a few groups to the Administrative College at Henley to see how other professions were training and shaping their leadership. He ensured that we should not be content with a hit-or-miss process in ecclesiastical leadership any longer but rather try to enable the individual to do what was expected of him. Though he was not closely identified with the church in his youth, Prince Philip assimilated not only the theology that lay behind our ministry but also the sanctions and incumbrances that surround the churches' mission. His light touch and very contemporary approach gave a quality to many a gathering that otherwise could easily have fallen flat. In addition to the importance that he attached to the training of clergy, Prince Philip also pressed for a sustained programme in which theologians and scientists should meet and attempt some form of mutual understanding. For the well-being of both church and nation he felt that reconciliation of the historic faith and contemporary scientific and medical attitude was called for: they were both essential to the integrity of our thinking. That the succession of consultations, continued in the 1970s between people of eminence in both disciplines, was productive of ideas and effective in forming new friendships was largely due to Prince Philip's insistence on the priority of the subject.

When the House was reviewing its purpose and progress at the end of five years of work, Prince Philip wrote in his own hand from the middle of a royal tour of South-East Asia, giving his comments on draft documents. His letter addressed to Anthony Davies indicates both his own and our determination to be unambiguous in our Christian position and precise in our thinking.

At Sea. As from
Windsor Castle

7 April 1972

Dear Admiral,

Thank you for your letter and for your comments. I have re-read your original paper and revised purpose carefully and then read my letter and your comments again.

I think the trouble about the clergy courses has arisen because neither the council nor the staff – nor indeed Robin – were convinced that this course was vital to the church and to the purpose of St George's House. You suggest that it was first mentioned in 1966. I can assure you that it figured in all the discussions I had with Robin from the moment he first mooted the idea of a conference centre. While I fully endorsed and supported the idea of a lay-theologian conference centre, I tried from the very outset to convince him that the in-service retraining of mid-career clergy was equally important particularly because of the experience gained in the lay courses.

As far as the 'purpose' is concerned I must frankly say that the revised version, in my opinion, is no improvement on the original. I think you should tear it up and start again. Indeed I think you would be well advised to re-edit the original purpose rather than write an entirely new version.

There is one point in your comments which I don't quite understand. In your last paragraph you say, 'God also speaks... through the evidence of creation...' Precisely what do you mean by this? The creation of what? What evidence?

As to the use of the word God, if you look at the revised purpose you will see in the first paragraph that it says 'that which God says to them...' As far as Christians are concerned (and this para is about Christians) it is that which *Christ* says which is important.

You use the word God again in the last para which refers specifically to Christian clergy – there is no mention of other religions, or non-believers. In this case you refer to 'the purpose of God in Christ'. Either you must refer to God's purpose for the world as a whole, or you should, in my view, refer to Christ's purpose for his church.

This may seem like splitting hairs but in a Christian setting it seems to me of the very first importance to concentrate on Christ's teaching, because it has a specific and clear message. God as a universal power is interpreted in a host of different ways by religions which all believe in a universal God. So I repeat that I believe the 'purpose' should only refer to Christ unless there is some point about universal theology – and I don't see one in the revised purpose.
Yours sincerely
Philip

One consequence of holding the privileged position of being Dean of Windsor which made it so interesting was the arrival of invitations to different parts of the world to speak and meet with others who had come to know what was happening at the 'House'. On one journey, having flown over the Pole we arrived at San Francisco at 9 p.m. their time and 4.a.m. ours, after at least a fourteen-hour journey, suffering

[189]

from jet-lag, only to be expected to join a reception and be on top form. That was no joke. We recovered after some sleep sufficiently to live up to our host's arrangements. On a further visit to Taizé I found myself with German and French colleagues pursuing ways and means of introducing the faith into differing situations. Off to the Caribbean in February 1968, Henrietta and I were able to attend gatherings in Nassau, Jamaica, Barbados, British Guyana and British Honduras. Since travelling always refreshed me, I found it no burden to meet groups with a view to sharing with them the progress towards church unity in England or the work of St George's House in applying our faith to the movements of thought at the time. The insular state of some churches overseas had to be seen to be believed.

On our visit to Belize, when Henrietta and I were trying to keep to a tight schedule, we were invited to board a light four-seater aircraft in order to fulfil an engagement on the Mexican border of the colony. The Bishop, Binny Vaughan, and his wife came with us. Soon after we were airborne our Spanish pilot told us that there were storms ahead and warned us that we would have a bumpy ride. Within a few minutes the tiny aircraft was in thick cloud and battered with thunder and rain. It was exceptionally alarming; we sat strapped in in terrified silence, the pilot having decided to fly immediately above the forest, leaving no opportunity for error, let alone landing. He soon informed us that he had lost his way and had no map. I had a tourist guide of Central America with precious little information in it, but just enough to tell me that if we flew eastwards we would be bound to hit the sea coast. Flying north, the pilot agreed to turn right, and in fact half an hour later we did see the shore. We turned right again, picked up a town on the map and landed back where we had started after two hours of the most perilous flying. God's providence was with us.

In Managua, staying with our ambassador, I preached and assisted at the ordination of a Baptist minister in order to assure him of our readiness to receive his ministrations to a rather beleaguered Anglican few. Nicaragua was even then beginning to polarize politically and socially between the right in support of the USA and the left looking for greater independence and a more vocal expression of the views of the great majority of very poor people. In such a situation anything one could do to enable the churches to work together for reconciliation was worth trying. At the same time we enjoyed much relaxation in the warm sunshine and warm sea that surround those areas.

Between courses at St George's House interspersed with enjoyable journeys overseas and visits to the cottage in Pembrokeshire, and with the daily life of the Chapel happily progressing, I began to realize the further potential of the Castle as a place that could well mount and accommodate an annual musical or artistic festival. By the end of the 1960s many a city or old-established borough had established its own celebrations in the form of a festival, or some similar event. Windsor, with the Castle at its heart and Eton at its feet, was ideally suited to a week of music-making and entertainment. There was a wealth of places for events: the Chapel, the Library, the Lower Ward, the Waterloo Chamber readily made available by Her Majesty, the Curfew Tower and the dungeon, before we started on the Town Hall, the Theatre Royal or the facilities at Eton College. Yehudi Menuhin and Ian Hunter agreed to become our artistic directors, John Piper designed the posters, Lord Gore-Booth and Colonel Johnston joined the board of directors, the one representing available talent and the other watching the interests of the Crown. Lord Caccia, Provost of Eton, co-operated willingly and Fred Coleridge, the Vice-Provost, joined the board. Michael Bedow, a financial director of Woolworth's, became our financial manager and Laurence West our general manager, taking all the administration off my shoulders. We were a good team and I enjoyed learning the ways – and indeed the costs – of professional musicians as we related them to the Castle and prepared their programmes. A Festival Club was made ready in the Curfew Tower and our dungeon became a bar.

When we opened the Festival on a fine evening late in September 1969 we had the best part of four thousand people crowded into the Lower Ward of the Castle to enjoy the Band of the Coldstream Guards beating retreat and then playing music conducted alternately by Yehudi Menuhin and Sir William Walton. A firework display from the top of the Round Tower completed the evening: it was never again permitted because of fear of fire. It was altogether a splendid occasion and the press gave us a good write-up. It was said that Windsor Castle ought to be the scene of competitive artistry as it was in the days of the annual joust of the Knights of the Garter. However, under my leadership the Festival never took on a competitive role; it did, though, engage differing talents in classical and modern music, in dance, drama and in popular lectures and exhibitions. Artistic and financial risks were taken, but in its opening years it proved a success. Every

[191]

room in the Deanery, St George's House and the hotels would be occupied, and the whole place became the scene of pleasurable meeting and entertainment. Those of us who lived within the setting of the Castle and the College at Eton were aware of being privileged people and were therefore the more eager to share these places and their historical associations with a wide circle of friends and hundreds of visitors. It was in this welcoming spirit that the Queen allowed her State Apartments to become the superb setting for Handel, Mozart and Beethoven concerts and much else. The Festival brought to Windsor a new dimension of public participation, but it also demanded a new partnership and financial commitment between Castle, College and town. This was readily forthcoming.

Partly as a consequence of the wider use of St George's Chapel and the Castle it was decided that the nation and the Commonwealth should join in Christmas worship with the Queen and the family on Christmas morning. When snow was lying on the ground we were televised in colour for the first time on Christmas Day 1970. At any time a broadcast is unnerving for amateurs like myself, and when it came to anticipating such an enormous coverage I was almost frightened. I found that my own part was primarily the address that I was to give and its message to a non-churchgoing, worldwide audience. However, I could hardly concentrate on myself. I had to sustain a quiet partnership with producers, technicians, engineers, organists, a professional choir and much else, not to mention such groups as the Military Knights and the Royal Household, who had their rights within the Chapel. For me the important thing was not so much what was said and done over the air as how the spirit of true dependence upon God and a rightful recognition of his intervention in Christ could be meaningfully portrayed that Christmas morning. The solemn moments of welcoming the Queen and her family to worship, leading in prayer and preaching, singing the National Anthem in her Majesty's presence and then conducting the party out on to the great west steps, as on several other occasions, with cameras at every turn, was an emotional strain for me. One always fears on such occasions that one will fail at some point or another, but God sustains those who try to convey his love and his purpose. I look back with gratitude to the several occasions when we could share something of our traditions at Windsor with the wider community through radio or television.

◁ *Leaving St George's Chapel after morning service, Christmas 1970*

The Deanery, with tourists peering over the front gate, and which was in part taken over for enlarging St George's House, is a conglomeration of large and small rooms with the showplace study on the first floor. From it a passage and catwalk over the slates lead to the clerestory off the Quire and to the Aragon Chantry. That was a useful vantage point from which I or any other member of the family could attend any service we wished to without being there. It was also the means by which the Queen, without it being known, watched the laying up of the banner of Winston Churchill. From the study a passage leads to the top of the stairs from which our bedroom, the spare rooms and the children's rooms were reached. Throughout the development of the life of the Chapel Henrietta had enabled our home to play a full part. Not only did she entertain a constant stream of visitors but also took many opportunities to visit the consultations, to meet with wives and friends attending them, and to make a contribution to the discussions of the day. Another part of the fascination of being Dean of this Royal Peculiar was its total freedom from parochial or diocesan demands. Until Henrietta and I were liberated from parish or diocesan work we did not realize the extent to which initiative was stifled for the average parson by routine maintenance work.

The latter years at Windsor were thankfully not wholly determined by this new venture of St George's House nor great occasions in the Chapel. It was in the midde of our time at St George's House that Henrietta was made a JP. This was no new experience for her family, as her father was a magistrate in Oldbury, and her sister Anne Fry together with Bill her husband were magistrates in Yorkshire, Kenneth her brother joined the Buckinghamshire bench, and it was to be only a few years before Rachel, at the age of thirty-two, was made a magistrate at Westminster. Henrietta's sitting on the Windsor bench brought a new dimension of local life into our sphere and at the same time made another link between the Castle and the town, a bond which was often in need of strengthening. To our surprise, on one occasion she was sitting when the magistrates had to decide whether or not a pop festival should come to Windsor. The organizers, having been refused by the local authority on the grounds that such a gathering was unbefitting to the dignity of the town, lodged an appeal with the magistrates. The magistrates' inclination was to endorse the decision of the Council, but when no less a person than Lord Hailsham appeared as counsel for the applicants, they were convinced of the proposal. Sittings of the court were not usually so colourful, but rather of a routine nature with each case requiring patience and judgment. Over the years Henrietta gave increasing time to the bench, the local probation service and the administration of the licensing laws, at intervals having to relearn the changing road traffic regulations. These were also times in which the family was becoming independent and also sharing in the pleasures and duties of the Chapel and Castle. Robert, after a period in merchant banking, had joined the staff of P & O. Edward was still at Cambridge, later to serve the banking world in East Africa, Bahrein and Saudi Arabia. Both Eleanor and Mary, having done spells in Malaya and India respectively, returned home, Eleanor to her Montessori course and Mary to Girton to read medicine. Kenneth Wilson, Henrietta's father, had grown increasingly supportive of our family, our work and our interests; his death in the early autumn of 1969 was inevitably sad. However, it was an occasion in which the whole family became aware how much he had accomplished not only for all of us but also for Worcestershire and the chemical industry. When I preached in Worcester Cathedral at his memorial service, little did I realize that before long I would be there in another capacity.

For Henrietta and myself the marriage of our oldest child stands out most. Rachel, having developed the literacy schemes of the South Bank, announced her engagement to Michael Benson. We had not known his parents, Sir Henry and Jinny Benson, for long, but our paths had crossed in meetings at Cumberland Lodge. As a very senior accountant Sir Henry was much in demand. It was through a weekend consultation on Christian living for younger people in the City and the professions that Michael found his way to Windsor and to meeting Rachel. His mother had long been involved in similar courses arranged by Eric Abbott, the then Dean, at Westminster Abbey. Not only Rachel and Michael, but our two families soon found much in common. I married the couple in St George's Chapel. That was a marvellous setting in itself but the kindness of the Queen in allowing us to use the Waterloo Chamber up in the Castle and being present herself at the reception made this an unparalleled occasion for the family.

== [11] ==

All Change

In the early months of 1970 I became clear in my own mind that Windsor did not require new initiatives but a sustained period of consolidation. I had tackled the major issues assigned to me some nine years earlier and brought the Chapel into wider usefulness. I was aware that I was beginning to repeat myself in the sequence of courses at St George's House, and I remembered that Michael Adeane had told me that I was not expected to leave my bones in Windsor. I had ten or twelve years of useful ministry to look forward to, and it became increasingly clear to me that I must get off the touch line and into the game. I had been in an advisory capacity long enough, and my experiences all through the years suggested that I was a better initiator than sustainer, better at implementing new ideas than at consolidating them, and potentially more fitted to reshape and rebuild ministries than just to carry them on. This had proved to be the case in Singapore, where in a way we had to start from scratch; at Sheffield, where I had been closely involved with a bishop who was himself a great innovator; and at Windsor, where the situation had called for something new and there had been openings for developments. I felt a great sense of challenge to try and do in the context of the wider church some of the things we had accomplished in the sheltered confines of Windsor Castle.

When Father was offered the bishopric of Lichfield and my brother Frank the archbishopric of Melbourne, each felt that he was being given a clear call. Neither of them was associated in any way with the processes of appointment, and each was ready for a move. From the start each felt that he could discern the hand of God leading him into a new and readily acceptable role. It was not quite the same for me. I had had the interest and privilege of talking over episcopal appointments at Downing Street, and as Dean I had been in regular touch with the Queen. I reckoned to be knowledgable about senior clergy, their abilities and their appointments, so all in all I was well up in what went on behind the scenes. At the time Ted Heath was Prime Minister and we got to know each other reasonably well. I had been in touch with him or his appointments secretary many times from Windsor. So when the first moves towards my becoming a bishop were made, they differed rather from the usual pattern.

The very first thing happened while we were on holiday in Wales. Henrietta and the family had gone down to the sea and I was alone in the house when the telephone rang. Surprisingly, it was a call from Balmoral. An invitation to a bishopric was on the way. Would I keep in touch? Shortly afterwards I had a personal letter from Ted Heath saying that the see of Worcester was vacant and that he felt that it was time that I left Windsor and took on a diocese. However, he would not convey a formal invitation until he had cleared the matter with the Queen. Here, then, was the chance for something new, but when it actually came we found that it posed a real dilemma: should I stay on at Windsor where the opportunities clearly suited us, or was it time for a change back into the diocesan and parochial life of the church? In the event the tug of Windsor proved stronger than I had expected, but as taught by B.K.Cunningham in the 1930s, I began to work through the pros and cons. In doing this I was soon helped by advice from many quarters. I was particularly grateful to Robert, our oldest son, who wrote at some length.

> I think you ought to accept Worcester for a number of reasons. The first is I think it offers you a chance of good episcopal work – Worcester is not just a quiet country diocese, as you know, but is full of industry as well as old – and would give you the type of job and interest that you want. I speak from ignorance, but I do feel there is no need to doubt Worcester as a dicoese – it probably has just as many challenging aspects as a heavy urban industrial diocese like Manchester but perhaps less obviously manifested. The church sometimes makes an error in thinking that the only problems are the visible ones of slums, unemployment, etc, and alas where these are not rife need no attention.
>
> Secondly, I feel that fears about being removed from the central organization of the church are equally groundless. If people want your advice and opinion on running the church, and they rightly seem to be wanting it at the moment, then the advice is just as valid

no matter whether you are based in Worcester or Windsor or even Winchester. And it is not as if it is impossible to go to London regularly from Worcester.

Thirdly, I feel that if you really have set your sights on a senior diocese, a move to Worcester would be an excellent training and place to prove your episcopal capacity, and fitting you much better for what some think would be a better job. I also feel you would be making a mistake to turn this post down in anticipation of getting a supposedly better one once you have made up your mind to leave Windsor – this last point I think is the most important, because if you have decided you want to leave Windsor, then I think the sooner we leave the better. I personally wouldn't mind your leaving Windsor at all; I should love to see you a bishop and I think Worcester is probably exactly what's wanted now.

I have always valued the family's view, but the decision was made more difficult by Leslie Hunter, who had advised me so well over twenty years. He took the opposite view, feeling that the bureaucracy involved in a diocese and with the central church was not my scene. 'I am, however, full of friendly curiosity to learn your decision,' he said at the end of his letter.

Most of all, though, it moved me to hear from the man I had come to respect very deeply not only for the integrity of his religion but for his ability to judge men and situations. Before I received any official advice on whether or not I should pursue the Prime Minister's suggestion, a letter from Prince Philip at Balmoral Castle, full of wisdom and insight, reached me down in Wales. It certainly summarized my own predicament.

> Dear Robin,
> I gather from the Queen that you are confronted with an awkward choice! When we chatted briefly at the Orangery Party I didn't realize that this had been going on for some time and that you were under any pressure to make up your mind.
>
> I hope we shall have a chance to talk about this when I get back, but I thought I would put some comments on paper meanwhile in case they are any help.
>
> In the first place you can take it that neither the Queen nor I would want you to feel that you should stay at Windsor for our sakes. I know this sounds rather unkind, but what I mean is that we would not want to stand in the way of your opportunity to serve the church in a more responsible way. It has been simply marvellous

having you at Windsor and your help and guidance for us and for our children has been invaluable, but frankly I think the church needs your services more urgently than we do!

The point at issue is where your services to the church would be most valuable and I would say that this is an extremely difficult one to answer. In the conventional view there is little doubt that the bench of bishops, the diocese of Worcester, would place you at the centre of church affairs.

I have no doubt at all 'conventional' advice would be to accept this answer and it may well be right. My knowledge of the upper management of the church is extremely limited.

Against this I think you must set the influence which you would exert over several generations of clergy who will be attending St George's House in one capacity or another over the next years. I doubt whether there is anyone in the Church of England today who is in a better position to make the next generation of bishops think about the vital issues of today and tomorrow. There is certainly no one who will have made personal contact with so many of the more intelligent rank and file and with so many influential laymen. By this unique contact and by your selection of the content of consultations, you have already established a link between the church and the modern world which can only be described as an immensely important service to the church.

Perhaps I have somewhat 'over-egged' the St George's House pudding but I am very anxious that it should be properly weighed in the balance. I suspect more people assume that you could do more as a bishop without appreciating what you are doing at Windsor – and you are not likely to tell them yourself!

All this may sound as if I am urging you to stay at Windsor – I'm not. I'm only anxious that you should not underestimate the future contribution which you could make from there. Doubtless a compromise has occurred to you. By retaining contact with Windsor and with your many other related interests in London, you might hope to have the best of both worlds. I don't think this would work and it would make a nonsense of going to Worcester. It may not be a demanding diocese, but if experience as a diocesan bishop is important, then you will have to give your time and energy to gain that experience. If you, in addition, want to make any impression on the diocese you will have to devote more – not less – time to it.

As I see it the problem resolves itself into whether you can contribute more to the church as an archbishop or in one of the great dioceses, or through the development of St George's House. If it is the former and experience of a smaller diocese is essential then go to Worcester. If it is the latter, I am still not entirely convinced that it precludes 'high rank' eventually, but I am probably wrong.

Of course I cannot put one factor into the balance and that is the personal inclination of yourself and your wife and family, and this factor, it seems to me, should be decisive.

If there is anything about Windsor which gives you any cause for anxiety or which may adversely affect your work, then I think a move is imperative. Equally, if there is a positive personal attraction towards Worcester and the people there, then that too should be decisive. This may sound selfish, but remember you have a choice. If you had been told to stay at Windsor or to go to Worcester then obviously personal inclinations have to be suppressed and you have to make the best of it. If there is a choice and it is evenly balanced then the personal factor should certainly be weighed because you will most certainly do better work for the church if your mind is fully at rest about all other matters.

Reading this through I am half inclined to tear it up because it hasn't come out quite as I hoped and I doubt whether it will be very helpful. However I am sending it because if nothing else it may help you to appreciate the importance of St George's House and its growing influence on the church in the future. I think we talked about 'influence' at some time and I just want to repeat that I don't mean that St Geroge's should start a new fashion in theology or a new system of administration. As I see it, St George's can make people think of issues that have otherwise been neglected, it can draw attention to weakness and deficiencies by making it possible for people to discover them for themselves. People should be able to look back at their experience at St George's and say what they learnt there and not what they were taught there.

Yours ever,
Philip

To clarify matters I went to Balmoral at the invitation of the Queen. The understanding with which I was greeted and the warmth of welcome in a sense made it all the more difficult to consider leaving such a rewarding position in the Royal Household. But over some long talks and wholly delightful excursions on to the moors in chase of either grouse or deer I left with a much clearer picture of where our future should lie. Alone in the night train from Aberdeen to London, before going on from Paddington to Fishguard, enjoying a picnic supper supplied by Balmoral, I pondered on the isolation of a diocesan bishop when compared with the close-knit community of Windsor Castle. Here I was proposing to exchange the partnerships and supportive groups around St George's Chapel for the individual responsibility of a bishop and the necessity of building up a fresh team of helpers around the job. And there would be enormous problems to face. Even then, in late 1970, there was also an air of unrest in the Government, economic stability was very unsure and the church itself was entering an era of having to face up to major changes. I did not sleep much in the train that night.

The appointment was published a few days later. The mixture of letters, the majority congratulating, but several doubting the wisdom of my choice, underlined our hopes and fears. Robin Mackworth Young, the Queen's librarian, interestingly pointed out that my situation had not been without precedent. He drew my attention to a correspondence between Queen Victoria and Randall Davidson when Davidson felt that it was time to leave St George's to move, and Worcester, strangely enough, was one of the two dioceses offered to him (the other being Rochester). I had made the decision rather as Davidson did. I was particularly glad to receive a personal and helpful letter in which Michael Ramsey generously acknowledged our 'lovely happy and creative ministry at Windsor'. He was worried nevertheless about finding the right successor. In this he was right: the matter of a new Dean and in the same appointment a new head of St George's House was much in my mind.

It was no good pretending that in going to Worcester I could just wash my hands of anything to do with the question who was to take on the varied work at Windsor. I remained in close touch with both the Queen and the Prime Minister – with the latter because he had to submit any proposal to the Queen, as had been done at the time of my appointment. There was fortunately time to think and make discreet inquiries during that autumn of 1970, and by the New Year it was agreed that since the leadership of senior groups and gatherings at St George's House was to be an essential element of the work of the Dean then he should probably be someone who was already a bishop. If the courses were to develop, in particular those for clergy, then a man who had seen the situation from the episcopal bench would be a great advantage. If the gatherings of laymen and women from various spheres of Government or commercial organizations were also to develop, then someone was needed who could command respect in those areas. Launcelot Fleming, Bishop of Norwich, accepted the invitation and it was a great pleasure to hand over the reins to him.

The Queen graciously recognized my years at Windsor in the New Year Honours of 1971. To become a Knight Commander of the Royal Victorian Order was a most special pleasure, and to receive the honour in mid-career rather than on retirement, which had been the case with my predecessors, gave me a continuing link with the Queen and an added distinction with which to go to Worcester. As is customary when members of the Household are honoured, the actual conferring of the honour did not take place at an investiture but at a private meeting with the Queen. She graciously handed me the star and riband and said some kind things in the course of conversation. Even that short meeting and gift of the knighthood was not farewell. A few days later we had the added pleasure of entertaining the Queen and Prince Philip to dinner with the family. The evening went by all too quickly as we recalled so much that had happened in the nine years that we as a family had been allowed to live in the middle of the Castle. It rounded off many happy years.

Henrietta had known Worcestershire all her life from Park Hall, her old home, and many of her family lived in the county. Through her I had also come to know the communities and countryside of this part of the Severn valley, which was to be my diocese. The Malvern hills standing up in the West, Bredon to the south and the Cotswolds to the east, with Birmingham and the Black Country to the north, formed the boundaries of a varied basin in which industrial towns, market towns and a lovely countryside are divided by the river. Right in the centre lies Stourport, with Hartlebury next door, where we were to live, and further down the river the cathedral city of Worcester, which has stood there since Roman days. The Teme valley, with villages and farms, running away to Tenbury and Herefordshire, and the Vale of Evesham following the Avon almost to Stratford, link the area firmly to the Midlands. Beautiful churches, many with church schools, serve this mixed community of town and country, industry and farmlands which give both diocese and county a happy balance. From the cathedral one can see the hills of the west and south; from Hartlebury the smoke of the industrial area was sometimes apparent.

Both places were strategically well located, in the centre of the diocese, and from them I too became familiar with Worcestershire.

Over the centuries the City of Worcester has dominated the Severn valley and the areas of the rivers that flow into it. From Somerset to Staffordshire the vast diocese held together for nearly a thousand years until Henry VIII divided off Bristol and Gloucester under their own bishops. The industrial areas of Birmingham were carved out by Bishop Gore in 1909 to form a new diocese, and Warwickshire with Coventry as a see city gained its ecclesiastical independence immediately after the Great War. Worcestershire as a county remained, a well balanced and manageable area. The northern part took in about half the black country. Both people and clergy in that part of the old county which included Dudley, Netherton, Cradeley, Amblecote, Halesowen and Stourbridge were markedly strong in character and independent in attitude. These qualities had been bred as a result of hard work in mines, iron foundries, steel mills, chain making, glass blowing and other physically demanding jobs. What are now the Metropolitan Districts of Dudley, Sandwell and Walsall, with more than a million people within them, looked to the two large centres of Wolverhampton in the diocese of Lichfield and Dudley in the diocese of Worcester for their economic and cultural life. To the south was the Severn valley with the market towns of Bewdley, Stourport and Droitwich but also with the very distinctive carpet-making town of Kidderminster. The eastern area had been designated for population expansion. Bromsgrove and Cateshill, where many people worked with British Leyland over the hill at Longbridge, thrived independently, but Redditch, from being the home of needles and fishhooks, was fast becoming a well-laid-out new town five times as big as it was, and taking in the light industry overspill at Birmingham. To the south, roughly following the Avon, were Broadway, Evesham and Pershore with the cluster of commuter villages around. They also had their own speed of life and their own traditional market gardening concerns. To the west were Malvern, with all its schools and the huge Royal Radar Establishment, and Upton upon Severn, which attracted a professional community around them.

From the very moment we went to see the situation at Worcester at first hand we were encouraged. Mervyn Charles-Edwards, the retiring Bishop, was welcoming, and ready to give any advice or help in taking over both the diocese and our new home – which was to be another castle! He had been much loved and trusted by the clergy and was full of sensitivity towards the laity, the towns and the villages.

He had also been involved in a considerable controversy over where the Bishop of Worcester should live. Hartlebury Castle, between Worcester and Birmingham, had been the home of the Bishop of Worcester for a thousand years, but it was an enormous ancient monument and there was great bureacratic pressure from the Church Commissioners that the Bishop should move out of it. Moreover, Eric Kemp, the Dean of Worcester, was convinced that the diocesan should be seen to live in a modest dwelling and if possible in the community of the Cathedral Close. However, Mervyn Charles-Edwards thought differently and had some strong arguments on his side. Not only was there tradition, but Hartlebury Castle was central to the diocese, it had plenty of car parking space and could provide big rooms for diocesan occasions. Moreover, after some thirty rooms had been leased to the County Council for a Crafts Museum, and a separate trust had been set up to preserve and make good use of the state rooms, it could be a manageable house. So he won the day. We were momentarily daunted by the thought of another 'castle' and it seemed a great deal for Henrietta to manage, since she was also to be the executive officer for the state rooms. However, despite this, it soon became clear that here was a 'family' house both for ourselves and for the diocese, and certainly no more extensive than the one we were leaving.

As from Christmas 1970 I gave my mind to getting ready for moving to Worcester. The diocese had hoped that I would have been able to come earlier, but it proved impossible to abandon the courses, both lay and clerical, that had already been planned for St George's House. I gave as much time as possible to my last long clergy course: on it, over four weeks, we had a first-class group of some thirty clergy, some of the best from all over the country, many of whom have now accepted a wider ministry with greater confidence.

I also got two opportunities for reflection, one which I did not choose and one which I did. Having developed rotten veins in my legs I went to Sister Agnes' Hospital in London and had my varicose veins stripped; this gave me ten days for reading, interrupted only by kindly nursing and visitors to wish me well, followed by another ten days so-called convalescence at the cottage in Pembrokeshire. To go there in January was strange, but the wind, the rain, the sea air and the long evenings in front of the log fire made it just the invigorating holiday Henrietta and I both needed. Henrietta had also been working hard getting ready for the move and tidying up her duties in the Windsor area, at Cumberland Lodge where she was chairman of the house management committee, and on the bench of magistrates. Her transfer to the Worcester county bench pleased us a great deal and enabled Henrietta to carry on in that particular sphere.

As a more definite preparation for consecration to the office and work of a bishop I took myself off to Westcott House for several days of real quiet. There was no official retreat in progress but there was the daily round of worship, with Peter Walker, the Principal, now Bishop of Ely, ready with spiritual advice; he helped me do some inner spring-cleaning to refresh my faith and my outlook. In those days I rediscovered what the Bible stresses as an experience, a sense of finding strength where you had known it to emerge from before. Was that not the case with Jacob who had to return to his altar after his dream? Was it not the experience of Joseph and Mary going back to find their son Jesus in the temple rather than among the people? And of the disciples who heeded the word of Jesus when he told them that he would meet them in his resurrection on the familiar shores of Galilee? I also found that time in the place where I had been originally called and tested for ordination was wholly renewing. Just as God had made up the deficiencies in my ministry since I left for ordination thirty years earlier, so he would do the same for me as a bishop of his church. Those days also served as a reminder of men on whose example I had tried to base my thinking: B.K.Cunningham, William Temple, Billy Greer and indeed Edward my father. Perhaps he was smiling as I came to take over the diocese next to his own. Cambridge once again had proved formative in my thinking. And there was the added pleasure of having Mary, our youngest, at Girton to talk with. She was making headway with her degree in medicine and had a growing friendship with James Burnell Nugent, then at Corpus Christi College, whom she was to marry two years later.

With days of reflection behind me, I returned for one night to Windsor. Up early next morning, I went to communion in St George's and quickly looked back on those formative years. Soon we were off to St Paul's Cathedral for the rehearsal. It was a non-occasion. Neither the Dean, the Canon in Residence nor the Precentor turned up. The Head Verger, together with David Carey the Provincial Registrar, always a kindly helper and adviser, did their best. I learned my movements and was not going to worry about other participants in the great service.

Returning to Westminster we got organized for my 'confirmation'. In cassock and gown I was led into St Margaret's Church. A table and chairs were set in the choir where Sir Harold Kent, Dean of the Arches, David Carey, the Provincial Registrar, Eric Kemp for Worcester Cathedral and a young solicitor, my advocate, were seated. David Edwards, the Rector, read the litany – always an impressive act of prayer and one which contrasted markedly with the air of unreality which otherwise characterized the occasion. The dialogue which followed between the Provincial Registrar and the Dean of Worcester was in the first place to prove that I was Robin Woods and not somebody else, then to indicate my acceptance of the Queen's mandate, and lastly, to clear my character as a person duly elected and fit to serve. I had seen no signs whatsoever of any form of election, and by then it was a bit late in the day for any negative answers to be given. I gave the blessing and signed Robin Worcester, not Robert: at consecration I was changing my baptismal name.

Across the river at Lambeth we were warmly welcomed by Michael and Joan Ramsey. The family soon started arriving and we felt embarrassed at having five children plus one husband to stay: Rachel and Michael, Robert, Edward and Eleanor were all at work in London and Mary had come up from Cambridge. We had so much to talk about upstairs in our rooms that we only just made evensong in the chapel. Being by this stage already rather prone to laughter, the 'children' could hardly take their eyes off the Archbishop's eyebrows. Both during and after dinner Michael Ramsey was warm, talkative and obviously enormously well-informed on almost any issue. He engaged the attention of all of us as he talked about matters facing the thinking Christian: race relations in England, apartheid in South Africa, the armament industry, South Bank theology – and on top of all that his memories of William Temple and Father. It was a memorable evening for the family, and it was well after eleven o'clock before he remembered that I had properly come to talk over being a bishop with him. At that late hour he and I went to his study and mutually decided that it was fruitless for us to discuss the matter: we knew in our own mind the kind of episcopacy that was needed in the church and in the nation at that stage, and that was surely enough. But he bade me take time off, keep my rules of prayer, and watch against accepting too many engagements. More importantly he discouraged me from pursuing ecumenical 'joinery' and pressed me to keep to the mission of the gospel through my social contacts and above all those which I had built up in Sheffield and Windsor in Government and in industry.

On arrival at St Paul's Cathedral next day we were overwhelmed by the vast gathering of friends from Singapore, Sheffield, Windsor and from the depths of Pembrokeshire. Worcester diocese was there in quite substantial numbers together with the mayors of the city and the larger towns. I now recall only the most moving act of worship, commitment and spiritual strengthening in my life. David Paton preached on the place of leadership in today's society. He and I had been in close touch but separated by great distances since pre-war SCM days; there was something sad about the fact that he was not better used by the church. I had hoped that Frank would come from Australia to be a presenting bishop, but that was not possible; I was well guided through the service by two close friends and advisers, Leslie Hunter and Oliver Tomkins, in this role: they led me away to a side chapel to be vested in a rochet and brought me back to answer that formidable set of questions which are put to a new bishop, asking for a confession of faith and a statement of motives. They are gruelling questions, setting the priorities for episcopal ministry that cannot be forgotten. Silence, prayer and the laying on of hands followed with moving simplicity. Seventeen assisting bishops and just over four hundred family and friends participated in a general communion. After the blessing the Archbishop led me by the hand, down the choir, through the nave to the top of the great west steps of St Paul's, there to be met by a battery of photographers and inquisitive crowds. The occasion was overwhelming, yet at the same time friendly and personal. The photographer of the *Sunday Telegraph* caught me with the Archbishop in a moment of almost hysterical laughter; the picture was published right across the English-speaking world with a variety of captions insinuating some private joke between us. There was no hidden cause; we had both enjoyed the consecration. Martin Sullivan, the Dean, had been kind enough to lend us St Paul's Deanery for the day, so after shaking hands with countless folk we gave lunch there to the family, bishops and friends, a great party of some seventy people, and then returned to Windsor after an eventful twenty-four hours.

The next day, Sunday morning, we were further greeted by a lovely gathering of friends from the Castle, Eton, and the town. I was aware that I entered the Chapel no longer as Dean, but I was saddened to

[207]

find that Bryan Bentley, the senior canon, had ordered the Dean's chair to be removed to demonstrate that I had no further authority. Our life in partnership with the Foundation had finished; our new commitment had begun. It was my fifty-seventh birthday that week, as I took on the biggest job of my life. How lucky I was when so many begin to look to lesser work or even early retirement at such a time!

Before we moved house ten days later we had much to occupy us. Secretaries and staff came over from Worcester and the interest and responsibility of clergy care and clergy appointments started at once. The children arrived at differing times to glean what they could of furnishings and oddments that we would not be taking down to Hartlebury in order to use them in the London flat in Thurloe Square, in which Robert, Edward and Eleanor made a home. Although the days between consecration and taking over the diocese were full, I was delighted to be asked to accompany Prince Charles on a visit to St John's College, Nottingham. There had been many occasions on which we had talked about ordination and the ministry, and he was keen to visit a theological college, before I left, to see something of the selection and training of men and women for parish work. The re-opening of the college after its move from North London seemed a fitting time for a royal visit. We flew there and back in an aircraft of the Queen's flight, with the Prince sitting in the co-pilot's seat. We also had time to discuss the manpower situation and the availability of leadership in the parochial life of the church: he was always ready to assimilate information and consider problems that faced the institutional churches. Michael Green, the Principal, and Denis Wakeling, the Bishop of Southwell, both friends over the years, were there to meet us, along with the Lord Lieutenant and the Lord Mayor of Nottingham. We were guided through the college buildings to a lively meeting with the men and women in training: in their hall they were given a well-informed but light-hearted address by the Prince. He pointed out, among other things, that those being trained at St John's were being prepared for ministry, not just in selected congregations, but within the community of the English people, who were looking to the clergy for leadership. It was the last occasion on which I was on duty to assist a member of the Royal Family, and appropriately one which gave Prince Charles some idea of the kind of issues I would be dealing with in my diocesan work.

◁ *With the Archbishop of Canterbury on the steps of St Paul's Cathedral, February 1971*

The very next day I went to Buckingham Palace to do homage. I arrived at the side door informally, as I had done so many times, to be informed that I was expected at the Grand Entrance. From there I was conducted to the room in which I had been with Father nearly forty years earlier when I went with him as his apparitor or manservant to do homage on his appointment to Lichfield. Roger, Bishop of Chichester, the Clerk of the Court, and James Mansel, deputy and sub-Dean, were there officially, together with Peter Walker, the then Home Secretary, who was also MP for Worcester. We were joined by Michael Adeane, Martin Charteris and Johnny Johnston and we went in together; they all said that they came in for the fun of it, and indeed by then we were all old friends. As I knelt before the Queen, she put her hands over my hands and I recited the oath of allegiance word for word, as it was administered by the Secretary of State. The wording had been unchanged since the days of Henry VIII. Departing after a glass of sherry, I returned to Windsor for two more nights.

My journal for Sunday 28 February 1971 reads:

Windsor: H had actually dismantled much of the house, but in the end this proved to be a tremendous Sunday for people coming in and out. It was our last Sunday and our last proper day here. To HC at 8.30 sitting with the family in the stalls, having now no place in the ministry here! Mattins at 10.00 was the occasion of my saying good-bye. The Queen Mother and Prince Charles came, the Queen being away, and there was a large congregation for the service in the nave. The QM particularly asked that it should not be a 'blubbing' occasion and it certainly wasn't. I preached a light sermon on the job as demonstrated by the Garter Jewel. The Bible, symbol of a faith received; the crossed quills, signs of taking a decision for God and his church; the blue riband, a heavenly blue with a vision of heaven on earth. It went down well. At the end after taking out the QM and the Prince I didn't really get down to shake hands with as many as I would have wished. A number in to sherry including the Agnews, the Haigs, the Airds and some other real local friends. Then the QM and Prince Charles came back for lunch and we sat down to our last proper meal in this lovely home with them. She and I talked much of her doings and the church. Prince Charles and H always got on well, and the whole table turned into an easy conversation piece. After coffee in the drawing room our last Sunday lunch at Windsor was finished. Quite a crowd outside the garden gate to see the Royals away. All so typical of our happy life with them at the Castle.

Hartlebury Castle. The west front from across the moat

We arrived at Hartlebury during that week and settled into the house that had been the home of Bishops of Worcester for so many years, and therefore the base for ministry to the West Midlands. It breathed history, but in a different way from Windsor Castle. The Italian bishops who lived in it during the fifteenth century had taken it over largely unaltered from those who built it as a fortified manor house a century earlier. Latimer, later to die at the stake during the reign of Queen Mary, and other great reforming bishops, had guided the diocese through the dissolution of the great Benedictine monasteries of Worcester, Evesham, Tewkesbury and Gloucester from there. Bishop Hurd, the confidant and adviser of George III, had added the superb library in the latter years of the eighteenth century and filled it with books which his friends Pope and Dryden had helped him to select. For the last two hundred years there had been a succession of which the diocese was proud. Wilson Cash, the great missionary whom I had known as a young man, was the last to occupy the whole of the castle, which was part of our new inheritance.

[211]

After his appointment in 1954 it had taken Mervyn Charles-Edwards six years to win the battle for retaining the castle as the home of the Bishop, living while he fought in a variety of temporary homes. As a result of his efforts we found ourselves with the best part of the castle in which to live. It was a house of eight or nine bedrooms, four bathrooms, a flat, and two other staff houses enclosed in part by the moat and a pleasant garden. The study, which for me took the place of the King Charles room at Windsor, was a splendidly proportioned panelled room looking out over the moat to the Abberley hills beyond. The private chapel, built in about 1380 but furnished by Bishop Hurd in the Strawberry Hill Gothic style, was next door to the study. A small sitting room for Henrietta and the family led through into the garden. The official architect had managed to fall down the polished oak stairs, so he had readily agreed to open up that end of the front hall to give more light; the secretaries had rooms formed out of a spare 'morning' room; the dining room looked west over the moat and beyond it a pleasant kitchen was a real family centre. Whereas at Windsor there was no way in which you could make yourself heard in the kitchen from the study and vice versa, that was just possible at Hartlebury, though for a good deal of our communication internal telephones proved invaluable. The state rooms were under the same roof. They included a 'saloon' which we made into a large drawing room, the great hall that could accommodate a gathering of up to two hundred people, and the Prince Regent bedroom, which was superbly equipped with furnishings from his time including a huge four-poster bed. Best of all was the Hurd library, which I have already mentioned. It was such a beautiful room that I seriously considered occupying it as my study; however, sensibly the state rooms were administered under a separate trust and were there for the use of the diocese or community as a whole when the bishop did not need them. It was a marvellous and adaptable home into which we moved early in March 1971.

Rather regrettably, in the Church of England the consecration of a bishop and his installation in his cathedral are two entirely separate occasions. The enthronement was a happy domestic affair for the diocese and county in a superb place of worship. The site of Worcester Cathedral, by the Roman crossing of the Severn, was selected by the first missionary monks who arrived in the seventh century. On the mound standing above the river successive great churches were built as the mother house for the Benedictine monastic movement in the valley and as a cathedral for the bishop. The Norman contribution is to be seen in the two most western bays of the nave, the main portion having been burnt down at the end of the thirteenth century, but the jewel of Norman art is in the crypt, one of the most beautiful undercroft chapels in Western Europe, with its little forest of pillars and circular arches. With its huge central tower, two pairs of transepts and its long nave, it was left to successive generations by its Gothic builders as a great cathedral church which the Victorian restoration fortunately in no way damaged. From my throne in the choir I came to enjoy the weekday worship and music, and from the dais in the nave I always felt in close touch with the congregations on Sunday. There is a restfulness and sense of prayer about the long interior of the cathedral with proper places for being busy in the cloisters and remaining monastic buildings. The view of the cathedral from across the famous county cricket ground over the river must have been painted or photographed hundreds of times, and on approaching the city from any direction the building stands solid but welcoming among the spires, towers and streets of the city.

Eric Kemp the Dean, now Bishop of Chichester, and Christopher Robinson the organist, now at St George's, Windsor, had put together a splendid and novel service. After I was welcomed at the main door we were plunged into the music and tradition of Elgar, so closely identified with Worcester. There is little to beat his anthem 'The spirit of the Lord is upon me to bind up the broken hearted'. It was sung that afternoon and has remained an inspiration to me ever since. After the prayers of all the congregation for the years to come it was difficult for me to match the mood of expectancy in my address. I took the text from II Timothy I.7, 'God gave us not a spirit of fearfulness but of power, of love and of discipline', and spoke of the confidence that comes of believing and the community in Christ that could unite the towns and countryside of the diocese. The clergy present sitting robed and forming a great white block of men filling the choir, the mayors and councillors and representatives of the civic life of the county sitting at the head of the nave, and the thousand and more men and women selected and sent from the parishes stretching away to the west end were a tangible reminder of the varied tasks that lay ahead. I realized there and then that the clergy were entitled to a firm lead in faith and action, that local government was looking increasingly to voluntary cooperation of a sort that the churches could provide and that the great body of the lay people were frighteningly reliant on their bishop and his clergy.

Both in the service and afterwards Worcestershire seemed to take us to itself in a most real fashion. Old friendships were also renewed, since in some ways we were coming home. Lord Cobham, the Lord Lieutenant, a friend over many years, greeted Henrietta at the party which followed my installation as 'darling', and Peter Walker our MP and others, including Gilbert Ashton, headmaster of Abberley, Sir Tat Brinton, Sir Derek and Rosamund Holland Martin, all joined in welcoming us back.

One of the many advantages of living in an old-fashioned large episcopal residence was the availability of space for entertainment and consultation. The state rooms of the castle were retained for the Bishop, but without the support of the Church Commissioners, who felt that they were not appropriate to a modern bishop's house. The Great Hall, which could accommodate two hundred for a concert or a conference, was a good place to meet in; the saloon, with a fine eighteenth-century ceiling and plaster mouldings on the walls, was a comfortable drawing room which fifty or more could use without pressure; and the Hurd library, one of the loveliest rooms in the West Midlands, was always available for boards, committees and staff meetings. Henrietta with a willing group of volunteers managed these rooms, which were well equipped with their own catering facilities.

Being able to entertain gatherings from small committees to diocesan synods up to two hundred strong in one's own home made the castle a very real centre for diocesan life. The many occasions on which we were able to entertain and consult with the rural deans and diocesan staff, the Bishop's Council and the diocesan synod itself were enjoyable 'family' occasions. Early in my time the church had to take several major decisions, which were properly referred to the diocese for comment and voting. The Anglican-Methodist unity scheme, admission to communion of members of other churches, the future of private patronage and the parson's freehold were all matters of real importance. Each main issue was always in danger of dying the death of a thousand qualifications and had to be worked over by so many interested parties that frequently no common mind could be found and good recommendations went to the wall. The synodical procedure is good in principle, but I fear that its cumbersome machinery could strangle the church and make it less able, rather than more able, as an institution to adapt to change. It is surely better to decide – even wrongly, and then ask for forgiveness – than to make no decision and receive no grace. By the same token, we are known to be an episcopal church, but when major decisions are removed from the responsibility of the bishops, leadership becomes compromised and bishops are distrusted. Had it been left to them, we would by now have had a united church in our country. It might have been Protestant, but it would have been girded for further unity with Rome.

We did, however, build up trust starting with the deanery as the unit of church life that eventually must matter most under the diocese. Eighteen deaneries covering some two hundred and thirty parishes were rationalized into twelve good and viable units. I was never short of good men to be rural dean,and I now realize how much is due to the quiet and unostentatious parish priest who knows his colleagues and his lay leaders in an urban or rural area. Successive rural deans in key areas like Dudley, Kidderminster, Evesham and Worcester city itself became not only indispensable officers of the diocese but close friends in the general venture. Without their knowledge and the confidence that they came to enjoy, pastoral reorganization would have been impossible. Over and over again I was made to realize the centrality of a parish priest and the place of the vicarage in a community. Just when the policeman was taken away, the village school was threatened with closure, the local bus was being axed, came the news that the parish parson was not to be replaced. To enable a congregation to face up to relating to its neighbouring parish and to share the services of a priest was often a long and laborious process. But it did in fact often bring out the role and indeed the ministry of lay men and lay women which had lain dormant for far too long. The expertise and patience of the rural deans and my immediate staff was to become essential.

I set myself the task of visiting every parish not less than once every three years. Confirmation services provided most of these occasions, but undoubtedly any such visits were the real heart of the job in hand. There is nothing more gratifying after the frustrations of commmittees to visit a parish and find a variety and frequently a thoroughness of care and teaching progressing in what one might have expected to be a difficult situation. Dotted around the Malvern hills, up the Teme valley, over towards the Avon or certainly in the Black Country, the vicar and his people were providing an opportunity for young and old alike to be involved in worship and service to the locality. The integration of the ministry of bishops, vicar and lay officers in a parish seemed essential to any progress in the average parish, and the visit of the bishop was often the enabling factor.

The changing role of clergy and the changing pattern of the parishes was a challenge to find new methods, but also a deterrent to some who would otherwise have contributed much to the ordained ministry. Of course one would not want to go back to the days of Oliver Goldsmith's Vicar of Wakefield, who was first the father of a family, secondly a farmer and lastly a priest, but in some strange way it is clear that for many generations the strength of the Church of England lay in the rather independent individual who had had a university education. Even as recently as the 1920s and 1930s those of us who were 'called' to the ministry saw it as a means to use our personal abilities and gifts in bringing Christ into the lives of as many as possible. We also saw it as the response of privilege, and thus as a means of bettering society, whether at home or abroad, as the opportunities presented themselves.

I realized from the start that a bishop's staff, not his shepherd's crook, was the key to effective selection and therefore effective leadership. I arrived to find colleagues with me with whom I was able to work well; this did not always happen with a new bishop, but I proved singularly fortunate. Among them, happily, was Nicholas Allenby, who on leaving Sarawak and North Borneo had settled in our area, becoming assistant to the Bishop. I soon realized that I could leave much to him, including the direction of ordination candidates, and I treated him as a suffragan bishop of my own choosing who could advise on policy and help with the care of the clergy. He was a disciplined Kelham man and I came from the rather more relaxed tradition of Westcott House, but though in that respect our backgrounds were different, we both had common experience in having been missionaries in the Far East and therefore understood the need to adapt resources and take clear decisions. Peter Eliot and John Williams, my two archdeacons, were both splendid in totally different ways. Peter, with experience in the army and the law and with a wide knowledge of the world, was a ready friend to the clergy and one who was held in high respect by the county, as was Lady Alathea his wife. Peter and I had both been at Westcott House and we both enjoyed a liberal approach to theology and churchmanship. John Williams, on the other hand, was an extremely faithful and highly efficient professional clergyman. In many ways he was of the old school of archdeacons, and enjoyed wearing gaiters; with his Welsh and rather independent personality, in the diocese as Archdeacon of Dudley, and then later as a Canon in the cathedral when he became Archdeacon of Worcester, he brought a stern but whimsical approach to pastoral and administrative problems. He knew the need for discipline; he understood finance and he had the gift of friendship. He certainly made a great contribution and had a talent for guiding large parishes, many of which he knew in detail. His considerable help to me was in calling men to the ministry and guiding them through their vocation. As archdeacons should be, he was the eyes and the ears of the bishop!

Poor administration and delayed decisions have always irritated me. I was lucky to have a diocesan office that had been well established and grew in efficiency, gaining the confidence of the parishes over the years. Bill Hook, succeeded by Douglas Smith and later by William Bell, was one of a series of laymen who understood the needs of the parishes and the personal idiosyncrasies of the clergy while at the same time being skilful enough to help in introducing modern methods of management and finance. Many clergy became fearful that the presence of lay officers meant that they would be 'managed' or have their independence threatened. However, I had found that lay leadership in many ecclesiastical matters was superior to that of the clergy and that the patient and considerate lay colleague, either man or woman, was essential to the staffing of the diocese. As a result of such help I was able to delegate decisions and duties that have often bogged down a bishop and kept him away from his real ministry. For more than five years I depended heavily on William Bell; he was a natural staff officer.

Quite early on we entertained Alexander Stewart, the American Bishop of Worcester, Massachusetts. As I was the Bishop of Worcester, England, he visited us when he could and as a result we developed close contacts. He came over soon after my arrival and was keen to share his experience. However, his diocese was considerably smaller and his clergy on the whole more uniform in approach than we were. Even in the early 1970s he wanted to introduce me to his computerized administration. He boasted that with his electronic aids he could keep abreast with every detail in every parish; he was up to date with clergy families and clergy pay and at the press of a button could even 'know what any one clergyman was doing at any one time'! This way of being a bishop was something new to me, and in Worcestershire it would hardly have worked, as Bishop Stewart found to his surprise.

During his visit he went to meet the deanery synod of Upton upon Severn, a rather remote and very rural area. 'Why,' he asked the rural dean, 'do you not make better use of your synod in your scattered area?' 'But, my Lord,' came back the answer, 'don't you realize that it costs £5 every time our synod meets? Our resources don't run to more than two meetings a year.' The Bishop could not believe our backwardness or the way we counted our pennies – but would we have been better off with more money and better administration, like the US Episcopal Church? We talked long into the night comparing the American and British scene, not only when he was in Worcester but when I went over to Massachusetts. During two or three visits there in later years I became much more appreciative of the Episcopal Church. It was totally free of any state or secular sanctions: its churches and resources were sparse but very well organized, and its payment and care of the clergy left us standing. I learned much from sharing an ordination and some confirmations with Alexander Stewart. 'Robin,' he once said, 'always arrive at a parish church before the people are around. Then you will learn the real situation. Moreover, it is more important to greet the congregation as they arrive than to say good-bye as they leave. They will listen much better.'

In 1974 Bishop Allenby, the assistant bishop, came to retire from ministry altogether and at that point I was faced with a major problem. It was urgent that I should have a suffragan bishop in the diocese as a second in command. For ten years, both Bishop Simon Stewart, who had come from Uganda, and Nick Allenby had made an impression on Worcester by their service in the diocese, but they formed the last of the line of overseas bishops to come to our aid: there was no longer a flow of bishops returning from the 'mission field'. At the same time, the population of the diocese had grown, and there were well over two hundred clergy increasingly in need of personal help and advice. Worcester was comparable to many another diocese which enjoyed a regular suffragan bishop. Added to all this, there was an even more telling development. Dudley had become a metropolitan borough, and the people there felt that there should be episcopal presence and care in the context of the Black Country. Undoubtedly the most demanding part of our parochial mission lay in that area, since there was great stability at that time in the country parishes and market towns. The Archbishop agreed in principle to a suffragan, and the officials at Westminster were sympathetic, particularly in view of the way in which the new local government boundaries had affected the population in the West Midlands. So I expected no difficulties. In principle the Crown was willing, and I made my formal approach to the Church Commissioners. They said no. 'Robin can perfectly well look after 250 parishes and less than a million people himself,' was their argument. It seemed out of character for Ronald Harris, Gerald Ellison and others to oppose me. However, Michael Ramsey, who had encouraged me from the start, overruled the decision, instructed the synodical committee and authorized the officers of the Crown, by whom alone the creation of a suffragan see could be ordered.

By an act of 1888 Queen Victoria had delegated the naming of a suffragan to the diocesan bishop concerned. The diocesan could nominate anyone he wished to the Prime Minister for appointment by the Crown. This system has worked well over the years and has been a major means of selecting and training men for the office of a diocesan bishop. Sometimes it could be abused – as it still is – by certain diocesan bishops who want to promote partisan pressures within the church. Let them be nameless.

So I was free to choose a suffragan. Surprisingly, during my time at Worcester I had to make the choice not once, but twice. The decision was, and remains, a very responsible one, not only because once a man has been made bishop he always remains a bishop, but because the appointment is a major step in the rather slender career structure to which clergy naturally look. My first choice was Michael Mann, at the time a Canon of Norwich Cathedral. He had served in the army and the colonial service and had held various ecclesiastical appointments since his ordination. With his close interest in St George's House and what seemed to me the right ideas about the way in which the patterns of ministry should develop he seemed to me to be the man we needed. He was consecrated in March 1974. His selection proved to be a happy one and he ably identified and worked out the role of the Bishop of Dudley as the first to hold that title, principally serving in the heavily urbanized areas in the north of the diocese. That he went on a few years later to become Dean of Windsor was no surprise. We had shared the hopes and aspirations of Windsor together for many years, and I certainly did not grudge losing him so quickly to that sphere of work.

His successor, Tony Dumper, came from a very different background. He had been a fellow archdeacon with me in Malaya, and since he had had more experience of parochial ministry than either Michael Mann or I had, he offered a different approach to the

developing situation in Dudley and a fresh apporach to the whole
concept of mission for the diocese. I soon learned that both I and the
parishes had received a good friend and a tireless worker. Politically
a radical, and convinced of the rightness of the Campaign for Nuclear
Disarmament, he had much to give to our staff meetings. He cham-
pioned the often depressed parish priest, and imparted a new
enthusiasm to the further training of junior clergy and the promotion
of lay ministries.

In the past and to a certain extent even in the present century the
diocesan bishops have not always worked in harmony with the deans
of their cathedrals. Since the Crown had the right to appoint the dean,
the bishop could find himself confronted with an individualist who
for one reason or another could easily queer the pitch for him in his
own cathedral if he thought differently. Sadly, Father had become
disenchanted after his good friend Freddy Iremonger had been
appointed Dean of Lichfield by the Crown. Father was an easy-going
pastorally-minded bishop; Iremonger turned out to be an obstinate
man who was primarily interested in writing and broadcasting. Such
a situation never came my way. Eric Kemp was Dean when I arrived.
His tremendous academic record in Oxford (he was already a DD),
his knowledge as an ecclesiastical historian and his sympathy for the
Catholic tradition in the church might have made him angular. But
no, he was ready to make the cathedral serve the people of Worcester
and to meet the special need of the diocese. He always let me preach
if I wished and together we endorsed new services and new musical
events in the cathedral. When it came to the ordination of women
deacons or priests he was not happy, but fortunately for him the law
did not allow me to put my own convictions into practice. He left to
become Bishop of the enormous diocese of Chichester, where the
burden of administration has tended to stifle his theological and
liturgical abilities.

When he left, I made suggestions and was consulted by the
appointments secretary at Downing Street. To my surprise and
pleasure, Tom Baker, then Archdeacon of Bath and formerly Principal
of Wells Theological College, was suggested and appointed. His
coming brought not only a first-class preacher and teacher to the
cathedral but also a man who was deeply sympathetic to the major
crises confronting the diocese: ecumenical partnership, women's
ministry, amalgamation of parishes and much else. Through his
understanding the place of the cathedral in the life of the city and its

role in sharing in the hopes of the parishes steadily developed. I personally found in his quiet and knowledgeable manner a continuing partnership in the worship and life of the cathedral. This meant a great deal, since every bishop hopes that he will find in his cathedral his own base for prayer and mission. In my colleagues I had therefore men on whom I could depend. They also suffered my ways and methods willingly, but not without feeling able to improve my planning or correct my theology.

Having a dean with whom I could readily work and with the successful establishment of a suffragan see within the diocese I found our staff work greatly facilitated. The weekly meeting was attended by all of us – bishops, archdeacons, the dean, the diocesan secretary and my principal secretary. Heads of departments could be invited to sit with us, and the chairmen of committees came in order to familiarize themselves with policy; an accurate set of minutes was issued quickly after every meeting which tried to leave no ambiguities. Such 'staff meeting' government was not always easy, and at times over the years we had quite major differences: Eric Kemp did not share my views over the development of women's ministry; William Bell had severe reservations about the designation of clergy for sector ministries – hospital, school and industrial chaplains; John Williams was always more discerning than the rest of us about individual clergy and their abilities; and Tom Baker felt that the pace of amalgamation of parishes should be faster than I liked. However, after our meetings, whether at home or in diocesan headquarters at the Old Palace in Worcester, the Spirit always sent us on our several ways with a unity of purpose and with a sense of pleasure and fulfilment. As I watched our senior men I realized just how lucky I was to have them.

In addition, however, I and the staff also felt the pressure of intractable problems that would not go away. Whereas clergy who had their own personal hopes and difficulties always remained my prime concern, we also had to try to be of help to the demands of various educational establishments and activities. The hundred and more church schools were an asset of enormous potential but not easy to develop, with ideas about the need for school worship and religious instruction running against the churches in some areas. An Agreed Syllabus was required for the education authorities. Closely allied to this was our voluntary youth work in parish clubs or in helping local authority ventures as a matter of urgency. The archdeacons were the executive officers of these matters, and when he became an archdeacon Christopher Campling added the educational portfolios to his group of parishes. As director of education, Christopher was more of an evangelist than an administrator; he was and remained a teacher, but in the routine care of school and institutions we came to rely on our schools officer more and more. With a constantly declining number of clergy, the pressure on the staff increased, but throughout my time the way we shared the work at diocesan headquarters remained a stimulus and a pleasure, and was in no way drudgery or a cause for despair.

It has never been my inclination to take decisions single-handed, and I tried to share most responsibilities. However, there is one area which a bishop cannot delegate effectively: the selection, training, ordaining and placing of new deacons and priests. This, together with deploying more experienced clergy, fitting round pegs into round holes and square pegs into their proper parishes, is the most important responsibility of a diocesan. My father was not a good judge of men, and I'm told that I am not either. Admittedly, I tend to see the best in people and optimistically accept perhaps a better potential than is warranted by an interview. I tried, therefore, to make sure of obtaining detailed assessments of ordination candidates and unprejudiced comments on those who wanted or deserved appointments. The first item of our staff meeting agenda was invariably 'vacant benefices' – and with declining numbers of younger men we had a relatively narrow range to choose from. However, we did attract a good series of men and women for ordination and over the years I ordained some eighty men and fifteen women. To follow their individual progress and try to sustain each one of them was essential, but despite all our efforts there was a failure rate – about seven per cent. I suppose half a dozen of those on whom I had set trust and expectation abandoned their ministry, often not just over matters of faith but also because of domestic, family, financial or homosexual difficulties. Such pressures are not easy to contain when one is an assistant curate. Although I tried to make sure that good candidates for ordination kept coming forward, the staffing of the parishes remained a perpetual difficulty in a situation with declining manpower.

My arrival in the diocese in 1971 coincided with the realization that a major crisis was upon us in maintaining manpower in the ministry. The church was in disastrous trouble over the number of men coming forward for ordination. For years the diocese had carried on comfortably, confident of having a parson in every vicarage. Just when the church needed to explore new avenues of ministry in new towns, industrial communities, in schools and to a population that was so much better informed through education and the mass media, the supply of clergy nearly dried up. This malaise went much deeper than inadequate pay or an uncertain role; it represented the victory of materialism over spiritual values and of a consumer society in which the scramble for possessions took easy precedence over faith and service. Worcester was typical of the church in general, but that did not make it any easier to match reduced manpower to increased opportunities.

When I became Bishop of Worcester I found two hundred and sixty clergy serving some three hundred parishes and daughter churches. Within a few months of my settling down, the Sheffield Report, prepared by that good and kindly bishop Gordon Fallows, was published. It told the rural and affluent areas of the church to share their manpower resources with the urban, industrialized and less well-served areas of the nation. It was a rational and inevitable proposal, but it made severe demands on the southern areas of England, where in fact the strength of the church was greatest. We in Worcester were told that our population and resources warranted only a hundred and eighty-five stipendiary priests, and the next-door dioceses of Gloucester and Hereford were told the same thing. This was an enormous drop, and meant the end of a resident vicar for scores of country parishes and the non-appointment of assistant curates in areas where the population was heavy.

Some were ready to pronounce severe judgment on the demands of the Sheffield Report. They pointed out that it would spell the end of small personal ministries, particularly in the countryside; it would be detrimental to the individuality of both parish and parson, and it would reduce the church that traditionally 'covered' the nation to being just another denomination. Of course there were dangers in change, but facts had to be faced. 'Sheffield' was not just a bureaucratic reorganization; it was a response to the rapid drying up of the flow of ordination candidates that ran so well after the war: instead of some six hundred men coming forward each year to replace losses, we were down to half that number, and in twenty years the diocese would in any event have lost half its total clergy. Added to this, the endowment resources of the central church, though excellently managed by the Church Commissioners, would not meet much more than half the figure required for adequate clergy remuneration. The parishes had grown so used to their clergy being 'found', in every sense of the word, that they were not able, or in some cases even willing, to find cash for stipends. Stewardship was making its mark, but if the laity were producing the money they rightly claimed a say in the deployment and proper workload of their clergy and could not understand why they should not see a return proportionate to their contribution.

Within the diocese there were parishes and individuals who reacted vocally against change as if it were the personal foible of the bishop; but fortunately there were more who saw the crisis of manpower and the demand for sacrificial giving as an opportunity to get the real mission of the church into shape. We were like a horse-drawn wagon bogged down in ruts and needing to become lighter, more mobile and more adaptable in every respect. Added to the needs of residential parishes was the growing demand for clergy to be properly attached to our schools, hospitals, prisons, armed services and increasingly to major industrial units in the diocese.

We had begun to face these changes in the courses at St George's House. In the dioceses it took some years for clergy and longer for the laity to come to terms with the proposed amalgamations, uniformity of stipends, and group or team ministries. So while our staff meetings might plan matters down to the last detail, everything depended on the goodwill of incumbents, churchwardens and some-times a whole parochial church council. Until recently an archdeacon's job was ill-defined: in the last few years, however, he has had a key role to play in ensuring a smooth passage for parishes that have had to be amalgamated and clergy who have had to accept wider responsibilities than they had ever expected. Peter Eliot, John Williams and Christopher Campling, in very different ways, brought about pastoral reorganization in the Worcester diocese without causing too much 'aggro', and retained the confidence and goodwill of the clergy at the same time. Areas such as the Teme valley, very traditional in attitude to all its churches, did not lend themselves to reorganization. Our new town of Redditch, with some 150,000 resettled Midlanders, had to be introduced to a new shape of ecumenical territory from the beginnning. To be able to delegate the prolonged discussions and interviews to archdeacons whose judgment and tact I could trust made my job not only possible but pleasurable.

Having witnessed the effectiveness of industrial mission chaplains in Sheffield, I was gratified to find the foundation for such work well established in the diocese. Mervyn Charles-Edwards had seen the issue primarily in terms of Kidderminster, the largest single town given over to carpet weaving in Europe. With the goodwill of management and the growing cooperation of the trade unions, industrial mission in Carpets International, Gilt Edge, Kosset, Brintons and other household names meant more than just a goodwill visit from a parson to certain factories, but a regular weekly occasion for the chaplains to meet with shop stewards and works managers and then to be available for individual consultations, often on family or domestic affairs. Under Canon Roger Howes, a most remarkable relationship developed between the churches and the industry of the town. He trained successive priests who worked with him before going to various developing situations elsewhere. John Gathercole in Redditch New Town accomplished as much within a wide variety of heavy and light industries. The secret of such chaplains lay in continuity of work and regular visiting. The emergence of the churches in the new population of nearly 100,000 was as much due to the specialist ministry of non-parochial clergy as it was to those who established house churches and congregations in the enlarged village centres of the new town. As elsewhere, the danger of independent chaplaincy work was the development of parallel unchurched groups of Christian adherents. On the whole, however, the mission established a working link with the parish clergy whch led to a confidence in it and a good partnership between parochial and specialist clergy.

Looking back, one can see how Oxford, Cambridge and London had satisfied most of the needs of the Church of England up to 1939, but from the peace of 1945 onwards the privileged and professional families clearly became increasingly disillusioned about the church and their sons did not even begin to contemplate entering its ministry. No longer were the public schools the seedbed of the ministry. Again, there were those who felt that this was no bad thing, but there is no disguising the fact that one undoubted element of ministry is leadership, and that had traditionally been inculcated within the public schools where those who were to enter the professions, the services and the church had for years been educated. The percentage of public-school or graduate candidates for the ministry went down steadily down through the 1970s, to the great detriment of the church both at home and overseas. Long talks with my sons Robert and Edward, both believing Christians and both ready to support their local church and give time to it, made me realize that the traditional image of the parson with a very real role to play in any town or village was no longer seen as relevant to the new situation. The common impression of the ministry, particularly among the more educated, was that it was an area of voluntary social service or a way of carrying on an outdated ecclesiastical tradition. Until the Church of England sorted out its standing on faith and the necessity of a better trained professional priesthood and recognized the validity of ministry in other churches, the best men would not come forward.

As a result of this situation, at least within the diocese I tried at an early stage to get a fresh and more open approach to recruitment in our grammar and public schools, particularly in Malvern, Worcester and Bromsgrove, where we had headmasters deeply committed to the gospel and the church. We took a keener interest in the modes and methods of training, which then as now were too academic in approach. Since I was among other things chairman of the Council of The Queen's College, Birmingham, where experiments in ministerial training were being developed, it was comparatively easy for me to see what was going on. We entertained the candidates and their families at regular intervals, either at Hartlebury or at the Old Palace, and we became, I hope, aware of the personal and financial needs of the men and women as they came into a profession that would never have much material reward.

Behind all the administrative changes and pastoral patterns that were developing there lay the much more basic issue of the religion of our people. Undoubtedly there was and remains a latent reliance upon God, but too often even the religiously inclined do not know what to do about such a sense; they find that the church in the form in which they encounter it is irrelevant to their lives in the world and its image differs from their expectations. The uncertainty among clergy and teachers in our technological era with its much more liberal moral code was also increasingly apparent. Most clergy and the few candidates coming forward saw the religious factors as paramount, and not just the maintenance of the parochial *status quo*. Nevertheless it was not easy to preach, teach and witness consistently in an environment that was sceptical and which devalued the institutional. I did my best in the early years by delivering Lent Lectures at Hartlebury and then at Evesham and Malvern so that lay men and women and their clergy could have a fresh approach to Christian belief and ethical behaviour. It is for future history to judge the church in the latter half of the twentieth century, but in the middle of it, with the explosion of the means to communicate, it needed no great insight to see that the tasks of the clergy and indeed the role of the bishops were in danger of suffering the death of a thousand qualifications.

However, we were fortunate in the Worcester diocese, and never suffered a worse shortage than elsewhere of good candidates; those who did come our way were a rewarding, hard-working and responsive set of men and women. Where in a huge diocese like Southwark, Mervyn Stockwood had ordained some six hundred over twelve years, I had selected and ordained only seventy-eight. In our early years, ordinands would come as a group to stay at Hartlebury before their ordination. This was always hard work for Henrietta, Eleanor, who was then at home, and the secretaries, but enormously worth while, for it meant getting to know them more intimately than could be done through any amount of interviews. The family welcomed them, they shared our home, and I hope that they found a lasting friendship with their bishop. However much had been accomplished or not accomplished in their theological colleges, what mattered most was the character of the vicar, his home, and the parish to which they were sent. That is what was to mould the pattern of their ministry and made it effective. The newly-ordained would go to the larger parishes in the diocese; as long as there was a solid backing and a caring ministry here there was always opportunity for further developments round the periphery. I was fortunate to have men of real ability in charge of the major centres who could think and plan in the same terms as myself.

I felt that the great services of ordination once or twice a year, at St Peter's tide or Advent, had to be in the cathedral, and not in the parish churches to which the men were going. Both Eric Kemp and Tom Baker had the gift of mounting very fine acts of worship, full of meaning and devotion both for those being ordained and, almost as important, for their families, who were often complete strangers to such an occasion. The choir under Christopher Robinson and then Donald Hunt maintained superb liturgical music and involved the congregation in the worship. We had to take a great deal of care over our ordination services. Five or six hundred communicants was not an unusual number, and if the service was not going to drag, its pace had to be organized thoughtfully. Since I have never forgotten my ordination and it setting, I wanted to make sure that those whom I ordained would not forget theirs either.

═ [12] ═

Lords Spiritual and Lords Temporal

Wednesday became almost a routine day for going to London. By being driven to Birmingham I could get from Hartlebury to Westminster, door to door, in just over two hours. I came to find such days a pleasant break, with an opportunity to read in the train; and this usually provided occasions for sharpening my ideas by attending or chairing London committees. As one of the directors of Christian Aid I kept in touch with the deteriorating situations of poverty and malnutrition which produced such a gulf between the south and the north and which the Christian resources could only marginally help. My horizons were also broadened by continuing to be on the executive committee of the Church Missionary Society for some years. Watching Kenneth Slack at Christian Aid and John Taylor at CMS handling the resources of the church as we became increasingly more committed to the Third World at the very time when were becoming politically disengaged from it was an experience I wish other clergy were able to share. Once again I found my ideas of ministry and leadership being stimulated by seeing other and better men at work.

Sessions of the House of Bishops, when we were convened under synodical government, did not differ very much from the informal bishops' meetings. The presence of lawyers and secretaries in synod made little difference to the plainness and honesty with which we addressed each other in a way which, at least in my earlier days as a bishop, made us all close friends. When I first became a bishop, I found myself a member of a group of about forty – a few more when the Scots and Welshmen were with us – drawn very largely from a common background of a few colleges and a shared wartime experience. Quite soon, however, the new generation of younger bishops tended to polarize our interests and attitudes in a way which led to divisions. The Anglo-Catholics in particular felt that they had an axe to grind, and this preoccupation meant that we had to keep an eye on the chairmanship of synod committees to make sure that there was what the Anglo-Catholics felt to be a fair balance. This was a pity: it marked the end of an era in which the diocesans had been a very close-knit group of friends, utterly confident of one another's abilities and always supportive of one another, despite differences in stand-point. My journal recalls a 1972 meeting which was not untypical:

We worked on:
1. How synodical government was working and the chairmanship of it in particular;
2. Local government reorganization and diocesan boundaries;
3. Future church relations: very good speeches by Michael C and Oliver Bristol;
4. Urban mission and industrial chaplains;
5. What should be the role of archdeacons;
6. Legal fees;
7. Revision of the ordinal;
8. Hospital chaplains;
9. Clergy stipends and the diversion of large benefice incomes;
10. The next generation and the appropriate age for confirmations;
11. The appointment of a new Chief Secretary for the Advisory Council for the Church's Ministry;
12. Married ordinands and the middle-aged candidate;
13. The use of redundant churches;
14. A bishop for West Indian immigrants, etc., etc.

We had lunch together and resumed for a final hour or two. I had a word with Michael C who thanked me for 'enlivening and illuminating our discussion'. When I met Geoffrey Tiarks (Chief of Staff to the Archbishop), he told me that the Archbishop had said to him, 'I did not know that Robin had ability as well as enthusiasm.' We live and learn.

It was never very congenial for Michael Ramsey to chair long meetings with intractable agendas. So while the bishops' meetings one or two days three times a year were useful, at the same time they also proved frustrating. We had long-term 'annuals': the care and destiny of clergy who had come off the rails; the consequences of clergy shortages; how available ordination candidates were to be distributed; matrimonial legislation; Anglican-Methodist unity and Prayer Book revision. At any time Michael Ramsey could appear to be asleep, but this was not really the case. Discussions would suddenly come alive under his leadership when he made potentially boring matters issues of belief and spirituality. Throughout the *Honest to God* crisis he had proved a superb interpreter of the critical approach to the historicity of the Gospels. He understood the requirements of our people in any new liturgy or Prayer Book, he deplored dependence on Parliament for liturgical reform and steered our thinking through to the passing of the Worship and Doctrine Measure, which largely released us from domination by the House of Commons.

An insistence on the holiness of the church, divided or preferably united, and its divine mission to our nation and through Anglicanism overseas was an essential corrective which he gave. His personality and whole vocation to theology and ministry radiated his dependence on knowing and seeking the mind of God. I had never expected to be influenced to the degree that I was by Michael Ramsey, but that was his way: he guided the whole spectrum of Anglican allegiance back to a living theology, and although I had come from a liberal evangelical background, with his own liberal catholic background he guided me into an appreciation of a high doctrine of the church. Donald Coggan, who given his age could only undertake a relatively short primacy, was someone who was able to relate afresh the concept of a divine mission for one nation rather than instill renewal into the established church. His personality, so attractive and acceptable to those outside the general run of ecclesiastical affairs and indeed to those within it, enabled the gospel to be more quickly grasped and our church to be more quickly appreciated by the other communions. He could assimilate into his care the growing charismatic movement and help both the evangelical and the catholic wing of the church to grasp their role in the mission. More importantly he carried the church in our era when it was subject to material pressures and secular attitudes. Michael Ramsey and Donald Coggan were splendidly complementary. In process of becoming a dicoesan bishop and in consolidating the early years at Worcester I emulated both of them and was sustained enormously by their leadership.

When Michael Ramsey was succeeded by Donald Coggan, and Stuart Blanch was appointed to York, we all became aware throughout the nation that we had a complete change of style not only at Lambeth but also on the bench. The scholarly holiness and monumental theological application of one with as high a doctrine of the church as Michael had was replaced by the friendly demands for faith and

Christian conduct made by Donald Coggan. Here was an archbishop who more readily related to the latent religion of the English people; who was ready to develop the partnership of resources with other Christian churches that Fisher and Ramsey had inaugurated; and who also had first-hand experience of the Anglican Communion overseas. By his transparent integrity Donald Coggan was immediately understood by the clergy and laity alike. However, we did have questions to ask of him. The diocese of Worcester loyally supported his Call to the Nation, which he undertook so soon after he became Primate, but we felt that this approach, like national days of prayer, tended to oversimplify our material prosperity and presuppose widespread disillusionment in the nation without enough supporting evidence. Nevertheless, I found that both the archbishops who led the church through the 1970s were marvellously complementary in their approach to our diocesan problems.

Bishops' meetings also had their lighter and social side. They became the scene where the forty of us discovered our unity and ironed out our idiosyncracies. Dominating characters included Mervyn Stockwood (Southwark), probably wearing a loud shirt and striped trousers and making radical suggestions from his position within the Catholic side of the church; Gordon Fallows (Sheffield), full of wisdom and also quick to comment; David Say (Rochester), already a veteran on the bench but retaining a fresh approach to social and parliamentary issues; Ronnie Williams (Leicester), tiresomely traditional but usually right in his judgment; and Robert Stopford (London) with his cool judgment.

That was how it was like in the early days; however, it was not long before the bishops bore the inevitable marks of a generation gap. Traditionalism and paternalism were carried on in Robert Mortimer (Exeter), Basil Guy (Gloucester) and Faulkner Allison (Winchester). There was a refreshing new approach to the national issues both politically and ecclesiastically from Bob Runcie (St Albans), Stuart Blanch (Liverpool) and Kenneth Woollcombe (Oxford). Oliver Tomkins (Bristol) was invariably reliable in reconciling old and new attitudes and in identifying the importance of one or the other. My resolve was to learn increasingly from the younger group and not to be identified with those who were almost on the bench with Father. I did find myself wondering whether we matched up to our predecessors, who seemed to have such great stature in their time: Billy Greer, Leslie Hunter or F.R.Barry. They were great men in their day.

But having talked, prayed and laughed with my fellow bishops, I concluded, perhaps conceitedly, that we were as good a group of individual bishops as there ever had been. Keeping a close eye on all of us at bishops' meetings was George Reindorp (Guildford). He was quite unmerciful on those who felt they had to make a speech on every issue and put a tick against the name of each bishop as he spoke. Not surprisingly Graham Leonard (Truro) won the medal for speaking most often and too portentously.

It is perhaps too easy to make value judgments with hindsight, but the general impression I have of the ordering of the Church of England in the first ten years of synodical government is not a very happy one. It was not surprising that three distinct groups – bishops closely-knit and with wide experience; clergy rather arbitrarily elected from very different backgrounds; and elected laity who had time to spare – could not really reach a consensus of opinion over major issues. The very nature of attempting a three-tier parliamentary pattern spelt failure to adventurous plans and, to this day, does not lend itself to taking decisions which the body of the church urgently requires. The negative decisions on Anglican-Methodist unity, matrimonial law reform and the ordination of women did not reflect the will of the rank and file, who were maintaining and developing the parishes. Those who best represented the hopes and requirements of the 'man in the pew' were in fact the bishops. Had the major decisions required in the 1970s been delegated to the bishops, by now we would have a much happier church, a much more united national Christian body and a wider base for the ministry, including the ordination of women. The Church Commissioners progressed over the years and took many major administrative and financial decisions that strengthened the ministry largely because in the final instance the diocesan bishops had the required power.

Among other responsibilities I soon found myself deputy chairman and episcopal representative on the body set up to administer the new Parliamentary Act on Redundant Churches. Bill Harris QC was our chairman, a keen churchman and a friend of many years. We got on with our unpopular task and month by month over several years we settled the destiny of some six hundred mediaeval or more modern churches that were superfluous to requirement in today's spread of population. It was an interesting assignment: not much applied to my diocese, but there was much advice that could be given to vast rural areas like Norfolk or Lincolnshire on the one hand, and large-scale inner-city reorganizations on the other. Every single parish that looked like losing the use of one of its churches was considered individually. We discussed the assignment of buildings for preservation by the government-aided Redundant Churches Fund or their use for community or even residential purposes, and occasionally we had to plan demolition. All our recommendations had to be confirmed by the governing body of the Church Commissioners, and appeal was allowed only to the Privy Council. I found myself obliged to handle a great deal of this kind of work on behalf of the English dioceses.

Closely allied to the matter of the disposing of redundant churches was the recurring dilemma of replacing or selling the vicarages. With the levelling of clergy stipends to a figure that enable a good middle-class standard of living it was not surprising that many vicarages or rectories that were built to accommodate a priestly landed gentleman were not suitable. At the same time many hundreds of these houses were fine examples of domestic architecture over three centuries and provided both a home and a parochial centre for the congregation. To measure up the pros and cons of disposing of historic benefice houses and the building of new accommodation was the constant and difficult responsibility of the Church Commissioners. Where matters concerned with my diocese required my comment or consent I leaned towards retaining fine dwellings in the belief that they would find a new role in better years, but at the same time I always bore in mind the economic resources of younger clergy and the demands that were being made on the capital in central church funds. I hope that later generations will not judge the Church of England in the twentieth century too badly when they realize the wealth of property and land that has recently been disposed of.

All diocesan bishops are Church Commissioners, but only a handful of half a dozen do the work. As episcopal member of the Redundant Churches Committee I was *ex officio* a Governor at Millbank. Another monthly meeting meant more time away from Worcester, but there, in many ways, lay the centre for communication and decision taking for our work. After all, the Church Commissioners are the body which ultimately holds the purse strings and legally owns the physical resources of all the parishes of England, including parsonage houses and clergy pension funds, all of which was made possible by the substantial endowments in land, housing and financial capital that the parishes and church as a whole have inherited. Though I was there to be answerable to the Governors on the problem of redundant churches, I also took a proper interest in our policies of land management, farm tenures and provision of housing. I was never equipped nor invited to serve on the 'assets' committee, which actually evaluates and watches over the resources of the Church of England, but I soon realized what substantial work was being brought to completion by Gerald Ellison (London) and David Say (Rochester). Each of them gave years of sustained service to the Commissioners in that particular sphere.

As the optimism of the 1960s gave way to the pessimism of the 1970s, the churches clearly had to make some major adjustments. The decline in the economy and the crisis over employment approximately coincided with our move from Windsor to Worcester. The standard of living and material prosperity that had promised so many things was proving too good to sustain.

With strikes and threats of strikes in some major industries, and an awareness of the prospect of serious inflation, the Conservative Government under Ted Heath was in a state of such crisis that for a while, to maintain its authority, it was reduced to legislating for a three-day working week. Enduring this showed just how vexed the economic situation was, and at the same time it demonstrated clearly to the nation, and the churches, that the full employment and booming economy which had been taken for granted were not to be counted on. Inflation, the rise in oil prices, the beginnings of computerized industry and the rise of Japanese and other imports all made the nation unsteady in the early 1970s. The churches would have to learn that stewardship campaigns and competent investment in equities would no longer be enough. We were being thrown back on what should always be sufficient – the gospel. At the same time we were failing to discover our unity, which was essential to any move forward. Our congregations were declining in numbers, and those volunteering for the priesthood in the Anglican, Roman or Reformed churches were dropping so severely that a serious crisis of professional leadership did not seem far away. Nevertheless, this slimming down of the churches was not all loss. The clergy, and even more particularly the laity, were rapidly becoming aware of the 'priesthood of all believers', of the real role that all Christians, whether ordained or lay, could play in the ministry, and of our dependence upon the truths of the eternal gospel rather than on an 'established' religion. All this

[234]

was becoming more and more evident, and bode well for a future strengthening of Christ's church.

With this situation in view the British Council of Churches spent many months preparing for a Church Leaders' Conference in September 1972. I was invited to be present and had kept the date free. Even for me, born and bred as I was into SCM, going to a conference was not at all appetizing, but if I was to be true to my past and willing to share what the Windsor years had taught me, then I had to join others in trying to face up to the issues facing the Christian community, and indeed the stability of society. Staying for a week in Woodbrooke College and going to work in the Central Hall of the Selly Oak Colleges brought back many memories and family connections. About a dozen bishops were involved, along with the leaders of all the member churches. There were also many excellent clergy, men who were making a real impact on their situation: David Paton from Church House, Hugh Montefiore from Southwark; Peter Morgan from Enfield; Trevor Beeson and Derek Greaves. Together wih representative laity we made a gathering of some three hundred strong. Peter Walker, then Secretary of State for the Environment, whom I had come to know well through his connection with Worcester, gave the opening speech. His survey of changing Britain was competent but a little patronizing and opportunist – as befitted a good Conservative. There was an immediate reaction from Alec Lyon, a Labour MP, and so the gathering became politically rather polarized. It was David Jenkins and Ian Ramsey who clarified the real issues, declaring what God was doing with the nation and how he was 'inches ahead of the institutional churches'. Sir William Armstrong, then Secretary of the Cabinet, who had been closely associated with us at St George's House, gave a sad picture of his experience of the churches, but was remarkably reassuring about where Christian values could still change the sequence of events. How fortunate the country was in having him and Burke Trend at 10 Downing Street during those critical years; I felt fortunate and privileged to be able to enjoy their friendship.

Since the conference was near enough to Hartlebury we were glad to welcome weary participants to meals and time off. Betty Ridley; John Taylor, the head of CMS; Denis Wakeling, Bishop of Southwell, and Ian Ramsey all came over for shorter or longer times. Sadly, the pressure of work on Ian, then Bishop of Durham and the leading theologian of the younger generation, was all too noticeable. He was clearly too tired to carry on when he came to lunch on the Sunday of the conference. News of his death while sitting in the chair at Broadcasting House a few weeks later was a sad blow to the churches and it was a real personal loss to me. How long shall we take to learn the lesson not to run our best theologians into the ground by the sheer weight of episcopacy? Though it would be tragic if we stopped making first-rate scholars into bishops. Our need now is to discover how best to bring the insights of modern scholarship into the episcopal system.

The Church Leaders' Conference proved not only a meeting place for laity and clergy concerned with the direction in which the nation was moving but also a stimulus for the Christian forces in the land to take the economic and social situation much more seriously. In the face of uncertainty congregations had unconsciously enclosed themselves within their church walls, reduced resources had led to fear, and lack of progress had given the impression that the ecumenical movement was at a standstill. The gathering of leaders at Selly Oak that autumn re-energized much that was essential to the British religious scene.

Helping to keep contact between the churches, whether through such gatherings as the Church Leaders' Conference, through the various divisions of the British Council of Churches, or through our local councils of churches in the diocese again became a priority for my time and energy. The Church of England cannot go it alone, however much we may have inherited from the Catholic tradition and national status.

Whether I went up for bishops' meetings, General Synod, or other matters, London was by no means all work. I came to understand the readiness with which Father used to leave Lichfield for a day or two in London, returning with a smile. A not uncomfortable journey from New Street, often with the good old-fashioned breakfast on the train, and the pleasant luxury of a family base in Thurloe Square at the other end, made all the difference. Being able to be with Robert, Edward and Eleanor in the flat on a fairly regular basis meant that we were all in close touch and gave us a home in London.

On many an occasion my work would finish reasonably early and we could spend an evening together or go out to a local curry house in South Kensington. Rachel and Michael were blessed with our first grandchild in 1970; to be able to spend time in their home in Fulham was always a pleasure and an opportunity for me to acquaint myself with the outlook of the next generation. In addition, the old dining club known as 'Nobody's Friends' kept me in touch with judges, academics, parliamentarians and clergy who made up the hundred or so members. Three times a year this club has met for a hundred and fifty years, and continues to do so with a minimum of formality.

The fiftieth birthday of Prince Philip, royal weddings and other celebrations were also occasions for really splendid parties at Buckingham Palace to which both Henrietta and I were invited. These were evenings of enormous pleasure in renewing old friendships from the Windsor days. After a good dinner and much dancing at one such party, to which the 'official' life of the nation had been invited, I found Vic Feather, then head of the TUC, resting behind a curtain. By 2.00 a.m he was as tired as I was, and was relieved that it had been a good friend who disturbed him.

With plenty of work and interests already demanding time in London, in addition I became a member of the House of Lords. I might have spent quite a number of my early years as a diocesan without becoming a member. Before the era of compulsory retirement for bishops, dead men's shoes did not come thick and fast, but in 1974, some three years after I became a bishop, there was an avalanche of episcopal retirements and I found myself summoned to take my seat unexpectedly soon.

There are those who believe that the era of bishops in the House of Lords may be drawing to its close. The Lord Chancellor himself, Lord Hailsham, advised that in any newly constituted second chamber it would be inappropriate to include bishops. But one cannot but be surprised at such a curious recommendation from one who is a Christian, and an Anglican at that. Lord Hailsham undoubtedly had a good reason for his suggestion, but it was purely pragmatic. In his proposal he saw most bishops as being under such pressure from their diocesan work that they were quite unable to take advantage of their membership of the Lords. Yet I well remember the freedom with which Theodore, with a vast diocese, and Father, with some six hundred benefices, found the time and had the sense of commitment to go to the Lords regularly, to meet with those in Government and parliament and generally to be involved with the. legislature at Westminster. This is not always the case today. Bishops tend to be totally immersed in ecclesiastical pursuits, and politicians are increasingly reluctant to include spiritual and moral decisions as part of their responsibility. Church and state have been drawing apart ever since the failure of the Prayer Book Measure of 1928. However, my years at Windsor had shown me the enormous potential for good that there was in the partnership, and it was gratifying and exciting to be invited to take a place in the legislature.

It was on Wednesday, 11 December 1974, that I formally responded to the Writ summoning me to attend. I had already received memoranda from the Clerk of the Parliaments on the one hand and from the Archbishop's staff on the other as to how to behave and how to arrange my new duties. The events of the day started with a family lunch party followed by photographs, and a quick rehearsal with my two supporters, David Say, Bishop of Rochester and George Reindorp, Bishop of Guildford. After prayers had been said and the House had assembled, I set off, hat in hand, a Cambridge mortar board borrowed from the cupboard carried flat against my chest, in the wake of the Clerk, David and George. We went into the Chamber where we paused, bowed at the Dispatch Box, bowed again, went on towards the Lord Chancellor and bowed again. Kneeling before him, I handed him the Royal Summons. Then I went back to the Dispatch Box to take the oath of allegiance and sign the register. Having been led around the back benches, the three of us took our seats. There, as it might be in Alice in Wonderland, we stood, removed our hats, bowed, sat down, up again, hats off, bowed again, hats on; all in deadly silence, to be followed by shaking hands at the Woolsack to the murmur of 'Hear, hear' from those present. All the time the family and friends were gazing down from the public gallery on this antiquated procedure.

Nevertheless the welcome was real. I soon realized that I had to learn the procedures and traditions of the House in the conduct of debates before I could take any active part or make a speech. One early incident still makes me blush. On a routine afternoon sitting, when there were usually some forty peers present on any one day, after I had knelt alongside Lord Elwyn-Jones, Lord Chancellor, at the Woolsack, to lead the prayers, there was the usual pause to let others in before business started. Without being aware of the significance of what I was doing, I committed the unforgivable sin of walking across the floor of the House to speak with Nancy Seear on the Liberal front bench. My movement was met with horror: I should have walked round and not crossed the House. I beat a hurried retreat to the episcopal benches, which historically are on the Government side.

By sitting together we were able to converse and compare notes. Mervyn Stockwood was a ready challenger of many Conservative proposals. It was certainly to his credit that he mastered the difficult and constantly recurring problems of housing, local government, the National Health Service and issues connected with the wider hopes of the Welfare State. With his clearly identified allegiance to the Labour party he spoke as few others were able to. Ronnie Williams embodied the type of bishop who could adapt himself to his audience with a real touch. He always had a well informed and critical attitude, particularly in the field of legislation relating to matrimony, the family and the Common Market legislation. Then there was Gerald Ellison (London), who had made a well deserved place for himself in the House by his regular attendance. His mastery of the names and personalities of Government and opposition spokesmen was the envy of all of us bishops. He was also ready to speak competently at short notice in the rather routine debates on the economy or international issues; successive archbishops came to rely on his being their spokesman. David Say developed a real confidence in the bishops among many peers, regularly speaking with brevity and to the point for the church on a variety of issues.

However, it was when it was known that Michael Ramsey or Donald Soper were going to speak that both sides of the House would fill up. On the rare occasions when the Archbishop spoke, he commanded a remarkable sympathy and authority, although I am sure that he did not find the audience congenial to his tradition. As a theologian he was able to bring the historic perspective of the church to changing moral attitudes in the nation – and whatever else, his rising and falling eyebrows will long be remembered! Donald Soper, on the other hand, had the enormous advantage of years of being identified with the population around Tower Hill and the East End, and was consequently able to speak with an authority that was unmatched on either side of the House. He never accepted the Labour whip, just as we bishops too never took a political position either. All in all, being in the Lords was no easy task. With a heavy job well away from Westminster, it took time and energy to maintain the respect and authority of being Right Reverend Prelates, the form by which we were always addressed.

Although consultations at St George's House on legislation and the nation's life had given me a wider experience than most bishops enjoyed, the most thorough preparation I received for any participation in the Lords was through many years of close contact with the industrial missions up and down the country and through being chairman of the Industrial Committee of General Synod. For some time I had already found myself trying to interpret the situation in industry and employment, labour relations and trade unions, in two ways: trying to enable the church to understand the working industrial community and to enable the legislature at least to be aware of Christian values.

It proved to be a taxing assignment to have to watch over these interests in the name of the church on top of my routine diocesan commitments, and there is no way in which I could have managed had I not had the constant help of Giles Ecclestone, previously a Clerk in the House of Commons, David Muston and Paul Brett, who were secretaries to the Board of Social Responsibility at Church House. I admired their powers of analysis and speed of work and was enabled by them to make many a statement and prepare many a speech. They – and particularly Giles Ecclestone – knew what the bishops ought to be saying and were able to identify the real issues confronting legislation. I was especially fortunate in having such back-up; they not only provided factual information which was vital to speaking in Westminster but also gave me confidence in speaking of matters that did not primarily concern the church but were in fact moulding the social and working life of millions of people. Many doubted whether bishops should 'interfere' in secular issues, but since these issues were of the very texture of our people's lives, to relate to them seemed to be essentially part of a pastoral and prophetic ministry.

I gave my maiden speech in June 1975. Encouraged by many friends I entered the arena on the subject of 'Urgent economic and political measures consequent on membership of the EEC'. I had gathered my facts and formed my opinions carefully, but at the very moment when I was due to rise, full of trepidation, there was an interruption. The Government needed the attention of their Lordships on a statement being made in the Commons about the future of Rhodesia. More questions and argument followed, until the stir was eventually quietened down by Douglas Home. The orders for sittings were slipped in, and after that the Deputy Leader of the House signalled me to get started. It was not an easy moment, but bringing the House back to the main issue of the day made a good way in. I received the usual 'Hear, Hear' for a maiden speech – a comment which gave no indication of whether the peers either approved or disapproved. The

House is an extremely polite place compared with the Commons, and as is also traditional, the peers who followed made kindly and appreciative references both to my presence in the House and to the matter of my speech. Lord Eccles and Lord Elton on the Government side, both good friends, and Lord Wells Pestell, who always remained an ally of the 'Prelates', for the opposition, were generous in their remarks, as they were in the bar later on. I sat through the debate for some five hours until it closed. It is a sensible but demanding tradition in the Upper House that if you speak, you stay until the summing up or reply from the Government. At nine o'clock I escaped to Brooks's Club for an evening meal.

Taking a close interest in what was going on at Westminster was gratifying, as it recalled much of what we were doing at St George's House, and in the same way Windsor days had given me many friends in both Houses of Parliament: Enoch Powell and later Jocelyn Cadbury were across the lobby, and close at hand to meet in the Lords were David Eccles, Derick Amory, John Redcliffe-Maud and John Vaizey, to name but a few. They were all deeply committed to the aims established at St George's, welcomed me back and introduced me both to the Government and Opposition front bench. I was soon invited to attend the cross benchers' weekly meeting, and although I was very bad at attending, it gave me an insight into the working of the legislature and the pressures on the agenda of the House.

I spent more time with the all-party Industrial Study Group. Lord Rochester convened some twenty peers at regular intervals to hear talks and make comments on industrial issues facing the Government of the day. This kept us on our toes, and was informative, as the legislation on trade unions, the closed shop and numerous other issues came to be debated on the floor of the House.

There was always a bishop on duty to conduct the prayers at the start of the day's work. It was a pleasant duty, and formed a useful introduction to the structures and procedures of the House. One day, on average, in any week called for prayers in mid-morning when the Law Lords assembled in the chamber to convey a legal judgment in the name of the High Court of Parliament. The mace was carried in and the presiding Law Lord took his seat on the Woolsack in place of the Lord Chancellor. Few people were around, so with only the Law Lords in the Chamber we would read the psalm and kneel for prayer using the very appropriate collects before any decision was made.

[241]

Then, with barristers at the bar, a legal judgment would be given in the name of the House of Lords, the final court of appeal. My admiration for the care with which the Law Lords heard the appeals grew as the years went by, and they appreciated a bishop leading them in prayer and sitting with them at the reading of their judgments. Sadness has often been felt in the Commonwealth at the passing of the right of appeal to senior judges at Westminster from lands overseas. When their Lordships assembled in the afternoon for routine business prayers had already been said: the House had formally sat in the morning.

When I made a start at Westminster, Oliver Tomkins, a longstanding friend and advisor to our family, was nearing the end of a remarkable career: his great contribution to the World Council of Churches was followed by a period as Warden of Lincoln Theological College, after which he became Bishop of Bristol. During his years at Bristol he had developed his own position in the Lords and at the same time had convened a regular group of MPs from the Commons, not to be confused with the official 'Ecclesiastical Committee' of the House of Commons. This group became a useful and quite formidable source of information for the Commons about the church and for bishops about the thinking of MPs. To a lesser degree it replaced the unstructured relationships and common friendships that had existed for years, until quite recently, between bishops and those in Parliament. I inherited the leadership of this gathering from Oliver Tomkins. It met three times a year over lunch, always within earshot of the division bell, so that members could take their places when required. There were usually about two dozen of us, including half a dozen diocesan bishops. Since the group had come into being during the Labour administration of the 1960s we enjoyed the participation, among others, of Ted Short, Terry Walker, Ted Bishop, Richard (now Lord) Crawshaw, Ronald Lewis, Alec Lyon and Eric Heffer, the last mentioned leaving us in no doubt of his political and advanced Anglican views. From the Conservative benches under the leadership of Bill (now Sir William) van Straubenzee we received much help and advice from Eldon Griffiths, Michael Latham, David Mudd, Patrick Cormack and Ivor Stanbrook, not to mention Michael Alison, a well-informed conservative theologian, and John Stokes, a very conservative politician. Alan Beith of the Liberals was our cross benches representative and Enoch Powell stimulated us on almost everything; he was far too perceptive to ignore. In order to balance such a group of MPs I always enlisted the presence of Derek Pattinson, the Secretary General of the Synod, and Sir Norman Anderson or Oswald Clark, each at different times Lay Chairman of the Synod, to support the bishops, who were those of London, Leicester, Manchester, Rochester, Derby and, in later years, Winchester. We consulted on Prayer Book revision, unity proposals, parochial law and patronage, modes of appointment of bishops, educational and matrimonial legislation, and many other matters common to elected members of Parliament and elected members of General Synod. This group fortunately continues under the leadership of Ronnie Bowlby (Southwark). Our prime purpose was to establish a sense of partnership and mutual confidence between those in the Commons who were rightly concerned about developments in the church and ourselves on the episcopal bench. We talked freely and critically of each other's legislative progress, and vehement opinions were often expressed. Coming to know each other's attitudes at a time of increasing independence in the church seemed important. As long as Parliament and General Synod trust each other in their respective spheres, disestablishment will not come about by legislation. We are, however, in danger of lapsing into it through the increasing divergence of attitude between Parliament and the church over social matters. Such a day will be a sad one for the Sovereign, the state and the church.

The majority of the time in the Lords was inevitably taken up with routine legislation sent up from the Commons. We were a most useful committee stage for bills which often received too little care and attention down the corridor. On Wednesdays and Thursdays, however, motions were commonly introduced on basic social or national issues which certainy affected the church's work or Christian values. There were usually two or three of us bishops present, only just enough over the years to keep our end up and so small a group as to suggest to many that we could just as well be disposed of. 1976 and 1977 proved to be years when perhaps I spent too much time there at the expense of the diocese, but then there was talk of the reform of the Upper House and, more important, much proposed industrial and employment legislation. Baroness Young, for the Government, called the attention of the House at short notice to the problems of retirement. I was the duty bishop for prayers, and Lambeth expressed the hope that I would speak.

This I did with the help of Giles Ecclestone, but not before Lord Byers for the Liberals had covered the ground well and the front bench had interrupted the proceedings by making a statement on the Falklands. On the subject for the day what did seem to matter, as I said, was a more flexible approach to retirement age and benefit. Quite apart from avoiding the waste of a good deal of ability, it seemed to me that there was much to be said for phasing the period over which the average worker would cease work during the early sixties. To do this would avoid a sudden break, which often did damage to the individual and to family life and would create less of a stereotyped category of senior citizens, Further, it would lead towards a part pension and a gradual withdrawal from professional or manual work. I also pressed for the 'job swap scheme' which by then was being worked out by the Manpower Services Commission. Under this a man reaching retirement could obtain a phased benefit provided that his retirement led to a job being created for an unemployed young person. It also seemed important to press for the better provision of sheltered housing within housing estates, rather than in groups separated from where many families were taking up new homes. Many families wanted 'granny' to be nearby, and to estrange old people from their offspring was to invite less and less community care for them. 'In supporting the motion,' I said in conclusion, 'I would hope for a fresh examination as to how the state may give aid to preserving personal values right the way through; how we can promote flexibility in retirement and how we can think in terms of whole rather than disintegrated families.' Such a speech was always put to the test by the amount of comment it received. It was rewarding for me to have the support of Paul Gore-Booth, of Baroness Gaitskell, whom I had never met, and Lord Gowrie, who replied for the Government.

Much has been said elsewhere about two major controversies that broke out both in Parliament and in General Synod during those years, coinciding with my chairmanship of the Industrial Committee, but they were so important that it is appropriate to recall them here.

The Labour Government under Harold Wilson and Jim Callaghan had promoted new legislation which made the 'closed shop' obligatory upon employers where it was requested, with only a religious conscience clause by which to abstain from participation. Historically both church and society had supported trade guilds, distinctive standards and disciplines and a closed shop attitude to many professions, including the ministry of the churches. We had all recognized the need for exclusive industrial, commercial and professional groupings. It seemed all the more just, therefore, that apprentices, tradesmen and factory workers should have standards which they had set themselves and their own powers of group consultation. This could lead to clearer trade relations – though it could also lead to injustice and prejudice in the free labour market, and give undue restrictive power to the trade unions. In addition, it was clearly seen that a non-member of a trade union was resented as a free rider who avoided obligation but enjoyed benefits.

To justify such legislation a booklet was issued by the General Synod under my signature, but composed by Bishop Wickham and a very competent group of industrialists and trade unionists including Henry Marking, head of British Airways, and David Warburton of the TUC. The booklet was regarded by many as factually true but too radical. It did include some provocative phrases:

> The Trade Unions' role in the work place is not that of an invader but that of an institutionalized expression of the basic right of individuals to be represented where decisions are made... Any group, however, which has power needs to develop a due sense of responsibility on the exercise of it... The tension here between freedom and order may be acute but the Christian should be realistic about the need to live with conflicting claims... With the safeguards for individuals described above we judge that closed shops may be legitimately negotiated in our society.

That was too much for both church and Parliament. Ted Wickham and the Industrial Committee at Church House saw our contribution as the opportunity to engage the trade unions in responsible management and to give them the credit of intelligent application of the law. We may have been over-optimistic, but we did feel that the national interest warranted a trusting relationship with the world of labour. Understandably the reactionary element of the church and the media came out heavily against us. 'The Church Led by Guilty Public Schoolboys' was a headline in the *Daily Telegraph*. 'The Bishops are terrified of not appearing to be radical and sympathetic to the spirit of the age... the Bishop of Worcester declared that churchmen were inclined to rally to the individual but fail to understand the new responsibility of the collective to which the gospel calls.' This was a far cry from the reasoned opposition to my comments in the House of Lords as one who spoke for the churches and the thinking that lay behind our report.

The most resolute and misinformed criticism in the press was largely prompted by Dr Norman of Peterhouse, Cambridge. A few years later in his Reith Lectures this don identified 'Donald Coggan our Archbishop and Robin Woods, Bishop of Worcester, as principal "politicizers" in the church', at the same time denigrating those 'who become socially aware in order to assuage their middle-class upbringing and the more radical tendencies of the clergy'. With the Archbishop I was in good company. There will always be a rearguard action by those who see the Christian faith only in spiritual terms as understood by the individual and as providing only for personal religion.

A more cogent and acceptable critique of our stand came from Hugh Montefiore, Bishop of Birmingham. His views have consistently won my respect in many aspects of ethical practice and moral theology. He felt strongly that the main principle at stake over the closed shop was whether an individual's freedom of choice should be so curtailed that he either had to join one particular union or lose his job. He also felt that the individual's conscience and certain circumstances had to be allowed to dictate whether or not someone joined a union. 'The state,' he wrote to me, 'is there to administer justice between groups and individuals, and loss of job is a very heavy price to pay for conscience. As far as the church's relations with the state are concerned, I am sorry that a more prophetic role is not commended. A national church should help to keep the conscience of the state.' In general Hugh Montefiore was right, but there was more to be said, as I tried to point out in a letter to *The Times* which was given top place:

> First, the primary duty of leaders in the churches is to help Christian lay people to understand and to discharge their responsibilities in secular organizations. In the context of work this means, among other things, that a Christian should be in the lead in joining his union, staying in it, and helping to shape its policy, as well as giving it the loyalty appropriate to it. We have been saying this for years and there is no reason for being less emphatic at this moment. Secondly, Christian men and women, managers and workers in industry with whom I speak, are convinced that within their particular industrial community their role is to join in and not to opt out; they are certain they must be influencing decisions, even though that may result in compromise.
>
> If in spite of this a particular church member comes to the conclusion that his faith makes it impossible for him in conscience

to belong to a union, thereby rendering him liable to dismissal, we must, I am convinced, back him up… But to suggest that the church authorities should in advance offer blanket support to any claim to exemption on religious grounds would be one way of destroying whatever respect for that provision of the law the unions may have and not be helpful to our members playing their part in the union.

Some months later the debate on statutory industrial democracy came to a head and an attempt was made to involve the unions in some form of democratic responsibility. The Bullock Report recommended legislation to give employees, in companies employing more than 2,000, the right to representation on their company boards. A minority report called for representation on a supervisory board: a two-tier system. Once again I found myself involved, but as was wont to happen, I had a confirmation in the diocese on the evening of the debate. Dennis Wakeling, Bishop of Southwell, duty bishop that week, stepped in admirably. In the event the whole set of interesting and poignant proposals died the death of a thousand qualifications. Under pressure, however, from colleagues on the Industrial Committee and the Manpower Services Commission I did again write to *The Times* and again they gave it the honour of being top letter. In it I made the following points:

1. It is consistent with the Christian vision that society should develop in such a way that each person can exercise his God-given ability to make choices, to take responsibility and to share in shaping his environment. We believe that employees have a stake in their companies which is at least as significant as that of the shareholders and that this should be recognized both by law and by the urgent extension of opportunities for them to share in decision-making at all levels, including the highest.

2. There is a real danger that in the heat of debate about methods, the importance of reaching agreement on the fundamental principle of genuinely shared decision-making will be forgotten. We would hope that the end itself will not be lost in the welter of disagreement about the means.

3. The hundred largest manufacturing enterprises, we read in the Report, produced forty per cent of the total net output in 1971, compared with only twenty-five per cent in 1953. This growing concentration of power in the hands of so few emphasizes for us the importance of sharing it properly. The tendency of power to corrupt is fully acknowledged in the Christian doctrine of man.

Power in the hands of one group needs to be properly balanced by equivalent power in the hands of others if we are to approach justice in society.

4. We read also that around seventy per cent of employees in enterprises affected by the Bullock proposals are, in fact, members of unions. It is our hope that it will be widely and willingly recognized that the obvious bodies to take greater responsibility in balancing the increasingly centralized power of the larger employers are the trade unions, and that this should be enabled through appropriate legislation.

5. Law, however, that is not tolerable to the majority of those affected is bad law, as the history of the 1971 Industrial Relations Act amply showed. We believe that legislation based on the Bullock report should not be introduced when it is known that there is such opposition from both sides as to make the proposals unworkable and to prevent the achievement of the end of shared decision-making itself.

Further consideration of this deeply human issue and wide-ranging experiment in real participation is urgently called for in a cool and unemotional atmosphere, before effective legislation can be introduced.

I was conscious on many occasions of giving too much time to the Lords, the Church Commissioners, the Industrial Committee of General Synod and other calls in London, but I was encouraged by Henrietta and the family to fulfil all I could in addition to the concerns of the diocese. It was by no means all a matter of committee work, which can be frustrating and unfruitful; more often than not London days were rewarded by personal contact. For example, one afternoon at Westminster led into the annual dinner of the Engineering Employers Federation, an occasion to which I was invited over the years. There I found myself sitting next to Sir Michael Edwardes, at that time chairman of British Leyland. I was glad to get some first-hand information about the motor industry, which affected so many in the northern area of my diocese. This was not untypical of occasions that provided opportunities for me to keep in touch with thinking laymen, something that was essential to my way of working.

After a night at the home of one of the children, the next day I found myself faced with an unusual and totally different reponsibility as Bishop of Worcester. My bishopric automatically made me a Commissioner of the Crown for the appointment of the Archbishop of Canterbury. Donald Coggan had resigned, and my presence along with that of the bishops of London, Lincoln, Salisbury and Rochester was required by the lawyers to 'confirm' the 'election' of Bob Runcie. The absurdity of such a session, where we all sat in scarlet robes at a long table and swore that the archbishop was born in wedlock, was honourable and trustworthy, and had been duly nominated by the Sovereign, was all too obvious. However, the occasion was redeemed by the Lord Mayor of London, who also was obliged to be present: he gave us all a very good lunch in the Mansion House.

The procession of archbishops over the years during and since the War has brought both advantages and disadvantages to the church. Under William Temple we were all aware of consistent moral and religious leadership; under Geoffrey Fisher the church was to be given some spring cleaning and streamlining, though he also made an authoritarian stand on Anglican Prayer Book doctrine and ministry, which was the basis for his invitation to other churches to join the Church of England.

Not unexpectedly, there had been considerable debate in the nation and in the church as to who should succeed the partnership after ten years of Michael Ramsey at Canterbury and Donald Coggan at York. Stuart Blanch at York carried real weight; his teaching and speaking abilities were to remain outstanding. For anyone who wants an interpretation of New Testament themes the set of four devotional addresses given to the bishops at the Lambeth Conference in 1978 are a masterpiece, and I have frequently returned to them. When it came to the time for the Prime Minister to nominate to the Crown for the new archbishop, the new regulations accepted by Parliament and the General Synod had come into play. A properly constituted committee of those representing interests from both church and state was summoned. In the political and ecclesiastical circumstances it proved a far-sighted step to appoint Sir Richard O'Brien chairman of the committee to advise the Queen, through the Prime Minister, as to the man whom the church would like to see appointed. This was the first time I saw the new legislature for senior Crown appointments brought into play.

Since Bob Runcie had come to our parish at Wigston to see what local ministry was all about in the late 1940s, he had exercised an increasing influence on the new generation of clergy and laity as Principal of Cuddesdon and Bishop of St Albans. He represented an attitude beyond the original ecumenical movement of the between-war years and the impact of the SCM on younger men. His vision was not one of ecclesiastical unification or structural plans for uniting denominations into one national church but of mutual dialogue leading to a deeper understanding of theological and structural convictions. His vision of Anglican progress towards some sort of partnership with the Roman and Orthodox churches appeared to some of us to have too high a priority in his concept of unity, but it is much to his credit that he pressed for the uniting of the Church of England with the Methodist Church, never deviating from supporting difficult but necessary propositions. That the scheme failed was no fault of any archbishop. With the new impetus Bob Runcie has given to the Anglican–Roman Catholic consultations something very remarkable has begun to re-shape the ecumenical movement which may begin to heal the biggest of the Reformation break-ups. One can only hope that his open-hearted overtures to the Pope will not be rebuffed by the hard-line traditionalism increasingly shown by Pope John-Paul II.

I certainly had the goodwill of my staff at Worcester in giving time to Westminster and central affairs. Nevertheless, however much time was spent away, the diocese and our home were always my first priority. During the years at Hartlebury, from which I was never away for long, the family became established. We had never been seriously separated since Singapore days, but Hartlebury had proved a uniting base for us all, to which children and now grandchildren came and went. Rachel and Michael, having been married in our Windsor days, were blessed with three children during the Worcester days: the centre of memorable christenings in our private chapel. They had settled in Fulham, Catherine, Harriet and Charles all coming to know and enjoy Hartlebury. Mary, after completing her medicine at Girton, was at the Middlesex Hospital; she became engaged to James Burnell Nugent, who rather delightfully asked my permission to marry her, having established himself in the Royal Navy. Their wedding was in the cathedral at Worcester with the reception at Hartlebury. This was followed by James being appointed to an interesting succession of duties in the submarine service. His most recent appointment, after being Commander of HMS Olympus, has been to the command of HMS Conqueror, a large nuclear-power submarine, on completion of her refit after the Falklands episode. His links with the Navy, his technical knowledge of nuclear power and the making of a new home not far from Plymouth brought a new dimension into our family. Robert, by the mid-1970s a manager in the P & O Company, was settled down, having married Georgiana Garton; and his work brought us an interest in the Merchant Navy. He and his wife also settled in Fulham not far from Rachel, which gave us quite a covey of children and grandchildren in that area. Edward came home from Bahrein to marry Sorrel Voorspuy from near Eastbourne, only to take her off for a further period in the Gulf. Eleanor continued to keep guard on the family flat until she came home briefly to get married to John MacLachlan, a land agent in the Smith Gore partnership. All the children remained in close touch, giving Henrietta more than enough to care for in the arrival of our grandchildren. How lucky we were not only to have them all happily married but all of them also believing Christians and being involved and taking their part in their local churches. Equally, they continued to be interested in what we were doing. We frequently all spent Christmas together, Hartlebury providing a splendid rendezvous for three generations.

Not unnaturally Henrietta did not accompany me on many visits to London. She continued as a magistrate in Worcester and Droitwich and did much to help in the care of clergy wives and women's organizations in the diocese. In addition she was involved in many diocesan occasions in the state rooms of the castle, supervising the constantly increasing numbers visiting them when the place was open to the public, and arranging concerts and exhibitions to bring in the necessary cash for their upkeep. All these activities essential to my work were in her department. With such a home base I was able to travel round and undertake engagements in the diocese with an easy mind.

=== [13] ===

Home and Dry at Hartlebury

O God of unchanging majesty and steadfast love, we thank you for
your blessing on this diocese through thirteen hundred years until
now. We pray that we in our generation may be awake to your calling
and faithful to your service; through Jesus Christ our Lord who is
the same, yesterday, today and for ever. Amen.

Below the study window and down the steps that led from the sitting
room next door was a steep bank running down to the moat that still
surrounds the southern and western sides of the castle. It was easy
to take oneself off to the privacy of the garden or even to walk round
the other side of the water. An escape route from visitors, the
secretaries or even the family was useful and sometimes essential; it
enabled me to go and think and pray and sometimes read undisturbed
in the quiet areas beyond the brook that fed the moat. Father used to
do the same by having his own quiet in the garden at Lichfield. I
would also take odd hours off at home to work at shoring up the bank
or planting trees. I enjoyed building a bridge of old telegraph poles
across the stream and cutting paths through the undergrowth and
bracken that had overtaken the distant parts of the grounds. Planning
the renewal of the decaying birches, limes, plane trees and mulberries
in the avenues and groups around the Park gave me great pleasure
and refreshment. From such times in the garden or beyond the moat
I would return with a clearer mind for the rest of the day. Each
evening, before leaving the office, my principal secretary, Hazel Lee
and later on Diana Quinney, would leave the file on my table for
the next day's work with carefully prepared notes in readiness
for interviews, committees or services. To be properly briefed was
essential to my way of working, for a memory of people's names has
never been my strong point.

The many confirmations that came my way, particularly those for the independent schools, seemed of real importance. They provided a regular and consistent opportunity for trying to instil Christian responsibility into the new generation. Whenever possible, I would give a short talk to the parents and godparents, without their children, on their role in helping the newly confirmed; this was always worthwhile, but not easy to arrange. I took more than a hundred confirmations a year, and over and over again would find in the candidates and those who came with them a responsive congregation, of both young people and their parents. These were occasions when I gave myself as fully as I could in laying the foundation for another generation of believers and witnesses. Without them the church would fade away and many values become eroded. It was nowhere near possible to visit the deanery synods or chapters of clergy as often as I would have wished, but they certainly shared my concept that the kingdom of God and his rule in the whole of life matter more than the fabric or administration of the churches or even their regulations. Of course I was concerned about Sunday worship, and I wanted congregations to grow, but the state of the church needed to be seen in the light of a theology of Christian engagement for the whole community rather than an enrichment of the religious and cultural life of the few.

All these concerns, many full of interest and pleasure, were reviewed each month at our staff meeting. Though its composition changed gradually over the years I continued to find sustaining support in my staff. Certain spheres of diocesan life remained difficult. There were one or two non-viable deaneries that needed amalgamation or reshaping, particularly in the Teme valley and the areas round Upton and Bredon. Children's work became increasingly elusive. Since the diocese had over a hundred church schools it might seem that here was the clue to future congregations, and that should have been the case. However, even with the help of compulsory religious education and school worship under the 1944 Act things were not easy. Fewer and fewer teachers were able to fulfil these requirements. There were many Christians at work in our schools, but never enough with imagination and initiative. Christian teaching had increasingly become necessary outside school activities; weekday 'Sunday Schools' had begun to replace Sunday children's work, as that day was a family free-for-all. For those who had left school, where were we to fit in to the statutory but inadequate youth service?

These questions were delegated to our Education Committee, where circumstances and personnel changes made progress difficult. Although Christopher Campling, as my principal assistant in the educational world, wrestled with the problems, I felt that the area was the least successful in my period as bishop.

When it came to setting up fresh parochial arrangements in the country areas such as the Teme valley, running up to the hills and valleys of Herefordshire, an area dominated by a traditional attitude to the parochial ministry, work was easier said than done. I did find, however, that clergy when properly introduced and well briefed could take on amalgamated parishes with patience and understanding. One of my best younger priests with countryside hobbies and with an interest in buying and selling both horses and foreign stamps adapted his abilities outstandingly to the needs of very varied village communities. He was not untypical of a new generation of clergy. The break-up of his marriage and his consequent resignation was a severe setback to the work. That, however, was all part of my episcopal responsibility.

In the east of the diocese lay the ever-increasing urban sprawl of the West Midlands. Redditch New Town had by 1978 reached a population of almost 100,000 and the old industry of needles and fish hooks had given place to a varied conglomeration of light engineering concerns. The parish church had successfully linked up with the ecumenical centre which all of us from the Anglican, Methodist and United Reformed Church had conceived and established. On the outer fringe of the new town, shared churches were planned as far as possible. The Anglican-Methodist church at Matchborough was typical. Here we shared everything with our partners: sacraments, ministry, children's work and finance. We always regretted the failure of legal unity some years earlier. After a time the Methodists appointed a properly ordained woman minister: would this prove to be an embarrassment? In the event Elizabeth Mays proved to be a superb partner in the ministry of the area, and together with Raymond Adams, the team rector, made progress in the face of the Midlanders' casual approach to religion. Just to make things more complicated, half the housing was in the Coventry diocese. I was pleased to visit this church on a Sunday when it was the turn of the Methodist minister to celebrate the eucharist. Although I was bishop of the diocese I made it an opportunity to assist a woman celebrant, to preach, to lead in prayer and then to receive the sacraments at her hands. That is how it should be as we draw towards corporate unity. Not unexpectedly, however, some people, including the *Church Times*, took a poor view of my attitude. I felt that sharing in that way was an earnest of Anglican attitudes to our sister churches, both in the matter of shared sacraments and in the more vexed issue of accepting the ministry of women. I was particularly thankful at the time to have my suffragan bishop, Tony Dumper, my dean and my archdeacons all standing firmly behind my actions.

As the situation developed in the diocese and the economic recession began to have its own grave effects on our people I found myself back in touch with Prince Philip, who kindly expressed a wish to see for himself what was involved in the regular work of a diocese. After dinner with His Royal Highness one night in London where several of us in positions of leadership in the churches and in the non-Christian communities were entertained, I made plans with him for a visit not primarily to the city or county but to the diocese.

The anticipation of this visit to the church did, in a sense, take us 'to the cleaners'. Prince Philip had earlier written in a long letter:

> Secularization has not killed religion, it has merely changed the traditional concept of religion. The instinct is still there, but because the circumstances are different the expression of the instinct is different. God isn't dead except to those people who have an old-fashioned or inflexible view of him... God and religion are alive, but I think the important thing now is to make sure that the way in which we interpret the revelation of Christ is appropriate to the modern circumstance. Both in the religious sense and in the Christian ethical sense, I think it is most important that people should not be asked to subscribe to ideas which are opposed to the more obvious scientific facts. Any future faith has got to come to terms with the facts of life as they are generally known... Religion – I would have thought – is to influence men's minds, to establish God in men's hearts, and Christ, again I would have thought, has shown how this can be done. The way in which he tried to persuade people and the way in which the disciples interpreted his words and actions were contemporary with the environment and the attitudes of the time. The message itself – when it can be isolated – is timeless.

Since Prince Philip had expressed the hope of meeting industrialists, young people, and those at work in a new town, as well as clergy, we undertook a full day's visiting. The County Hall was the scene of his first encounter. After a short word of welcome from myself and the

Chairman of our County Council, he spoke to and entered into discussion with councillors, employers, social workers, careers officers and clergy on the trend of attitudes in our society. A pictorial exhibition had been prepared which made a good introduction to Worcester. From there we went by car through the city with many crowds in the streets and over the river to Malvern. There Prince Philip declared the new sports hall of the Girls College open and in so doing met teachers, careers officers and senior girls. We were only a few minutes late back at the cathedral where several clergy were gathered; there we had a short time of prayer and an anthem sung by our choristers leading into five minutes of meditation as we sat quietly in the choir. This moment of worship without any publicity reminded us of eternal verities.

Pressing on in an informal motorcade we reached Redditch. There the authorities of the new town together with the clergy of our different churches conducted Prince Philip through the large covered shopping precinct to the ecumenical centre, which provided a variety of social services as well as a dual-purpose church. It was to a packed house that he spoke on the work of the church today. 'Perhaps,' he said, 'because I have a special relationship to the supreme governor of the Church of England, I can offer some help today.' He went on to outline the priorities that Christians in particular must pursue. When he had unveiled a plaque commemorating his visit to the YMCA, we drove the twenty miles back to Hartlebury with much to talk about. We recalled St George's House and I became aware of the importance of engaging successive generations of clergy and laity and in reviewing their mission. The penetrating interest and gentle encouragement was not forgotten. By ten o'clock the royal train was parked in Hartlebury village station. It was looking beautiful and polished in the moonlight. We accompanied Prince Philip to his coach, bade him farewell and the train glided away into the night.

In both the industrial and the rural areas of the diocese, however, school leavers were increasingly joining the army of the unemployed. With increasing concern for the widening gap between industry and the churches, and the growing community of the workless, Hartlebury Castle became a regular rendezvous for industrial consultations. Roger Howes, as senior industrial chaplain, was a real expert at assembling management, trade unionists and civil servants with selected groups. The carpet industry, the glass makers of Stourbridge, the motor manufacturers and engineering firms in and around Redditch New Town, and the steel trades of the Black Country provided more than enough areas of concern in which it seemed that the church should properly be engaged. Campbell Adamson of the CBI and Vic Feather, General Secretary of the TUC, Richard O'Brien and Peter Walker, our MP, were among those who came to Hartlebury for different occasions and conferences. These could never take the place of sustained consultation, but they did bring people to face up to social and industrial change together under the auspices of Christian initiative. The church for once seemed to be sharing the engine driver's job instead of following in the guard's van.

Legislation and discussion during those years about industrial relations and the power of the trade unions was slowly being overtaken by the rising tide of unemployment. I personally moved between two poles: practical concern for the industrial situation in Dudley, the Black Country and the northern end of the diocese on the one hand and the theoretical debates that tended to take place in London on the other. The coal industry had disappeared from Worcestershire some years previously; the Coombe Hill steel works (Stuart & Lloyds) was running out of orders, and the British Steel Corporation works at Round Oak was closed in 1980 with the loss of nearly 4,000 jobs. At the same time the carpet industry in Kidderminster was being eroded by EEC competition, hindered in its operation by patchy management and outmoded machinery. The market gardening industry in the Vale of Evesham was in serious decline. All too often I found myself sharing the anxieties of management or the hopes of the career service and technical colleges. It was during those years when the employment crisis was looming dangerously ahead that the Manpower Services Commission was formed and I was approached by its Director General, Sir Richard O'Brien, with a view to my becoming the first chairman of the Birmingham board. At the same time I had a kindly message from the Secretary of State for Employment endorsing the proposal. To undertake it would involve a substantial commitment of at least two whole days a month, studying the labour situation and chairing the board. The area for which we would be responsible stretched from Solihull and Sutton Coldfield in the East to Worcester, Ludlow and Hereford in the West, with the Birmingham urban sprawl in between. My colleagues on the board were to be drawn from management, the trade unions, local education authorities, the careers service and selected civil servants. Holding the reins of such a team was not going to be easy. The routine work at Worcester and London was already quite enough, but Tony Dumper, and Oliver Tomkins, who had retired to Worcester and was assistant bishop in the diocese, along with the archdeacons and the staff, told me to do it. It seemed impossible to refuse.

It was in fact a pleasure getting to know my members of the board. They brought with them the experience of great and long-established industries: British Leyland, Lucas Industries, Cadburys, Royal Worcester Porcelain and the agricultural interests of Herefordshire. Barry Shuttleworth, regional organizer of the National Union of Public Employees, was appointed vice-chairman. He brought real expertise to our meetings in the whole field of employment and industrial change. We worked together and established a lasting partnership, with Barry taking an increasing lead in both the MSC activities and in the voluntary work of the churches. The careers service was in partnership with us, to our enormous advantage. Percy Walton, the senior careers officer of the region and a churchwarden in the diocese, had a most realistic approach to the vexed problem of school leavers without work, and his plans for youth training were some of the first in the country. In general, the careers service does not receive the attention it deserves, and being within the educational budget of the local authority, it is too easily short of resources. The MSC area office was substantial, with an administration occupying several floors of a Birmingham skyscraper. The succession of good special programme area managers and in later years Jonathan Sleigh, who was seconded to us from the Cabinet office as the unemployment rapidly increased to be our regional director, were all efficient, knowledgeable, and remarkably patient with their 'lay' chairman. We soon settled down to work, in early 1977 accepting some 50,000 unemployed in our area, rising to 350,000 in 1982. Throughout we could easily have felt overcome by events, and participants in a losing battle. In fact the schemes we promoted for school leavers, youth unemployed (sixteen- to eighteen-year-olds), the long-term unemployed, those who had gone more than a year without work, and other special programmes designed to assist ethnic minorities in the Birmingham area, were rewarding. The peak period of the work coincided with the summer months, when some 40,000 left school for work. It was our target to get them into jobs or further training by Christmas. For several years we reached our target by the end of the year, with anything up to

60,000 participating in MSC programmes. I found it almost alarming to watch the expenditure of nearly £10 million a year in our area alone in order to enable job opportunities to be taken up, or training schemes to be managed and supported. Each month I tried to visit either training workshops, or technical colleges running MSC schemes, or public service spheres with labour-intensive requirements such as the railways, hospitals, or the private sector of industry that worked training schemes and job opportunity programmes that we had promoted. It brought me into touch with areas of my diocese, and those of Birmingham and Hereford, that otherwise I would certainly never have come to know. However, there remained intractable problems with no immediate answer. The availability of unskilled labour and of young people coming out of school went far beyond the requirements of automated industry in a place as progressive as Birmingham. The real anxiety was in the number who could not get further employment when they had completed their courses or schemes. At the age of eighteen or nineteen such young men and women are very vulnerable to social forces that in idleness undo the good that has been begun.

Secondly, there was the specific problem of the ethnic groups. With over 100,000 Pakistanis, Indians and others who had arrived in the days when Commonwealth immigrants were seen as a welcome way of supplementing our labour forces, we now had tens of thousands of mostly young people from the coloured communities without work. Clearly Government policy was full integration in educational and working requirements. Equal opportunities for all races must remain our goal and the churches were hard at work to provide this essential social requirement. There were, however, pockets of racial communities in the metropolitan area which had to be given independent assistance, at least for the moment: their culture, family life and general attitude had been forced into separation by the economic recession. Out of fairness to their own traditions and potentialities we provided training workshops specifically for ethnic groups, although I had always hoped to keep all the schemes multi-racial and to use them for integration rather than emphasizing the racial issue, but here there was no alternative. Separate training was also costly to the taxpayer, since the courses were often small and sometimes inefficient. However, without them those who had suffered from 'last in, first out' would have been severely penalized.

[259]

As the economic situation deteriorated and firms were not investing in the new technology, I watched with sadness British Leyland drop from employing 130,000 to a work force half that number. Lucas Industries, the pride of central Birmingham, fell from 70,000 to 32,000, and Guest Keen Nettlefold from 60,000 to half that. Smaller units were in a similar crisis situation. To make matters worse, the great companies were not in a position to undertake training schemes or admit apprentices: it was too costly for them. We saw then that this situation was likely to prove disastrous for the future of our engineering industries. To help us face these problems in the West Midlands we were allocated the service of Jonathan Sleigh. After taking his degree at Oxford he entered the civil service and found himself in the Treasury. From there he was appointed to the staff of the first Downing Street think-tank, from where he came to us. At that stage the unemployed community was so big that its magnitude had become difficult to comprehend. In our area, twice the number of people to be found in the city of Worcester, largely between the ages of seventeen and thirty, had no jobs. As chairman I backed up Jonathan, who set about improving the quality, variety and length of training schemes. Well before the Government would consider extending admission to the eighteen- and nineteen-year-olds and before they agreed to more sustained training in view of the breakdown of apprenticeships, he saw the opportunity and foresaw the needs of the next two decades. Much imaginative work went into extending the Youth Training Schemes, but in the end we were overtaken by numbers and the lack of financial backing. Even then the budget of my board exceeded £12 million per annum. However, that was not enough for the problem that had been created. The Conservative monetarist policy with a consequent refusal to find resources for the refurbishing of public utilities never allowed unemployment to be radically remedied, and the private sector remained – as it still remains – quite unable to cope on its own.

Things were difficult enough for us at that stage, but in 1981 the element in the leadership of the Manpower Services Commission, which had supported us well and had advocated many good schemes, was changed. Jim Prior was replaced by Mr Norman Tebbit and Sir Richard O'Brien by Mr David Young. Our new pharaohs did not look kindly on the more radical and socially demanding schemes that we were embracing. Both Jonathan and I approached the end of our joint work together: it was time for me to retire, and he knew he would be posted. However, rather than wait for that he chose instead to leave government service and be ordained. It was a delightful surprise for us in the churches but a severe loss for the civil service. In the summer of 1982 we prepared a joint statement on the future of the MSC and the care and training of the unemployed and sent it to *The Times*. What we said has hardly lost any of its relevance:

> In the West Midlands, it is now part of everyone's conventional wisdom that high unemployment is here to stay. People believe neither those politicians who tell us that imminent recovery will mop it all up, nor those who assure us that policy changes can do the trick. We offer our own thoughts on the basis of finding the instincts of people rather more persuasive than the eschatology of politicians. Like most of those whom we have worked with and for over the last few years, we do not believe that the unemployment problem can be wished away in the foreseeable future; but we do believe that we can learn to live with it better than we are currently managing.
>
> We cannot agree with the common assertion that we should 'come to terms' with our high unemployment figures if all that means is tamely accepting them. That is an attitude that shows lack of imagination and a lack of an active social conscience. Anybody north of Watford knows that being out of work saps individual morale, undermines families and destroys whole communities. Yet all around there are social needs unfulfilled and work waiting to be undertaken. We think it right to say bluntly that the sort of coherence of policy for which we look is unlikely ever to come from politicians or local authorities unless and until they are prepared to admit that we have a long-term problem.
>
> An imbalance between the supply of labour and the supply of jobs can be addressed by tackling the one, or the other, or both. Our preference for the instincts of non-political people pre-disposes us to think that it is probably easier to adjust the rules under which people seek jobs than it is to conjure genuine new jobs out of thin air. It is in labour supply policy, if anywhere, that the sense of coherence which people seem to hope for will principally be found.
>
> Most people appear to accept the Government's word for it that real jobs cannot be invented; but they find it hard to believe that a Government that was prepared to mobilize anything and everything remotely relevant to recovering the Falkland Islands could not mobilize enough resources (of willpower as much as money) to civilize the business of living with a shortage of jobs.

In the conclusion of the article we went on to discuss in detail such questions as how more incentives could be provided for work-sharing, how the retirement age could be lowered, how the quality of the national labour force could be improved in the long term, how the rebuilding of the infra-structure of our decaying cities and our collapsing public services could be shored up by more use of unskilled labour, and how more *capital* could be made available for projects of real community value. However, our article was not accepted for publication, nor was it appreciated by the authorities! We were too radical. I found this failure to think more deeply most disappointing, but despite it felt that seven years on the Manpower Services Commission had been well worth while, if only to show that the churches had a deep concern for those outside their normal circle.

Largely as a result of my experience on the Manpower Services Commission and partly because there was no other area chairman in the Lords I was invited by Lord Aberdare, Chairman of Committees, to join the newly appointed House of Lords Select Committee on Unemployment. The Commons already had such a body but it was felt that the Lords could make a significant contribution towards helping to solve the problems facing the country in this area. I was both honoured and humbled to be invited: the first bishop to be selected for such a committee for many decades. Our 'select' committee, as others, had the authority to summon anyone in the United Kingdom to appear and to give evidence; its discussions had the standing of the House and were reported verbatim in *Hansard*, and we could incur substantial expenses if travel or other means would enable better work to be done. Once again, I found that time would be the main problem since the committee would meet weekly. Again I consulted my diocesan staff, and again they gave me their whole-hearted support.

I soon found myself at work with and enjoying a growing friendship with those who had direct experience of our problems and who knew a great deal more about the economic structure of the nation than I did. Baroness Seear was appointed our chairman; she was known to be a superb analyst of social issues and was an enormously hard worker, a ready listener and one who could draft statements and present matters with clarity in or out of the Chamber. Rarely can there have been a more acceptable chairman for a group with very wide political differences. From the Government we had Lord Carr of

Hadley, until recently Home Secretary, Lord De la Warr and Lord Vaizey. The latter had become a dynamic Principal of Cumberland Lodge, and I had already become good friends with him; he had crossed the floor of the house since his elevation to the peerage by Harold Wilson and became a protagonist for Tory policies. He was not an easy man: impatient of others to such an extent that he was liable to walk out of our meetings. But he was an original thinker and a most attractive personality. We all felt a real loss when he died the year after the publication of our report. Of the Labour peers Lord Lee of Newton was able to advise with the wisdom of years of trade union leadership, though he became increasingly infirm. Lord Melchett, with his family experience of ICI, had now espoused a clear socialist position, and together with Lord MacCarthy, an Oxford don with incisive left-wing economic view, represented those who regarded Mrs Thatcher's policies as wholly disastrous for the nation. Their alternative policies were very cogently argued. From the liberals we had our chairman, Lord Kilmarnock, and Lord Rochester. The latter in particular could speak from a direct involvement that was not common in the House; in his position as personnel director of the ICI works in Cheshire, he had established working trade relations that led both sides of industry to be mutually concerned about youth and adult training schemes. He had much to contribute. Of the cross-bench peers Lord Spens acted as a kind of ferret searching out intractable causes of unemployment, though his enormous size does not fit the simile. We enjoyed the solid common sense of Lord Wolfenden with his intimate knowledge of young people and the social services. There was little left for me to fill in except from the pragmatic angle of working in areas deeply affected by the recession and giving plain information as to what was happening among the rank and file of the unemployed.

The evidence that we heard from economists, socialists and educationalists including several employers and trade unionists of great integrity over a whole year is all available in *Hansard*. Our consequent discussions, whether in a committee room at Westminster or in one of our residential meetings at Oxford, are also recorded in full. I was disappointed not to visit other scenes of unemployment. We decided to examine the Northern Ireland situation on the spot, but before we went the security people were called in to vet the visit. The only person not to be passed was an English bishop: I appeared to be a security risk! So I was politely asked not to go. Diocesan work did not permit to me to accompany the members to see the situation in Germany, which was also sad.

The report which we produced reflected our common mind. It was no mean achievement of the chairman to obtain a unanimous statement from so diverse a political grouping. This was partly due to the fact that we faced up to really basic issues, like the meaning of work for individuals, the difference between the requirement of a wage and the desire for personal and family fulfilment. We agreed that the old Protestant ethic of work which saw idleness as culpable was now inadequate, that the era of so-called full employment was over and that leisure and time to spare for the whole community, following automation and technology, were social factors that we needed to accommodate. This situation, we felt, called for a new flexibility in working arrangements and rewards; there was a need for readiness to adjust to domestic and world-wide needs. We did not report in generalizations but in clearly-defined financial, social and geographical statistics. Furthermore we tendered advice to the Government on the damaging social consequence of unemployment as it affected marriage and family life, as it caused new health hazards and as it tended to promote mental depression or even suicide. The cost to the nation of these by-products of the recession is not always appreciated.

The 1982 Report of the Select Committee of the House of Lords on Unemployment, published by HMSO, stands, then, for future generations as an inter-political party statement of diagnosis and remedy built on patience and mutual trust. Here was a genuine consensus of opinion and advice in the face of a grave national malaise: in my mind and in the minds of many others it remains one of the most competent and far-seeing statements affecting the future patterns of working life for the nation. Part of the press release that we presented highlights its findings:

> We proposed action over the next two to three years which should reduce the number of the unemployed by about 1 milion, at a net cost to the Exchequer of less than £1.95 billion above present expenditure commitments.
>
> We described the existence of 3 million unemployed as an affront, a prodigal waste of human resources, the source of much personal misery and a stumbling block in the way of prosperity. We calculated that the fiscal cost of unemployment to the Exchequer is about £5,000 per year per person unemployed; social costs, such as

burdens on the National Health Service, the social services and the judicial system, amount to another several hundred pounds per person; and these are additional to losses of output and the personal burdens of the unemployed and their families. We considered that the money spent on paying for unemployment could be spent more profitably on employment and training without fuelling inflation.

We further hoped that education or training should become the norm for sixteen and seventeen year olds, but opposed the Government's proposal to make training compulsory by withholding supplementary benefit; we recommended instead that there should be a small financial incentive to choose training rather than unemployment.

We envisaged:

1. The enlargement of the Community Enterprise Programme to 75,000 places and Community Industry to 15,000 places – primarily to give work experience to the young unemployed.

2. Creation of 100,000 jobs through the voluntary sector and up to 300,000 jobs through the public sector related to improving the infrastructure of our cities and communication – these jobs, paid for by the Exchequer for a minimum of three years, would occur mainly in those services for which there is a recognized need for additional labour.

3. Creation of 90,000 jobs on capital investment projects, especially in construction and civil engineering, where the case for capital expenditure is good on investment grounds.

We recommended ways of encouraging early retirement, including an extension of Job Release and a new scheme of pairing whereby two people over sixty are employed half-time in place of one person full time.

We were concerned that the public employment service was being cut at a time when the demands on it were highest. Everyone unemployed for one month should receive a full interview with specialist counselling staff. To make this possible, we recommended that registration of the unemployed at job centres should be voluntary for one month but compulsory thereafter.

We also made numerous other recommendations including assistance to small businesses, encouragement for new technology, more effective careers education, aids to specially disadvantaged groups, and promotion of formal employment in place of the black economy through (for example) tax credits and enterprise allowances.

That the Government refused to take the House of Lords Select Committee Report seriously or even find time for an adequate debate on its recommendations was an affront to the hard-working chairman, Baroness Seear, and to those who had put in three years work. It was also particularly regrettable that no advantage was taken of the significant fact that here the two political parties had agreed principles and made recommendations. Here was an agreed statement by Tories, Socialists and members of the Alliance parties, hammered out in considerable detail for the good of the nation, being almost immediately shelved by the Department of Employment. Having obtained a close view of the labour situation on the ground in the West Midlands and having shared in the Committee's deliberations, I came to realize that a *laissez-faire* economy would not put matters right, nor would the private sector of industry ever be able to recover the level of employment needed. I found myself increasingly sharing a political view that was not so much to the left as one which required a consensus approach to our social problems rather than the confrontation politics of the Thatcher regime. There clearly was little benefit in doctrinaire socialism and the proposals for further nationalization of industries as was advocated by some on the committee and some on my board of the MSC. That would undoubtedlly have led to worse troubles. On the other hand, if the monetarist policy was to produce such hardship among so many of our people, that also was unacceptable for my Christian hopes. There remained the army of unemployed and disillusioned young people together with decaying city centres and collapsing public services. Within these situations there were potentially thousands of jobs to be taken up by many low-skilled people. Much work is crying out to be done in large and small units, but with the lack of Government money on the one hand and the obstinacy of trade unions in not accepting remuneration at levels below negotiated rates of pay on the other, many a community feels bitter and rejected. This tragic impasse has to be broken sooner or later. My sympathies therefore became allied to those on the Liberal and SDP benches in the Lords and indeed in the constituencies at home. I am not surprised that a number of bishops, now recently joined by David Jenkins at Durham, have felt that we must speak out in our dioceses in support of neglected sections of our nation and in the hope that there may be a fresh appraisal and agreed policy whereby the available work and resources in our country can be shared out more equitably.

Participation in various debates, largely on trade relations, require particular care on the part of the bishops, and the office at Church House was kept very busy advising and preparing material. Little did I think that I would find myself one day backing up Lord Scanlon, who had become a Labour life peer with strong views on current Government policies. He moved a motion calling the attention of the Government to the need for assistance in the remaining Industrial Training Boards, technical and sixth-form colleges. I felt that as chairman of a large area of the MSC I had to report on the failure of the authorities to utilize available resouces in these areas of youth training and stress how vital it was that the Youth Training Schemes should be extended and geared in with the facilities we already enjoyed. My friends told me that it was the best speech I made over the years, but it was largely to an empty house – though, as usual, it was well reported in *Hansard* and over Today in Parliament. In thanking me, Hugh Scanlon mentioned that he never thought he would be supported by a Prelate. Times are changing, and the contribution of the episcopal bench on social issues is becoming increasingly relevant to all political parties. The way in which the bench of bishops has impinged on the government of the day has varied, but it is clear that William Temple and his generation had much to say in cautioning the government; in the 1970s bishops and government were gratifyingly close; today the ambiguous situation that prevails between church and state is not helpful to either party

1980 had been set aside by the diocese as the commemoration of its founding thirteen hundred years earlier. Over so many centuries there was a tremendous history to commemorate. Our historians had argued as to whether Bosel was consecrated Bishop by St Augustine and sent to the Severn valley in 679 or 680, but pragmatically, I found it easier to have the programme later rather than sooner, so we settled on 680. To mark the start of the celebrations we had been able to plan in advance that the Queen should visit Worcester Cathedral for the distribution of the Royal Maundy gifts in Holy Week. Ever since we left Windsor, Henrietta and I had been hoping that the Queen would come to see us at our new home. Over the years Prince Philip, Prince Charles and Princess Anne had all been to Hartlebury as part of visits to the churches and communities of Worcestershire, and a visit from

the Queen would be a crowning delight. Strictly speaking, the Maundy gifts should have been distributed at Westminster that year, but I had outlined our centenary hopes to Sir Philip Moore and he was kind enough to see that the Royal Maundy Service would be with us.

The preparatory visit of David Say, Bishop of Rochester and Lord High Almoner, enabled us in the diocese and others who would be in the cathedral to see the significance of the occasion. For centuries the Sovereign in London and the Pope in Rome had followed Christ's example in washing his disciples feet and therefore in humbling himself before the people on the eve of the crucifixion. In lieu of washing the feet of poor subjects, the Jacobean monarchs had instituted a royal gift of money to the poor and needy, and to this day, with the help of her Almoners, the Sovereign reflects the attitude and the care shown by Jesus. Those who were to receive the Maundy money and those who were chosen to represent our parishes in the cathedral were therefore carefuly introduced to the significance of this act of worship in which the Sovereign takes a leading part. The cathedral under the care of Tom Baker made meticulous arrangements, and the Mayor and city fathers cooperated to the full in their preparations. We were delighted when the Queen decided to lunch with us, after our close connection in the years at Windsor.

Soon the day itself was upon us. For the last time in my life I dressed in gaiters and a frock coat, slightly sad that such distinctive dress had virtually ceased to be required. The sun was shining after several days of rain and we were all ready for the great occasion, the city packed, with thousands in the streets. The royal train arrived strictly on time and the procession of cars reached the cathedral to rousing cheers. It was a moving moment for Henrietta and me to welcome the Queen and Prince Philip and those in attendance to our own cathedral. Together with the Lord Lieutenant, the Mayor, Peter Walker, our MP, and others we walked over the green to the door, there to hand over the royal party to the Lord High Almoner and the Dean.

The service itself was much more an act of worship and commitment than I had expected. The Foundation of the Chapel Royal largely took charge to start with; Prince Philip read the gospel with clarity and conviction; and twice the Queen walked round the packed cathedral giving the Maundy money and the purse to the 108 recipients. The prayers were wonderfully appropriate to the commemoration of the coming together of the disciples and the washing of their feet at the

◁ *Visit of HRH the Prince of Wales to the family, 5 July 1979* meal before the crucifixion. We added a moment of thankfulness and intercession for our diocese in its centenary year and the two verses of the national anthem with trumpets, the organ and combined choirs rang out as thrillingly as ever. I gave the blessing, much aware of all that God had given us and would continue to give us in the years ahead. The gathering for photographers at the door of the nave brought back many memories of great occasions on the steps of St George's Chapel. Here the Queen and Prince Philip were with us in our own cathedral after nine years of expectation.

At the Old Palace, the Queen met the diocesan staff and many others. I personally was very touched when she gave me her posy of flowers 'in memory of your father who was my first Lord High Almoner'. Then the walkabout in the High Street began. It was solid with cheering crowds; bouquets were presented in abundance; and with both the Queen and Prince Philip readily greeting hundreds of ciizens we made our way slowly to the Guildhall. There the Mayor and city fathers welcomed and entertained the Sovereign. The logistics of getting away before the Queen in order to receive her at home were complicated, but with the help of police cars and back-door escape routes we were on the steps of Hartlebury Castle to receive the Queen and present her to the family gathered for the day. Rachel and Michael, Robert and Georgie, Mary and James and Eleanor were with us together with their children. We were sad that Edward and his family were still in the Middle East. Our family was enlarged by the royal party for the day, including David and Irene Say. We had a relaxed and happy luncheon. During and after the meal we were able to talk of old times, recalling Father and the Maundy occasions under his care, and also bringing back many memories of my Windsor years. But as before, we lost no opportunity for a good talk about the present state of the Church of England and its mission.

Before the party broke up both the Queen and the Prince spoke with all the family. Catherine Benson, our oldest grandchild, gave the Queen the centenary medallion. Time by then was pressing and regrettably the usual official photograph was overlooked. However, a tree was planted in the garden, we exchanged farewells, and in a fleet of shining Rolls-Royces our unique visitors left for their aeroplanes. All of us who remained sat down with a sense of enormous.pleasure and contentment.

Easter and the few days afterwards provided a break in our centenary celebrations. Rachel, Michael and family stayed on with us after the memorable Maundy Thursday; a whole day was given to going to see Robert, Georgie and their family in their new home in Berkshire; Edward had sent us the first photographs of their first child from their rather isolated home in Saudi Arabia. After a few days we left for Shepham Mill, near Plymouth, for the baptism of the latest addition to the family of James and Mary. To have the baptism of Anthony Burnell Nugent in the control room aboard the submarine was a privilege of James as captain. For those present it was a squash among the pipes, valves and control gear, and with the base of the periscope in the middle I was just able to find about a square yard of space to stand in. The little service was wholly appropriate, and also provided the opportunity to pray for and meet with the ship's company.

The centenary celebrations carried us through a memorable year. We had planned to light a series of bonfires on our principal hilltops and to ring the bells of all our towers on the evening of Ascension Day. It was to be an evening of local pleasures, bonfires, bells and beer on village greens, a convivial project planned with real imagination. However, surprisingly the weather was too dry for safety and the bonfires on top of the Worcestershire Beacon on the Malverns and the Abberleys had to be cancelled. Still, splendid fires were lit on the top of the Clents and Bredon Hill, and with the bells pealing from below it formed a marvellous backcloth to a whole variety of parties; there were gatherings throughout the valleys of the Severn and the Teme. By dint of careful map reading and fairly quick driving we visited the parties at Broadway, Bredon, Knightwick and Far Forest, enjoying hot dogs and sandwiches and beer or tea, depending on the convictions of the local church.

It was on Sunday 18 May 1980 that we reached a real milestone in the life of the diocese. Three years earlier we had called the first working party to plan for the occasion. Our purpose was to recall the arrival of the first missionary bishop in 680, together with his monks, in the early days of the Benedictine mission. Since they arrived and established a bishopric, a cathedral and one of the greatest monasteries of the land on the banks of the Severn, the church of Christ had grown and spread north towards St Chad and his followers at Lichfield, west to find the disciples of St David, south towards the Bristol Channel, and east to meet the vast neighbouring diocese of Lincoln. Those had been the beginnings of our diocese; through the centuries we had witnessed progress, setbacks, martyrdoms and divisions in the

church, but now had come the signs of reconciliation. What we sought to do was to commemorate in one event the whole church in the Severn valley.

The Archbishop and Lindy Runcie arrived on the eve of the celebration in time for a pleasant evening of reminiscing and discussion of current affairs with other guests from the diocese. In the morning the sight of crowds streaming through the streets of the city and over the bridge to the famous cricket ground made us speechless. There were so many people that a police car had to guide us through. Arriving an hour before the service was scheduled, we found that four thousand people had already been admitted. By eleven o'clock we were nearly ten thousand on the cricket ground. With massed choirs in the stands and to the accompaniment of a temporary organ, music heralded the arrival of representatives or whole congregations from every parish in the diocese. As celebrant I conducted a eucharist which was quite unique in my experience. Laity did the reading and the Methodist District Chairman led the prayers, together with Sandy Landale, Lay Chairman of our Synod. The Archbishop preached with real discernment; he manifestly appreciated his welcome and he spoke a word to the diocese which was not forgotten. Royal Worcester had produced plates for the centenary and our glass industry in Stourbridge a hundred flagons for the wine, which was all set out on a huge altar table in front of me and the other bishops present. After the Prayer of Thanksgiving a hundred coloured golf umbrellas went up, dotted through the huge crowd, to indicate the points at which people could receive their communion. Some nine and a half thousand did so in some twenty minutes with the choirs singing throughout and the sun shining from behind our cathedral on the other side of the river. It was an amazing sight to look across our field full of people reverently partaking in thanksgiving. I called the whole place to silence for the closing prayers and the Archbishop gave us his blessing. The Lord's supper had become the Lord's picnic. The spontaneous expressions of goodwill and enjoyment as we walked through the city streets to the Old Palace, there to meet with representative laity and clergy, were all most moving. Later that afternoon, when all had departed, I sat in the garden overlooking the moat and thanked God for his goodness and providence over us all in our day. I was weary but very thankful.

With John Mushon, a youngish priest from Stourbridge, in charge of all the centenary arrangements, we were not allowed to stop at

◁ *Diocesan eucharist in commemoration of the thirteenth centenary, Worcester County Cricket Ground, 18 May 1980*

triumphalism or great acts of worship. Each parish had been invited
to send an indefinite number of its younger parishioners to spend
forty-eight hours in and around the cathedral. There they would find
a bed and accommodation in a neighbouring home or church hall,
food, entertainment and instruction in many aspects of their Christian
living. We called the whole operation over Pentecost and the Bank
Holiday 'Springfire'. Careful preparations were made to accommodate several hundred young people in the city, and on that Whit
Sunday afternoon groups from all over Worcestershire began to
arrive. Throughout the Monday 'workshops' on religious drama,
worship, children's work, art and craftsmanship went on in the
cathedral. The Lady Chapel and several of our beautiful side chapels
were labelled as places where people could find help in particular
interests, with clergy ready to advise as requestsed. The afternoon
was given up to a colourful historical pageant, a huge evening meal
was served in the cloisters, and the closing eucharist started the
evening party. My role in all this was marginal. I watched it going on
and felt privileged to preside at the service which was superbly
informal. No robes, no processions; just a gathering of two thousand
sitting on the floor of the nave around a dais with the altar table. As
the summer evening faded and the lights went on, having given the
blessing, I found myself for the first and last time dancing down the
nave, around the huge pillars and exchanging partners every few
yards. Everybody, young and old alike, joined in the merriment of
faith, including our superb musicians who achieved an amazing
transition from the voluntary that concluded the service to contemporary rock music that suited the company. The difficulty was to
empty the cathedral in the early hours of the next day.

As another part of the celebrations we had arranged a service for
all our MPs, mayors, county councillors and leaders in the secular
community to hear an address by Philip Potter, head of the World
Council of Churches. Here was a chance to get the image of the world-
wide ecumenical movement across to a critical audience who needed
some real information about where the church in the world was going
– if only to counter the common attitude that the WCC were Reds
under the bed. Sadly, with only a few hours to go we heard that Philip
Potter could not leave the bedside of his wife, who was ill. As we
were thinking and praying for them and for ourselves we heard that
she had died. We sent our sympathy in place of welcoming him to
our celebrations. At incredibly short notice, Harry Morton, the head

of the British Council of Churches, came down from London. He spoke as one of a line of prophetic leaders in the church: he outlined not only our future needs but the means that God provided for their fulfilment. It was a pleasant surprise to have him with us: years before, he and I laboured together for Anglican-Methodist unity and together had been early directors of Christian Aid. His visit, followed soon after by that of the Cardinal Archbishop to preach to a monastic gathering, added a serious depth to our celebrations and put the diocese and its mission into relationship with the Roman Catholics of the area. However, the Cardinal's address recalled our people to the spirit of St Benedict which gave us our beginning; a useful word, but one which did not give our two churches any significant lead in working together

In the diocese during those summer months, when the weather was kind and all the churches and indeed secular organizations were joining in public celebrations, I visited nearly all the deaneries, conducting services or confirmations at least four times a week. With the help of Nick Allenby, Oliver Tomkins and Tony Dumper it proved possible to respond to almost every invitation to commemorate the arrival of the first bishop and his preaching to the people in the presence of a bishop. I shelved all other responsibilities for those weeks and was made very much aware of the readiness of the local community to respond and the latent religion of many a town or village. Would that we could continue to offer an enthusiastic ministry in the parishes and schools! There may not always be the people in local ministries able enough to provide consistently good teaching, and attempts at pastoral care may often be less than ideal; but men and women are rising to the occasion. What the centenary celebrations really brought home to me was the need to help the people to find enjoyment and enthusiasm in their involvement with the church and to enable the clergy to regain something of their first vision and primary vocation. Somehow the centenary met a particular need and awakened a new sense of advance in our parishes.

As a break, in June we enjoyed a week on Islay. We returned for the month of July, which included the Lord Mayor's banquet for bishops, always very enjoyable, as well as being the occasion for much informal conversation away from the pressurized atmosphere of General Synod. Then came the service of the Order of St Michael and St George, in St Paul's Cathedral, at which we continued our annual commemoration and reading out of the names of those diplomats and others who had died. It was always a solemn but happy service, and year by year I got to know the 'Grand Crosses', the Knights and the Commanders of the Order. It was also an occasion for prayer and dedication of our diplomatic missions all over the world.

Back again in St Paul's a week later we joined in thanksgiving for the eightieth birthday of Queen Elizabeth the Queen Mother. London was jammed with people, so we went by underground and found ourselves walking through the crowds in the area with friends, diplomats and members of the Government. The service was marked by quiet beauty and prayer and by an address by Bob Runcie which was a masterpiece of commmemoration and exhortation to the whole nation.

That evening, as one of the patrons of the Elgar Society, I went with Rachel to join Prince Charles in the royal box at the Albert Hall for the start of the Elgar Festival. The fact that he and I are both devotees of Elgar has been an additional link between the Prince and myself, and a further tie with Worcester where the great composer lived and worked.

For the next day, Wednesday 16 July, my journal simply lists the occupations of a typical day on the job:

    8.15 Left Putney (Rachel's home)
    9.15 Clergy interviews at the House of Lords
    9.45 Talk with lawyers over Hurcott Wood
   10.30 Chaired Christian Unity group, Methodist Central Hall
    1.00 Lunch with Peter Morgan
    2.15 Meet Ronald Allison, Buckingham Palace PR man
    3.00 Select Committee on Unemployment
    4.00 Train out of Euston
    6.30 Supper with Vicar of Netherton
    7.30 Preached Centenary Celebration service, Dudley
   10.30 Home. Worn out.

A memorable summer both at home and in London was completed by several weeks at the cottage in Pembrokeshire. With members of the family coming and going and with time to think we began to discuss our future and possible retirement. We were aware that we had completed nearly ten years in the diocese and that the work was showing no signs of flagging, but that our stamina was not unlimited and moreover that too many bishops outstayed their welcome. The time therefore seemed right to take the decision to do another year but no longer, and to retire at the end of 1981, when I would be nearly sixty-eight. The family was clear in their support for such a plan; my brother Sam, having been Archdeacon of Christchurch, New Zealand for some ten years, seemed sensible to have retired while he was still active. Frank, we felt, had done a superb job as Archbishop and Primate in Australia, but by the time he had to retire, compulsorily, at seventy, he had worked too hard and too long. Though it was not an easy decision, we did conclude that I should not look to much more than another year. As the ministry does not stop, I realized that it meant a serious break, but this was a conclusion that I came to with a clear mind. By September the winter's engagements were fully planned and I was felt ready to acomplish as much as I could in my last year at Hartlebury.

Rather than being preoccupied with my future, my immediate concern was the future pattern of episcopal leadership in the West Midlands. The boundaries between Worcester, Lichfield, Birmingham and Coventry bore little relationship to the communities within the metropolitan district or the smaller but traditional townships within it. We were sufficiently close and interwoven to make good use of one financial structure and one good professional parsonage board, with less duplication of diocesan services. The clergy also needed more scope for movement between town and country, and urban and industrial missions, like chaplains in the health service, rightly took no notice of diocesan boundaries. By establishing suffragan sees at Dudley, Wolverhampton, Warwick and Ludlow we diocesans met pastoral needs to a certain extent, as the districts in our area felt their need to become more individually aware of their church and the contribution it could make. We had some distant and far-reaching ideas about a province in the Midlands under a presiding bishop, but the historic claims of Lichfield, Hereford and Worcester, all founded before the Norman Conquest, meant that they could not lose their individuality as dioceses, whatever the advantages of a single unit. To make no adjustments was unhelpful for the new towns of Telford and Redditch, through whose areas diocesan boundaries ran, and short-sighted for Birmingham, which needed some rural areas in its diocese. What applied to us applied also to Manchester: if the Church of England is to remain in any sense a service to the whole nation it

[277]

will need both to be united with other churches and to have its resources redeployed. Synodical government is generally not helpful to regional planning.

It was partly through meeting Bishop Lesslie Newbigin on several occasions and partly through a continuing concern for the role of the British Council of Churches that I accepted an invitation to join the BCC Trust for Religion and Society. This high-sounding title in fact denoted a group composed of fairly senior churchmen who had been invited by the British Council of Churches to look into the future impact of the institutional Christian bodies on the differing moral and ethical issues confronting society. To do this it was essential to have the formal cooperation of the Roman Catholics and useful to have one or two who had served in Westminster on parallel causes. I was particularly glad to find myself under Lord Blake and with Lesslie Newbigin as chairman, working with David Jenkins, at that time Professor of Theology at Leeds, Tony Dyson, Professor of Pastoral Theology at Manchester, Caroline Miles, a Roman Catholic and Chairman of the Oxfordshire Health Authority, Derek Pattinson, Secretary General of the Synod, Paul Rowntree Clifford, President of the Selly Oak Colleges, and Gerald Priestland, the Religious Affairs Correspondent of the BBC. To this group was added the headmaster of Ampleforth, Sir Michael Quinlan, now at the Department of Employment, Peter Hodgson, a nuclear physicist at Oxford, and Lady Oppenheimer. Meeting either in committee or in an open forum four or five times a year we began to unravel and clarify the Christian attitude to such widely separated issues as the Christian and the health service, work and unemployment, nuclear power, the mass media and similar selected fields of enquiry. We soon learned that to be of any use to the leadership and thinking of our respective churches, particularly at Lambeth or Westminster Cathedral, we had to be selective in our subjects and thorough in our enquiries. Working individually and in groups we have set ourselves a long-term target involving the publication of books and booklets on these matters, as well as sharing our findings with those who need such help. Two books, written by Paul Rowntree Clifford, *Politics and the Christian Vision* (1983), and *Government by the People?* (1986), have already appeared from SCM Press. My experience in the House of Commons Group, the Select Committee on Unemployment and my clear memories of undertaking similar but less thorough exercises at St

George's House has served me in good stead. It is plain that Christian convictions lay behind much of the Beveridge plan for the Welfare State and behind R. A. Butler in his working out of the 1944 Education Act. Such conviction seems to be absent from Government circles as new legislation is prepared with substantially less moral and social conscience. It becomes all the more important, therefore, that the churches should somehow remain alert as these and other issues are considered. Although we tend to get overtaken by events, we do fully expect to remain more than a think-tank: a resource group for the churches.

It was in the nature of the job that I should constantly be turning from the wider concerns of the national church to the domestic interests and possibilities of the Worcester diocese. The last full autumn that we enjoyed was marked in the first instance by the finale of the centenary events at the home of the bishopric. We had determined some time previously that Hartlebury Castle should also make a major contribution to the centenary celebrations. Henrietta and I, together with our immediate circle of helpers at home, had followed up a casual suggestion by Elizabeth Johnston, wife of Sir John, the Comptroller of the Lord Chamberlain's Department at St James. This was that an exhibition, mounted at Windsor and consisting of works or art and craftsmanship actually done by members of the Royal Family from Tudor times up to the present, should come to Hartlebury Castle. Acting on it with our encouragement, and the goodwill of the Queen, Elizabeth collected together personal works of art or literature actually produced over the centuries by Kings and Queens and their children. 'Royal Performance', as the exhibition came to be called, included a manuscript composition of some music by Henry VIII, embroideries from the Elizabethan and Stuart eras, designs from the reigns of the Georges in the eighteenth century, several items by Queen Victoria and Prince Albert, works by Queen Mary, and from our day pictures or work by Princess Margaret, Prince Philip, Prince Charles, Prince Andrew and Viscount Linley. Sir Hugh Casson PRA, a good friend over the years, came not only to work with Elizabeth Johnston in setting up the exhibition but also to declare it open. It was an enormous success. £11,000 was raised for charities in three weeks and we found ourselves crowded out of house and home. Security control, duty admission staff, the bookstall, the cafe and general management were largely on Henrietta's shoulders. It was a totally new experience for many of us in and around the diocese to see and appreciate the talent in successive generations of the Royal Family. Under our roof, thanks to the generosity of the artists and owners, was a splendid mixture of differing skills, style and attitudes but all inspired by the same real and obvious enjoyment of the particular project.

Although I was aware that time was limited, I did not find that my programme of work differed from that of previous autumns. The urge to remain in the diocese did, however, conflict with interests at Westminster. Still, engagements worked out satisfactorily and I was able to include some days shooting at Park Hall and elsewhere. What concerned me particularly was the status and future of the ministry of the women workers I had encouraged and licensed in the diocese, and who were doing such excellent work. With the cooperation of Tom Baker at the cathedral we arranged an evening ordination service when any or all of our stipendiary women workers could be made deaconess. The law had not in fact changed, permitting women to be made deacon and priest, but we felt, particularly in view of the increasing pressure to ordain women priests, that the time was appropriate to have those women exercising an essential ministry in the parishes, with a status at least as responsible as that of deacons or curates. In fact they were generally much more important to the mission of the church than the average rather inexperienced curate. The service itself was quiet and dignified. Four women were made deaconess, presented for the occasion by Diana McClatchey, wife of the rector of Hartlebury and my director of women's ministry. Through her initiative and perseverance we now have a regular flow of women serving in parishes, schools and hospitals. I hope that the Worcester diocese will be in the forefront when it becomes legal to ordain and appoint women in the ministry, both stipendiary and honorary: they have so much to give the church.

Christmastide followed, with the family united at Hartlebury for the last time over the festival. The house was almost overrun with children and grandchildren, making a party of sixteen altogether. Only Robert and his family were away, by then established in Dubai. After carols in the cathedral on Christmas Eve and visits to certain clergy in particular need, something I always did at Christmas, I preached in the cathedral at midnight and assisted in the morning in our own parish church. Bishops are not really wanted in the parishes on the great festivals; it set one free to be about at home! Christmas dinner reverted to midday for the sake of the small children, and the afternoon chaos of presents and games in the state rooms was both noisy and memorable in that setting. We realized that we should never be in such a house another year. After two days shooting at Park Hall and with Kenneth Wilson at Sudely, we enjoyed a week of winter holiday in Wales before returning and coming down to earth in a bishops' meeting at Lambeth.

The Lenten season was marked by the beginning of the final round of visits to parishes, often with a confirmation as part of the occasion. It was both rewarding and humbling to see the work in progress of so many clergy whom I had had the privilege of appointing, and to share with them and their wives something of their successes and frustrations. In the country parishes there was all too often anxiety about the future of the parson in the place. I was already well aware how unsatisfactory it was for a vicar to have to hurry from church to church on a Sunday when he had several parishes to care for, and I became more convinced that if the Church of England in the villages was to survive it required a fresh plan for priestly care. To leave it all to one professional in half a dozen villages was destroying the fellowship of the country churches, but it was a forlorn hope to anticipate a resident parson in each place. There was, however, the will to keep the churches alive and not allow them to be seen as redundant. To consolidate this faith it was essential that there should be non-professional honorary priests, ideally in every village. The recruitment and training of a voluntary part-time ministry will be a major demand on the diocese in the future. I hope and believe that for each congregation there can be a 'lay person' who is ready to become the licensed president at the weekly eucharist for the parish. In this respect it is as well to remember that the Methodists have always insisted that even if no minister is available, the Lord's supper can be authentically celebrated by a layman. We now need to anticipate such a situation with selective training and the licensing of both men and women for part-time ministry. Their oversight and general direction would be in the hands of a stipendiary rural dean. Such a pattern could develop relatively easily if our church had the courage and the sense to ordain women. They have been the 'priests' for many a family over the years; now it is time for them to be so openly.

From visiting the parishes and talking over their future with wardens and others I returned home full of optimism: the resources are there if we care to use them. In addition to facing the immediate matters of staffing our parishes I was able that last springtime at

Worcester to visit Jerusalem for a week, taking Rachel with me, since she was then thinking very hard about the ministry. I returned in time to give a series of Lenten talks at Hartlebury and in the cathedral. They seemed to meet a need for both clergy and laity who did not find 'spiritual' food in their locality.

In March 1981 routine work was happily interrupted by the wedding of Eleanor to John MacLachlan. With her teaching and other work she had fully expected to stay on in Worcestershire, but in a matter of months she became engaged to be married to John. He is a land agent in the Smith Gore Partnership, with his home and work in East Anglia, and as a devout but liberal Roman Catholic he has brought many new interests into our family circle. Their wedding, using the new rite from the Alternative Service Book, took place in the cathedral. It was a model for any marriage thanks to the preparation of Tom Baker, the Dean, and the local Roman Catholic ministry. The reception provided one of many occasions for a good party at the Castle during our last year. Then came Easter and several months about the diocese; I was also able to complete or hand over many matters in which I had been at work in both Birmingham and London. At the last meeting of the General Synod which I attended, in York, Bob Runcie was kind enough to recall not only my service to the church but also that of Father and Theodore.

After the Synod we came to London for the reception for the members of the Order of St Michael and St George at Clarence House and another great service in St Paul's Cathedral. Those weeks also saw the wedding of Prince Charles and Lady Diana. He had done us the honour of coming up to Hartlebury for a night, and during his stay we were able to share his interests – and he told us of his plans. We found it almost embarrassing to be a family party of eight invited to both the Wedding Ball at Buckingham Palace and the historic service at St Paul's Cathedral. At the party it was particularly gratifying to meet the new Princess and spend the evening with a large company of the Royal Family and their friends. We talked and danced, we had dinner and an early breakfast with many whom we had come to know at Windsor and more recently. By three-thirty a.m. the party began to disperse, just as daylight was returning.

At the cathedral two days later we were again there as a family. I was seated up in the sanctuary together with Michael Ramsey and Donald Coggan, both past archbishops, Cardinal Hume, and Harry Williams, who had kept up with the Prince since Cambridge and it was appropriately he who was invited to lead the prayers. The Royal Family and close friends were under the dome and our family were in seats at the head of the nave, able to see and hear the whole service with ease. The pride of the nation was mixed with a sense of prayer and hope for the couple on whom so much could fall. To be in London that day was exhilarating; to be in St Paul's was an occasion the family will not forget.

Fortunately the holiday season was then upon us, and I was ready for a break. Throughout those summer days at home and in London I realized only slowly that I was not well in myself, and a severe rash round my waist was not responding to treatment. The doctors diagnosed a malignant skin cancer which demanded fairly immediate and exhausting X-ray treatment. I was directed to the Skin Hospital, part of the Middlesex, and had to go there weekly for six consecutive weeks. This I did among my duties at home, in the Lords, and at the Royal Wedding, and much else had to take a back place. When the treatment was completed and I was cleared for the present, we were glad to get down to Wales for some weeks, there to be able to think and prepare for leaving the diocese.

This we did at the end of the autumn. Having visited most of the deaneries and many individual parishes we came to say farewell in the cathedral. The hymns were my favourites and the anthem was by Brahms. There was little fresh to be said: what I had expressed over the years had clearly been taken in and a partnership of ministry had been established. Both at the final diocesan synod and at the cathedral service Henrietta was warmly thanked and we were given gifts with the warning not to grow old or to stop work, neither of which was our intention.

= [14] =

The Fragments that Remain

'Since golden October declined into sombre November and the apples were gathered and stored' were lines that had remained with me ever since I took part in T.S.Eliot's *Murder in the Cathedral* when at school. They now came into my mind as the autumn of 1981 drew on and the date of our removal was upon us. For those last weeks at Hartlebury there was inevitably a sense of declining opportunity, of work undone and of wondering whether or not we were doing the right thing. Since I had been appointed before it was made obligatory for bishops to retire at the age of seventy I had the option of staying on indefinitely, but in making that regulation the church and the judiciary had been right in principle. As I now see from my journal, some years after the event, I was clear at the time that the diocese was ready for a change and I was ready to make a break with the routine duties of a diocesan. It was too late in life to take the fashionable sabbatical leave and it was clearly irresponsible to stay on until I was carried out! There was an insistence in my thinking and in my praying that to hand on to a younger man would provide a good means both of seeing more of the family and of pursuing spheres of work that would remain in my care. It was not difficult to leave the administrative side, as it was now in good hands and in any event would continue to develop; I had no regrets in casting off the responsibilities of synodical government either in the diocese or in London. It was much harder to break the personal links that had been forged on the bench of bishops, in the House of Lords and above all with the helpers and friends around Hartlebury Castle, the cathedral and the Old Palace. There was also the sense of abandoning so many to whom I had committed so much in the ongoing life of the parishes, the voluntary organizations and the industrial and employment spheres of the West Midlands. The decision to retire produced the inevitable love-hate relationship to the proposal. There was the happy expectation of so much which has proved to be true, and the real sadness at losing further direct responsibility in the diocese and church at large.

When it came to the Archbishop of Canterbury and others kindly expressing gratitude at my last meeting of the General Synod and again at the last debate in which I took part in the Lords, I was particularly glad that the episcopal tradition in the family was recalled. It is true that with two bishops in Father's generation and with two bishops among his sons, the Church of England had a run of Woods in its councils for nearly seventy years. At the diocesan occasions of farewell I felt entirely unworthy of the appreciation that was expressed, an appreciation that was heightened in the cathedral by the unveiling, on the steps of the high altar, of a super-efficient motor mower which would demand my walking smartly behind it. At all the occasions in the diocese, deaneries and parishes, where people made speeches, their appreciation of Henrietta's part in the work was made abundantly plain. 'Behind every good man there is a better woman' was expressed with regularity. Indeed she had made Hartle-bury Castle a home not only for the family but for the parishes as well; she had supported the Mothers Union and women's work and both unofficially and officially, through the Parsonages Board, she had developed a knowledge of and care for the homes of the clergy.

In seeking a new place in which to live we had been aware of many factors to influence us. We clearly hoped to keep up with many friends and relations in Worcestershire and the West Midlands; we did not wish to be too far from 'The Wood', that lovely stretch of meadows, water and woodland at Park Hall that had remained in the family; we needed somewhere where the children and grandchildren could continue to share our life and interests; and a garden to work at was essential. Clearly we did not need a town house, but we did resolve that we would be within walking distance of a church, a post office, a shop and a pub, and since shooting and painting had always been my recreations, leaving the Severn valley, with which we were so familiar, was not to be taken lightly. With all this in view, after looking at a dozen and more redundant vicarages, we were glad to find an eighteenth-century farmhouse at the top of the village at Tirley, about a mile to the west of the Severn and not far south of Tewkesbury. It was a manageable house with small enough living rooms to heat reasonably, four bedrooms and an attic that was adaptable for children

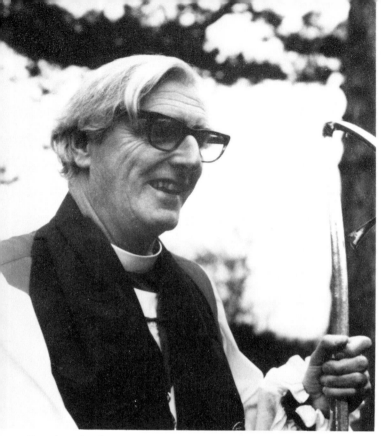

Leaving the final parish confirmation, September 1981

Torse End from the garden

and grandchildren. There was also an old barn, disused stables, a small orchard and a field: space for cars, possessions and activities. Yet it was not easy to leave Hartlebury and to be away from the ready availability of the chapel next to the study, the walk round the moat before breakfast, the garden running down to the water that Henrietta had virtually created, or the trees and vines that we had planted. Fortunately, however, there was no closing down of ministry: my pastoral job would go on, but in different terms and from a totally new base.

Whereas both at Windsor and Hartlebury we had had spacious drawing rooms where we were able to entertain, at Torse End the sitting room was small and compact, not large enough to contain the piano. For the first time since Cambridge days I found myself with the piano in my study, a good rectangular room with plenty of shelves on the west end of the house. Once again I was able to regain something of the pleasure of playing and to begin again to enjoy making music, and in a very amateur way pursuing harmony and improvisation; this has been particularly satisfying ever since I was taught their rudiments at school. I did once or twice play the enormous organ in St George's Chapel which, with its seventy stops, had two consoles, as if one man could not make enough sound on his own! I never dared to have a try on the organ in Worcester Cathedral, though over the years I did help out occasionally at informal services in a parish church that otherwise would have had no music. Now to make music at home was starting up afresh an activity that had been in the family for generations. It also provides occasions when grandchildren on holiday can be given some encouragement and pleasure, since piano lessons at school can easily become a chore.

At the same time as recovering music, albeit increasingly with the aid of records and tapes, I also again took to drawing and water-colour painting. I have never become prolific in works of art like Cuthbert Bardsley, my neighbour at Coventry in the 1970s, but I did find that with a few lessons, reading tutorial books and watching June Mendoza, my portrait painter, at work, I soon regained my interest in perspective and landscape painting – something again that I had been taught at school. Since my study is now genuinely my own and not required to be tidy for visitors, the shelves and walls are covered with a mixture of pictures of the family and my own inadequate paintings. Up the staircase, as at Hartlebury, there are some Cotmans and several beautiful nineteenth-century water-colours, mixed up with my own coastal scenes of Singapore, the hills and estuaries of Pembrokeshire, Canterbury Cathedral from my room at the Lambeth Conference of 1978, views towards Bethlehem or in the temple area at Jerusalem, all done at odd times on various travels. To have the outlet of music and drawing has been a stabilizing influence in my life. Moreover, any talents that I may have inherited, and painting in the family goes back to Joseph Woods, who was a member of the Norwich School in the 1820s, have now also shown up in the children. Robert and Rachel can both draw and several grandchildren show a real aptitude for the piano and other instruments. For us, to pass on an appreciation of good pictures and a love of Bach, Handel and the great composers is an essential bridge over the generations of family life.

Clearly there was plenty to do in the early months with a new home, an interesting garden, and quickly developing local interests. I took the occasional confirmation to meet the needs of the diocese and had the continued interest of completing the work and report of the Select Committee on Unemployment at Westminster, on to which I was co-opted as a 'permanent witness' after officially losing my active role in the House of Lords. However, all this did not provide any real occupation. Nevertheless, before we took up wider invitations to be of use we marked our break by having some weeks in the Gulf with Robert, Georgiana and their children. Their comfortable small house on the outskirts of Dubai with the desert beyond, with a garden and swimming pool, proved a relaxing centre for a holiday, from which we made expeditions into the desert, the Indian Ocean and elsewhere. Among these was a cruise around the Gulf of Arabia in the last of the long line of British India steamers which took us to Bahrain, Kuwait and Qatar, in all of which places we were entertained by the shipping community, colleagues of Robert, the General Manager of P & O and its subsidiary, Overseas Containers Ltd. A most kindly and well-educated Scot who was Chief Engineer, and his Latvian assistant, soon gave us the run of the engine room while on board, where a splendid old Boxford diesel stood twenty-four feet high, with its cylinders like grain silos and the throttle a two-handed bar that could bring the thundering pile up to a hundred revs per minute. That would mean twelve knots, our maximum speed. Immediately afterwards I spent a further week in Jerusalem attending planning meetings for the Ecumenical Institute before returning to Torse End, which was now home. From there I could undertake as much or as little as I pleased in the service of the church.

One day Henrietta, between sitting in court as a magistrate and doing the household chores, surprisingly returned from Gloucester having bought five black ewes and seven baby lambs. They were bought both for their interest and the prospect of their wool and meat, as well as for their mowing capacities in the orchard and field. Their arrival opened up a whole new venture. Instead of a few black sheep dotted round the diocese, we were to have our own flock at home. Our neighbouring farmer, Ray Hartland, of true Gloucestershire stock, whose dialect was in delightful contrast to those of Birmingham and Worcestershire, brought them back from market in his trailer and through him we became friendly with shearers, cattle markets, abattoirs, and most of all with others who have small flocks of sheep. Borrowing a black ram for a few weeks in the autumn is not as easy as it sounds. 'Put him in on Guy Fawkes' Day and take your lambs on April Fools' Day' was the advice given us. Henrietta now became both the shepherd and the sheep dog. Being set up in this way as smallholders we were duly registered by the local agricultural authority and thereby became participants in the largesse of the Common Agricultural Policy. What was actually more important was being accepted as members in a local farming community in addition to being identified with our neighbours in the village. We were therefore not without our interests, our family, our animals and pleasant surroundings when we came to settle and take up the ministry afresh.

By the autumn of 1982 the pattern of life for a retired bishop was taking shape. With the establishment of our new and very different home I was able to take up aspects of the ministry where help was needed. This was clearly first in our new parish, to which we were welcomed by Paul Dack, our rector. We found that he had three country parishes hugging the west bank of the Severn: Tirley, Hasfield and Ashleworth each have a vigorous independence, no unity of benefice or mission, but welcoming and isolated congregations in their lovely mediaeval churches. To expect cooperation between villages in most areas is still asking too much. Tirley took the side of the Roundheads while Hasfield raised soldiers for the King, and the inhabitants are still well aware of the fact that Tirley has no stately home or manor house; the others do. It is not surprising, therefore, that each village community feels independent from its neighbours though they are all bracketed together under one parsonage, and each congregation calls for its very own service each Sunday. The logic of united worship or Christian endeavour is not even considered. To be the unpaid curate in this situation with no responsibilities but many opportunities to help and teach in the small but welcoming congregations, including the Methodist chapel, is rewarding, and highly instructive about the basic culture of our present rural population. My role in the parish, which enables each community to have a little more priestly help, is wholly satisfying. However, our church is down by the river, a little way off from the village, and is cold and sometimes flooded in winter. So early on I felt the need for a place of worship here at home, particularly after having a private chapel both at Windsor and at Worcester. Thanks to the help of Robert and James over a weekend we erected joists and made a new floor in the loft of the barn. With a small altar table, a circle of chairs, and low rafters that hardly permit standing even for the gospel, we again have a place of prayer for a weekly eucharist and family prayers when appropriate. Either with Paul our rector, or particularly when any grandchildren are with us, we meet in our 'upper room'. It keeps our priorities right: perhaps it is a far cry from Worcester Cathedral or St George's Chapel, but it is just as real.

Since there are little more than a thousand souls in the three parishes it must appear that the rector does not need help, and in many ways he can well manage, as he is able, friendly and hard-working. However, the pressures of secularism, the fact that the children are taken away to a central school, and the contemporary reluctance to respond to institutional church life leave the ministry isolated: some form of group activity is essential, and our newly-found partnership has, I believe, been of benefit to us both. Does not this demonstrate how urgent it is for clergy and laity to find a new pattern of ministry, particularly for our villages? Our group is not untypical: people's expectations have not really changed since they had to share a priest; the danger of defeatism among church and chapel supporters is all too evident; the burden of repairs for our ancient churches is generally too much for the locality; and, most important of all, the children and younger generation are both ignorant of the church and oblivious of its significance. Nor is the situation helped by the inevitable centralization of education, the difficulties of the village store in the face of supermarkets, the partial withdrawal of local police and bus services and the gradual replacement of the rural population by professional commuting families. In the face of this situation the danger is that the church just has the attitude of make do and mend. While in the past the villages have been a mainstay of the church in the land, if now only minor adjustments are made, the result can only be the slow running down of country congregations. This, however, need not be the case. The ministry now can be seen, and indeed is being appreciated by many lay men and lay women, as the activity of the whole congregation, clergy and laity together. The lack of a parish priest can prove to be a blessing to a parish when it is forced to rely upon a 'do it yourself' ministry, as we find in certain areas of Worcestershire.

In the first instance, however, there remains the fact that the Church of England continues to need a strong, full-time stipendiary ministry in both parochial and specialist roles. The challenging of both men and women to come forward for training and whole-time ministry should now engage more resources than it receives at present. At the same time it is important that such a career be adequately paid and structured: the stewardship of resources has shown that this is possible. But the villages and many a town cannot now wait for a future ministry. A crash programme to engage a non-stipendiary ministry is called for, and there is an urgent need for the bishops to be ready to ordain or license suitable lay people as priests in industry, schools, hospitals and housing estates, who will at the same time remain in their secular employment. There is much potential, and such people cannot be left to effect a nebulous lay witness to the gospel; if they are ready to serve, they should be commissioned and possibly ordained. For example, there was no vicar in the Worcester village to which the head of a well-known publishing firm, a practising Christian, commuted each weekend. I was glad to ordain him priest so that there could be a president at the eucharist week by week in his village church. Such a move could be made in countless congregations, and instead of an overstretched priest hurrying from church to church on a Sunday, an auxiliary ministry could emerge that in its turn would encourage others to come forward for children's work, youth work and the care of old people. The initiative for such a priestly local non-stipendiary ministry may well not arise out of a sense of vocation in an individual, but rather from proposals made by the local congregation. Training would not be as full as for the regular ministry, but then the licensing of such people would not envisage their working in a broad field or entering the stipendiary priesthood. Bishops would undertake not to license a priest selected and trained for a local ministry in the context of another parish or wider field unless he or she had become established and accepted in that ·new community. Another way of avoiding the traditional and legal difficulties of ordaining individuals to a limited local ministry would be to license, under strict conditions, lay people to celebrate holy communion. The Methodists have always held this position in reserve. However, although I would be prepared to see this as a way forward which would not damage any New Testament concept of ministry, it would be too controversial for the churches at this time. It may also be that we have become too dependent on sacramental worship.

I remain hopeful of a non-stipendiary auxiliary ministry, working in loosely-knit groups under a trained vicar or rural dean, but realize that there are serious disadvantages. It would discourage vocations to the regular priesthood and genuinely lay participation in worship and service. It would also mean the phasing out of readers as a separate category of ministry. As a church we are indebted to readers, both men and women, and have relied heavily upon them. However, their appointment robs the congregation of the essential character of being priestly in outlook and action as a whole. It is not that congregations should be deprived of someone to lead Sunday worship, but that a much larger body of lay men and women should be encouraged to participate in leading prayer and giving instruction. (In making these comments I am indebted to the report prepared by the Bishop's Council of the Diocese of Worcester, 1985.) Imaginative leadership is clearly called for in the replanning of the ministry, certainly in the countryside and increasingly in urban areas. I can only be thankful that in my old diocese and in the diocese of my new home radical thinking and planning is in progress.

Gloucester did not need additional episcopal help, but we were warmly welcomed by John Yates, the Bishop. At his invitation, moreover, I agreed to become the chairman and convener of a working party set up between the diocese, local doctors and the district health authority to make provision for the care of those suffering from cancer or any other terminal illness. The establishment of a hospice or some provision of home care for such patients was intended as a memorial to Bishop Basil Guy, who died of cancer while Bishop of Gloucester a few years ago. This unexpected and, to me, novel sphere of interest has proved absorbing, and I hope that it will be of real use to the county. Working with doctors and the health service disclosed to me something of the sustained dedication that there is in the whole medical field, and at the same time some of the difficulties in maintaining a health service in the face of financial stringency. The three parties to the venture, mutually guided and financially supported by the National Society for Cancer Relief, decided from the beginning that a Home Nursing Service on a voluntary basis was a prime requirement in Gloucester City, in the Forest of Dean, in Stroud, and lastly in Cheltenham. For a full year I enjoyed testing the attitudes of clergy and doctors as we faced the needs of some 600 terminally ill people who are in the county at any one time. I have shared in raising a substantial sum of money, and by the end of 1984 we were ready to appoint, house and maintain our first two trained 'Macmillan' nurses for work in the area of Gloucester City. We find their salary and expenses; the Health Service provides all the facilities, drugs and requirements. The care of the individuals who are sick, the sustaining of the families concerned, helping relatives to be prepared for a death in their home and seeing to the inevitable needs of the bereaved as they face their loss and their future has become the daily concern of our nurses; and it has given me a new parish! After years of supervising the ministry I find it refreshing to go myself to training courses on these matters run by doctors, psychologists and clergy. With the prospect of appointing a further five nurses to work in our county, it is all proving to be a most worthwhile sphere of activity.

Being able to plan my own activities and not being tied to routine work, I hoped to give time to some of those areas of concern into which I had been drawn over the last twenty years and which had never received the care that was due to them. It was shortly before I left Windsor, in the middle of the years in which Anglican-Methodist unity was so nearly achieved, that I received an invitation to become President of The Queen's College, Birmingham, and chairman of its council. Over nearly a hundred years Queen's had grown into one of the major Anglican centres for the training of the ministry. Not far away, at Handsworth, was the Methodist college for training their people. Determined that the ecumenical movement should not be just a prolonged conversation between the churches but also an avenue to corporate unity, the two colleges, with the approval of their churches, had entered into an agreement to unite on the Anglican site at Edgbaston, close to the university. Those of us who had witnessed the success of the United Church of South India knew that a basic requirement of any scheme of unity in England was a common training of the clergy in the churches concerned to unite. An additional hostel was built, and the Methodist students arrived in 1969, with their staff and indeed their traditions. By 1971 I had become aware of the religious and administrative issues that now confronted a residential college with some seventy students. I found John Habgood, later Bishop of Durham and Archbishop of York, as Principal, exercising a leadership and understanding for this unique venture that was increasingly appreciated by both the churches and the university nearby. We soon worked together as Principal and President, and under his care good relationships were inaugurated with the other theological college in the city, the Roman Catholic college at Oscott. Quite soon plans were made and implemented under which candidates for the Catholic priesthood came to us for lectures and short periods of residence, and we sent our people to them. The joint course for all students, both Protestant and Catholic, remains unique in British Christianity.

Queen's was the first fully integrated united college, and has remained the only one. When a diocesan bishop, I tended to see the colleges as providing men for filling vacancies and keeping the whole machinery going. From the vantage point of retirement I now see the colleges as central to our planning for ministry as well as for training men and women. They are increasingly becoming the workshop in which many differing forms of ministry will take shape for both men and women, those who want to devote their whole lives to the ordained ministry and those who will remain non-stipendiary or auxiliary. With such developments pressing upon the college we needed lay professional administrative help. This we found in Stephen Lloyd. At one time Lord Mayor of Birmingham, and deeply involved in both the industrial and cultural life of the city, over nearly forty years he, too, has guided the participating churches in the material, financial and indeed the spiritual needs of the foundation. Birmingham has never been short of independent leadership and competent administration in its development of universities and colleges. The debt of the churches to Stephen and other laity for carrying through an Act of Parliament and financial readjustments on behalf of the churches in the venture of The Queen's College is immeasurable.

Successive Bishops of Birmingham, Lichfield, Worcester and Coventry and Methodist District Chairmen gave us encouragement to develop the college in the service of the churches of the West

Midlands. It has certainly become a major interest, although I have never in any sense been in the academic stream of the church. John Habgood, for whom I was a presenting bishop on his appointment to Durham, has remained on call as adviser and friend. He was succeeded as Principal by Anthony Bird, a family doctor as well as a priest, by which the college was given a new approach to pastoral care; Anthony Bird's links with the medical world opened new avenues that were otherwise closed to our men and women in training. He gave a fresh impetus to clinical theology and the care of the sick. Following his time as Principal I had the interesting role of appointing the first Methodist as head of a largely Anglican foundation. The task was made easy by the availability of Gordon Wakefield, Methodist District Chairman of Manchester. A few Anglicans doubted the wisdom of such a step, but looking back over the six years of his direction at Queen's I can only feel thankful. He came not only with teaching and pastoral experience but as an established authority on Anglican spirituality, liturgy and ministry. To have someone who could look objectively at Anglican traditions and ways has proved to be a real advantage for the generations of students who have already passed through his care. Under his leadership his staff have been drawn from all the traditions in the college and now include a Roman Catholic tutor and a Presbyterian theologian. With such advantages it has now been possible to develop training facilities for those who are retaining their secular employment and require non-residential courses of instruction. This new development in theological college work is enabling a wide variety of men and women to receive tuition designed to meet their particular vocation or ability. Men or women, for ordination or lay service, expecting a salary or in an honorary capacity, white or coloured, Anglican or Reformed, 'bond or free', are increasingly being recommended by their local church authority for training in the service of Christ as their circumstances best permit. Such opportunity for training may soon become more local, but method and requirements need to be pioneered now. The care of these additional members of the college on an evening or weekend basis, the 'West Midland Course', is now the responsibility of Andrew Wingate, whom I ordained into the diocese of Worcester and who for a time followed Lesslie Newbigin in training the ministry for the Church of South India. As I have already indicated, this new style of part-time ministry for many more members of a strong congregation is surely a foretaste of things to come. It would be wrong, however, to overlook the advantages of the community life in small colleges that has meant so much in shaping the devotion and constancy of so many of our clergy. In general, by continuing to work for the college I realize that such an institution may, by God's providence, become an instrument in saving the churches from clericalism on the one hand and continued denominationalism on the other.

Having been closely identified with SCM in early years, towards the end of my time at Windsor I was drawn into the field of the churches' care for overseas students. At the height of the boom period of 1960s, some 60,000 students from overseas arrived to gain higher education in our colleges and polytechnics. A substantial proportion of these men and women had been given their basic education in missionary or church schools; hundreds had found a living faith and happy membership in one of the younger churches. They came from Africa, India and the Far East expecting to find the 'home' of Christianity full of welcome and enthusiasm. In all some 30,000 came each year to the London-based colleges. On landing at the airport they were often bewildered and an easy prey to the apparent helpfulness of left-wing political agents or to those offering unsuitable accommodation. The commendation of these young people by their churches overseas was only partially effective, and therefore it was important to have responsible and friendly advisors at the airports and docks. 'Lord, when saw we thee a stranger and took thee in?'

In this situation the British Council was doing an essential job, as it still does; in particular it has promoted both hostels and good accommodation, particularly for those from the Commonwealth. However, the churches clearly needed to participate in the care of these students if they were going to return to their homes with a sense of accomplishment and faith and not just with certain technical abilities. The students also remain important ambassadors of Western values, quite apart from the opportunities they may later bring to British exporters. Some of us, therefore, prompted by the major missionary societies, tried to answer this challenge. We inaugurated the Church of England Overseas Student Hostels Ltd, and with George Grinshaw as our general manager and with Leslie Burns first as welfare officer and later as warden, we established a substantial hostel in Paddington, which was opened by Prince Philip in 1968. We also entered into partnership with William Temple House in Earls

Court and learned much from the Lee Abbey hostels project. Many hundreds of young men and women over the years have been through our care, and although only William Temple House remains, as a result of economic pressures on the churches, we continue to do the churches' work for this rather isolated section of society. College chaplains and the Student Christian Movement properly remain the churches' agents in pastoral care for the many who cannot find room in hostels. Though greater opportunity to develop this side of the churches' mission has been curtailed by the cold winds of economic recession which have swept through both the sending countries and the universities, I shall continue to press for the dioceses or the central church to accept some responsibility for these largely Christian strangers whom we are called to welcome.

With travel in my bones and with memories of Egypt, India and the Far East, I had been particularly gratified in 1971 to be invited by the Queen herself to become the Prelate of the Most Distinguished Order of St Michael and St George. While at Worcester I was not able to do much more than preside at the annual service, but in these last few years I have seen an increasing number of the members, who are drawn from the foreign and commonwealth service; for the appointment carries with it the opportunity for an unobtrusive ministry among those in the diplomatic service. The encouragement I have received from successive Permanent Under Secretaries of State and particularly from Sir Michael Pallister and now from Sir Anthony Acland has been such that I have felt it important to visit our embassies whenever I have been abroad as one caring for the welfare and spiritual needs of our personnel, often in isolated situations. In Teheran, just before the revolution, at Jeddah, Tel Aviv, Cairo, Pretoria and Cape Town, as well as in Central America, over the years I have found many an opportunity to offer friendly but independent counselling. Further afield, meeting members in Australia and the USA has forged links endorsing the Christian values that lie behind the Order. Each year I now write to all the members, which means a letter going into most of our embassies and principal consulates overseas. In it I try to relate the thinking of the Christian churches to the international and social situation. With the reduction of chaplaincies in several areas of our diplomatic missions the ambassador or consul quite frequently has to act in a moral or even priestly capacity among his own staff, or in relation to the local British community. With this in view I have prepared and distributed to every embassy and major consulate a handbook to enable our representative to conduct such simple services as may be required. A British community overseas obviously wants to mark Christmas and other great festivals, and an appropriate service for a civil wedding, a christening or a funeral when no priest is available should not be denied to those in need. The handbook that I have prepared tries to fill this requirement as well as offering simple aids to Bible reading and prayer.

However, the principal activity of the Prelate is to arrange and conduct the annual service for members in St Paul's Cathedral. This occasion, with a pleasant party for members the evening before, has become increasingly worthwhile. In origin and intention the service is a commemoration of those members who have died in the previous twelve months, but it has also become an act of worship in our own chapel on the south side of the cathedral and an act of prayer and dedication in the main body of the cathedral for those who cared for the foreign and commonwealth service of the nation. This distinctively Christian service derives from the days of the crusades; indeed the Order is the English equivalent of the Papal Knights of Malta: to have an annual occasion when one particular section of the public service can reassert Christian values and hopes is a remarkable continuation of so much that lies behind the establishment of first the Empire and latterly the Commonwealth. To attempt any description of the dignity and splendour of the service, the trumpeters and bands, which for all the pomp are combined with a noticeable spiritual impact on the hundreds present would inevitably understate its value. With the Sovereign present once in seven years and her deputy, the Duke of Kent, as Grand Master always in full support and reading the lesson, and with the Lord Mayor in state it becomes essential for it to be not primarily a splendid piece of pageantry but an act of prayer to God, in whose hand our destiny as a nation resides. Knights and Commanders of the Order together with families, friends and many associated with our diplomatic service make the cathedral the scene of music, prayer and worship that stays in the minds of all concerned. The Christian world mission and the overseas service of our nation has been, and remains, remarkably held together by the Order, and to further that link remains the personal and pleasurable obligation of the Prelate.

Curiously enough, the Knights Templar and the Knights of Malta were not only the forerunners of the Order of St Michael and St George but have remained, under the Pope, the proprietors of the hillside between Jerusalem and Bethlehem known as Tantur. On this land now stands the Ecumenical Institute, a centre in the Holy Land for Christian consultation and research for all the churches. Founded at the request of John XXIII, the great reforming Pope, in the wake of the Second Vatican Council, which ended in 1965, a collegiate residential centre was built and maintained by the generosity of a few in the USA. Although vested in the University of Notre Dame, Indiana, a British trust was formed in order to ensure its use and development. I was invited to serve on this body and became the chairman in 1978. To have a share in enabling scholars, theological teachers and clergy to reside for a time in the biblical surroundings of Jerusalem, Judaea and Galilee is both demanding and rewarding. Over the years we have enabled some fifty scholars mostly from the theological seminaries or faculties, clergy with an aptitude for research, and lay people in the world of Christian education to pursue their own studies, to follow up biblical or archaeological interests, and more importantly to meet with Hebrew and Islamic leaders in the vexed area of the Middle East. Although there has always been a strong Catholic element in the management of Tantur, with the Rector of Notre Dame as prime mover, my principal helpers in making the Institute serve the needs of scholars and church leaders have been Professor Henry Chadwick and Edward Gumbel, the one a theologian and Arabist of international standing and the other a knowledgable administrator of missionary work for the Church Missionary Society.

By good fortune we were able to invite Professor Donald Nicholl, then of Keele University, to be head of the Institute. It was a lucky day for the Institute and a happy day for me when he agreed to go and take the whole venture a step forward. His deep and articulate faith, his open churchmanship as a Roman Catholic layman, his ready ability to relate to those of other religions and other traditions made him a Rector we are likely to remember. Over the last four years Donald Nicholl has enabled British, American, German and French theologians to appreciate what are the main contributions of the three great biblically founded religions. He has shown our churches that what matters is not argument or political discussion but kindness and attentiveness to others, holiness and prayer: these are the avenues towards reconciliation in the vexed scene of Israel and the West Bank; they also lead to inter-church and inter-faith understanding. Not that

Tantur has yet won through in Jerusalem, but it has begun to establish itself as representing the common search for truth, justice and social care. Of recent years, our annual advisory group has not only had to give leadership to the venture and encouragement to the scholars and others who go out but has also learned much to take back to the Western churches.

In most of my visits I have found that a day or so away from committee work spent in the hills around Galilee or quietly in a convent at Nazareth were a means of renewal that one wishes could be the lot of many more clergy. And it was unforgettable to spend time with members of the British School of Archaeology or the Ecole Biblique and go with one of the staff to Qumran, where the Dead Sea Scrolls were found, or to Masada, the hilltop fortress where the Jews held out against the Romans in the first century of the Christian era.

As our meetings at Tantur were drawing to a close one year, Henry Chadwick enquired whether I had ever been to the monastery of Masaba. When I confessed to knowing nothing about it, he sounded regretful, and since Rachel was with me that year and we had hired a little car for the week, we all drove off together. The road beyond Bethlehem soon became a track and the track gave place to hard sand and rocky desert, but after some ten miles of Henry's directions we came upon this fourth-century haven of Christian faith and devotion. For hundreds of years this community of men had borne witness to Christ through the eras of Muslim antagonism and Turkish domination. We never entered the actual monastery, a building clinging to the cliff face, as no woman is allowed inside and we could not leave Rachel alone. As it was, when we were about to go, a little band of Arab boys appeared in this desert place out of nowhere and asked if we were Americans. Not waiting for an answer, they threw stones at us and at the car. We scrambled in and drove hurriedly away. The West Bank is a tragically unpredictable place; its antagonisms will only be settled by patient understanding. Back at Tantur for a few more hours we were able to consult with the scholars who were spending a semester at the Institute, some local church leaders, and the Consul General, leaving them to carry on as much contact with Jews and Muslims as was possible, under the direction of Donald Nicholl. Until regular dialogue takes place between Hebrews and Arabs, brought together by Christian initiative, the warring elements in Israel and Lebanon will not show signs of reconciliation. Tantur works slowly and steadily in this cause.

Ruby wedding dinner party with the 'children'

John   James   Michael   Edward   Robert
Rachel   RWW   Henrietta   Georgiana
Sorrel   Eleanor   Mary

Being enabled to travel round the Middle East these last few years, on visits to our two boys in the Gulf, attending meetings at Jerusalem or bringing a little priestly care to our embassies, has been a most particular pleasure in retirement. Back in Cairo in 1985 after an absence of nearly fifty years I revisited the mission headquarters in Boulac and the school on the island in the Nile where I worked and taught in 1933. I saw again the scene of Temple Gairdner's mission to the Muslim community, and I found the Nile Mission Press, still at work producing Christian literature, but I was made to realize the enormous damage that we inflicted on ourselves, our friends and our culture when we invaded the Canal Zone in the attempt to preserve Western rights in 1956. In so doing we largely and indefinitely lost our credibility as Christians and as a nation standing for integrity. Those of us on the British trust for the Ecumenical Institute will continue to persevere in searching for religious tolerance and social justice in the Middle East.

In the Book of Common Prayer we are bidden in the Gospel for the last Sunday of the Christian year to gather up the fragments that nothing be lost, a command given at the end of the story of Christ's Feeding of the Five Thousand. It would clearly be possible to continue gathering up the abundance that God has given to our family. Every generation from Elizabeth Fry to the present day, spanning nearly two hundred years, has been aware of the power of God in Christ to meet the needs of the 'five thousand' in their contemporary situation. In becoming aware of the goodness of God and the sustaining power of the Spirit, each generation has to a greater or lesser extent tried to exercise the responsibility of ministry, either ordained or lay. It has been an inheritance that hundreds of Christian families have experienced, so perhaps it may be presumptuous to have written it down. Be that as it may, it now only remains to record that the next generation, at home and 'down under', are feeling their way towards fulfilling the family tradition of the ministry. Two nephews are ordained. After starting on a medical career, Theodore son of Frank is now at work as a chaplain in Brisbane, while Christoper son of Sam, dissatisfied with a responsible job at Reuters, is now a vicar in St Helens, Lancashire. Their decision to enter the ordained ministry came late by some standards, but the work has already proved happy and fulfilling for them. The decision of Rachel, our oldest daughter, busy as a magistrate in Westminster, concerned with the care of those on remand, with a growing family and a busy household, has taken us all by surprise. She has volunteered in the diocese of Southwark for ordination and has been accepted for the present for training as a deaconess and as a member of the chaplaincy team in the area.

The decision has made the family as a whole think afresh about the ministry and mission committed to us all. Further, it has prompted several to consider the auxiliary forms of ordained ministry in differing situations: Rachel hopes to exercise her ministry in the field of the care of delinquents and those in prison. Many of us now believe that women have an indispensable contribution to make not only in the context of a local church but also as recognized and licensed ministers in various sections of our segmented society. There are signs that the Church of England can, as it did at the Reformation, take serious notice of the new situation now confronting us and put these convictions about the role of women in the ministry to the test. If it does, it will find itself guided not only towards the ordination of women to the priesthood but also towards the renewal of priesthood itself. As Anglicans we are part of the family of the Catholic Church, and as such it is our duty to listen seriously to what other churches are saying, particularly the Roman Catholic Church. But if in the end we fail to do what we believe to be right on a crucial issue simply out of deference to the senior partner, it would be a failure of integrity on our part: an integrity which we hope to bring intact into the church of the future. We may not all agree about the ordination of women, though I am sure that it will come both within the Roman Catholic Church and our own in the foreseeable future, but we can accept the challenges to many common assumptions and be ready for change. To be able to adjust to changing situations is a sign of greatness; to try and recover the past may well be weakness.

However, to return to the family and the future of being part of the believing community: what matters now is not the machinery or the structure of faith and churchmanship but whether we actually do trust God. Can we be sure that he has the power and the will to secure the fulfilment of the vision he has given us for his world? Can we be confident that our praying for the coming of his kingdom will be answered in this world? I believe we can: through the fact of Christ and his resurrection. The incarnation was not merely a past event; it is verified every day in our own experience. In fruitful good brought out of seemingly barren evil; in faith sustained in terms of darkness or doubt; in victory over potentially hopeless situations, God's presence and his love for his creation is guaranteed. He is our hope in this world and the next.

Index of Names

Brown, John, 166
Browne, Revd Francis, 66, 67, 69, 70, 72
Buchanan, Bishop Colin, 183
Buller, Amy, 161
Burnaby, Dr John, 35, 36, 42
Burnell Nugent, Anthony, 271
Burnell Nugent, James, 205, 250, 270, 271, 290
Burnell Nugent, Mary, 109, 142, 149, 195, 205, 206, 250, 270, 271
Burnett, Canon Stephen, 126
Burns, Leslie, 296
Butler, Montague, 24
Butler, Lord, 83, 174–6, 279
Buxton, Ellen *see* Barclay, Ellen
Buxton, Thomas and Hannah, 2
Byers, Lord, 243
Byford, Donald, 84

Caccia, Lord, 167, 191
Cadbury, Edward, 49, 50, 51
Cadbury, Jocelyn, 241
Callaghan, Audrey, 177
Callaghan, James, MP, 177, 244
Campbell, Canon John Macleod, 10
Campbell, Dr Sydney, 144, 149
Campling, Dean Christopher, 222, 224, 254
Carey, David, 205, 206
Carey, Bishop Kenneth, 86
Carpenter, Bishop Harry, 181
Carr of Hadley, Lord, 262
Cash, Bishop Wilson, 30, 31, 37, 53, 211
Casson, Sir Hugh, 279
Catherwood, Sir Fred, 187
Chadwick, Professor Henry, 299, 300
Chadwick, Professor Sir Owen, 154, 175, 182
Charles, HRH Prince, 149, 150, 153, 174–7, 209, 210, 267, 279, 282
Charles-Edwards, Bishop Mervyn, 203, 204, 212, 225, 276
Charteris of Amisfield, Lord, 139, 210
Clark, Revd Kelly and Priscilla, 113
Clark, Oswald, 243
Cleave, Bill, 144
Clifford, Revd Paul Rowntree, 278
Cobham, Lord, 214
Cobbold, Lord, 153
Cockcroft, Sir John, 175

Coggan, Archbishop Lord, 162, 168, 230, 246, 249, 282
Coleridge, Fred, 191
Collins, Canon John, 43
Cormack, Patrick, MP, 242
Cotman, John Sell, 24, 287
Cotterell, Tom, 106
Couch, Sir Arthur Quiller, 36
Crawford, Lord, 178
Crawshaw, Richard, MP, 242
Cunningham, Canon B. K., 13, 43–5, 149, 197, 205

Dack, Revd Paul, 289, 290
Daniels, Revd Abraham and Sylvia, 98
Davidson, Archbishop Randall, 201
Davies, Rear-Admiral Anthony, 159, 168, 187, 188
Davies, Peggy, 159
Davies, Revd Rupert, 181
Davies, Sir Walford, 144
Davison, Revd Leslie, 181
De la Warr, Lord, 263
Denning, Lord and Lady, 177
Diana, HRH Princess of Wales, 282
Dudley-Smith, Bishop Timothy, 24
Dodd, Professor C. H., 41, 42
Dulverton, Lord, 166
Dumper, Bishop Tony, 219, 255, 258, 275
Dyson, Canon A. O., 278

Eagle, Bruce, 82
Eaton, Revd Albert, 82
Eccles, Lord, 187, 241
Eccles, J. R., 21
Ecclestone, Revd Alan, 120
Ecclestone, Revd Giles, 240, 243
Edward, HRH Prince, 149
Edward VII, HM King, 10
Edwardes, Sir Michael, 148
Edwards, Provost David, 206
Eliot, Lady Alathea, 216
Eliot, Peter, 216, 224
Elizabeth II, HM Queen, 135–8, 141, 142, 147, 148, 149, 157, 167–9, 176–8, 193, 195, 197, 198, 200–2, 210, 267, 269, 270
Elizabeth, HM the Queen Mother, 135, 136, 142, 161, 178, 210, 276
Ellison, Bishop Gerald, 47, 219, 234, 239